Remembering Ronnie Barker

Richard Webber is the author of many TV-related books including
Fifty Years of Carry On, Fifty Years Of Hancock's Half Hour and a
number of authorised Dad's Army titles, including the hugely
successful Dad's Army scripts, as well as books about Only Fools and
Horses, Porridge, Rising Damp, Some Mothers Do 'Ave 'Em and The
Good Life.

Also available by Richard Webber

The Complete *One Foot In The Grave*

That Was the Decade That Was: Best of Sixties' TV

Porridge: The Complete Scripts and Series Guide

Fifty Years of *Hancock's Half Hour*

The Complete A–Z of *Dad's Army*

The Complete A–Z of *Only Fools and Horses*

Rising Damp: The Complete Scripts

Some Mothers Do 'Ave 'Em

Dad's Army: Walmington Goes to War –
The Complete Scripts for Series 1–4

Dad's Army: The Home Front – The Complete
Scripts for Series 5–9

Porridge: The Inside Story

Rising Damp: A Celebration

A Celebration of *The Good Life*

Dad's Army: A Celebration

Whatever Happened to the Likely Lads?

Are You Being Served?: A Celebration of Twenty Five Years

The Life and Legacy of Reginald Perrin: A Celebration

The Best of British Comedy – *Only Fools and Horses*

The Best of British Comedy – *Last of the Summer Wine*

Fifty Years of Carry On

Remembering Ronnie Barker

RICHARD WEBBER

arrow books

Published in the United Kingdom by Arrow Books in 2011

1 3 5 7 9 10 8 6 4 2

First published in the United Kingdom in 2010 by Century

Arrow Books
The Random House Group Limited,
20 Vauxhall Bridge Road, London, SW1V 2SA

Addresses for companies within The Random House Group Limited can be found at:
www.randomhouse.co.uk/offices.htm

The Random House Group Limited Reg. No. 954009

www.randomhouse.co.uk

A CIP catalogue record for this book
is available from the British Library

ISBN 9780099545569

The Random House Group Limited supports The Forest
Stewardship Council® (FSC®), the leading international forest
certification organisation. All our titles that are printed on
Greenpeace approved FSC® certified paper carry the FSC® logo.
Our paper procurement policy can be found at
www.randomhouse.co.uk/environment

Typeset in Adobe Garamond by Palimpsest Book Production Limited,
Falkirk, Stirlingshire

Printed and bound in Great Britain by
CPI Bookmarque, Croydon, CR0 4TD

To Paula, Hollie and Peter – all my love

Contents

Acknowledgements	ix
Introduction	1
Chapter 1	9
Chapter 2	27
Chapter 3	43
Chapter 4	55
Chapter 5	68
Chapter 6	80
Chapter 7	94
Chapter 8	108
Chapter 9	124
Chapter 10	139
Chapter 11	154
Chapter 12	168
Chapter 13	185
Chapter 14	197
Chapter 15	215
Chapter 16	231
Chapter 17	249
Chapter 18	256
Notes	259
Career at a Glance	267
Theatre	267
Film	275

Television   276
Radio   285
Bibliography   289

Acknowledgements

It's only when you begin compiling the Acknowledgements section of a non-fiction book that you realise just how many people help in its creation and production. There are so many to thank who assisted in a whole manner of ways, including giving up time to be interviewed, supplying written contributions regarding Ronnie B., digging out old photos and generally providing advice and assistance.

Particular thanks go to everyone who was willing to share their memories of Ronnie, from old school friends and early acquaintances to fellow actors and those working behind the scenes, including John Adams, Ern Ames, Keith Andrews, Eileen Atkins, Alan Ayckbourn, Bea Ballard, Evelyn Barber, Humphrey Barclay, Lynda Baron, Stanley Baxter, Roy Beaumont, Susie Belbin, Alan J. W. Bell, Adrian Bishop-Laggett, Terence Brady, Patricia Brake, Sheila Brennan, Richard Briers, John Bristow, Keith Burton, Philip Casson, James Cellan Jones, Julian Chagrin, Heather Chasen, Ros Chatto, Robert Chetwyn, Roy Clarke, Dick Clement, Brian Cobby, Michael Codron, David Cook, Brian Cooke, Douglas Cornelissen, Judy Cornwell, Jean Crowther, Barry Cryer, Ian Davidson, Ann Davies, Shirley Day, Penny Delamer, Bill Denton, Bill Dudman, John Fawcett Wilson, Moira Foot, Sir Paul Fox, Penny Francis, John Freeman, Glyn Frewer, Martin Friend, John Gale, Ian Gardiner, James Gilbert (who has been so helpful on many of my books), Robert Gillespie, Colette Gleeson, John Gorringe, Sir Peter Hall, Clifford Hatts, Eira Heath, Donald Hewlett, Geoff Hicks, John Hills Harrop, Chas Hodges, Derek Honey, Rikki Howard, Terry Hughes, Christie Humphrey, Ivor Humphris, Michael Hurll, Mary Husband, Judy Jackson, Paul Jackson, Paul and Pamela Jocelyn (thanks for the photo), Miriam Karlin, Bob Kellett, Ian La Frenais, Irene Lamb, Gordon Langford, Adrian Lawson, Bernard Lloyd-Jones, Richard Loncraine, Sydney Lotterby, Rex Maidment, Ivan Mason, Francis Matthews, Bernard McKenna, Barrie Melrose, Ray Millichope, Warren Mitchell, Jim Moir, Rowland Morgan, Sharon Morgan, Alan Muhley, Simon Murgatroyd, Brian Murphy, Maurice Murphy, David Myerscough-Jones, John Nettleton, David Nobbs, Iris Noble, Denis Norden, Denis O'Dell, Denise O'Dell, Mike Olive, Michael Palin, Kenneth Parrott, Marcus Plantin, Jon Plowman, Denis Ramsden, Gary Raymond, Malcolm Rennie, Jill Shardlow, Alan Simpson, Ann Skinner, Ian Smith, Maddie Smith, Dame Maggie Smith, Harold Snoad, Robin Spicer, Sheila Steafel, Mike Stephens, Alan Stevens, Jean Steward, Ian Strachan, John Sullivan, Dusty Symonds, Josephine Tewson, Leighton Turnham, Denis Tomlin, Peter Vincent, Beryl Vosburgh, Chris Wadsworth, April Walker, Nelson E. Ward, Hugh Whitemore, June Whitfield, Frank Windsor and Geoff Wyatt.

Special thanks extend to a number of other people: Don Chapman for letting me utilise Ronnie's letter and directing me to his own meticulously compiled records at Oxford Library; Clive Eardley for his continued support; David Hamilton for letting me tap in to his encyclopedic knowledge of all things TV and for trawling through his archive of *Radio Times* magazines; Andrew Pixley, another fountain of knowledge, who cast his eye over my *Navy Lark* segment; Simon Hall at the BBC for putting me in touch; James Codd and his helpful team at the BBC Written Archives; the various libraries who helped in my research, particularly the Local Studies department at Oxford's Central Library; staff at the British Film Institute; Anthony Hayward for answering my numerous questions, and for those enjoyable chats over a cup of coffee at the upstairs café in Hawes; David Renwick for his detailed contribution, advice and for lending me some of his photos; Derek Ware for his interesting recollections; Mike Chew and everyone connected to the City of Oxford School Association, thanks for the notices in your newsletter and for putting me in touch with ex-school chums; Ronnie Corbett for taking time out of his busy schedule to chat about his great friend; Hilary Johnson for her continued support and valuable advice during the writing of this book; my agent Jeffrey Simmons and everyone at Random House, especially Hannah Black and Katie Duce, who shared my enthusiasm for the project from day one. The late Joy Barker's help was much appreciated when writing the hardback version of this book. Although she preferred not to be interviewed, she was always helpful and allowed me to publish several items of Ronnie's work.

Thank you to The Random House Group Limited and Hodder & Stoughton Limited for allowing me to use quotes from the following books:

Quotes on pp. 23, 89, 125 and 126 from *Ronnie Barker: The Authorised Biography* by Bob McCabe, published by BBC Books. Reprinted by permission of The Random House Group Ltd.

Dancing in the Moonlight by Ronnie Barker © Ronnie Barker 1993, reproduced by permission of Hodder & Stoughton Limited.

It's Hello – from him! by Ronnie Barker © Ronnie Barker 1988, reproduced by permission of Hodder & Stoughton Limited.

Introduction

It was a defining moment in Ronnie Barker's life. Sitting in the spartan rehearsal room above a workshop in Oxford's Cowley Road, he watched ardent members of the Theatre Players, a respected amateur dramatics group, put the finishing touches to their latest show. Momentarily, he was transported into the make-believe world unfolding in front of his eyes and knew he wanted to be part of it.

The seventeen-year-old had, like many, drifted through school unaware where his future lay: he'd considered – briefly – being an architect and was currently a penpusher at the local Westminster Bank; this was assuredly not his metier. But as the Players performed that evening in 1946, Ronnie was sure of one thing: he didn't want to spend the rest of his working days among the dusty banking ledgers; instead, he was keen to chance his luck in the capricious world of acting. Two years later he was on course to realising his dream when hired as an assistant stage manager in Aylesbury.

Over the coming decades, Ronnie Barker rose through the ranks to become one of the true greats of comedy, exploiting his extensive repertoire of talents to the full. Actor, writer and, at times, a seeming jack-of-all-trades, his incessant drive for perfection saw him, increasingly, take an active part in every aspect of production; yes, this may have ruffled a few people's feathers along the way, and Ronnie was aware that he was seen by some as pernickety; but his desire to produce the best possible product combined with his obvious knowledge and experience in the field meant he often resembled an assistant director.

While researching this book, I was told about a humorous Christmas card designed by the *Two Ronnies'* camera crew one year, depicting a scene being shot in the studio. A camera stands ready and waiting, with Ronnie at the head of the queue with his eye pushed firmly against the eye piece, followed by the director and, thirdly, the poor cameraman, unable to get a look-in. It was sent in jest, as most people not only liked the man but learnt much from him, too. But it represented what life was like on a show starring Mr Barker. Never the demonstrative type, Ronnie's style was to shepherd colleagues towards his way of thinking by delicately and subtly guiding them.

Although he sought perfection throughout his career, he was fastidious from an early age: even as a child staging little plays with his mates in back gardens in Oxford, everything had to be just so. And from the first days of his career, Ronnie Barker understood the mechanics not only of comedy but of how a show should be structured; although he learnt so much in repertory theatre, the classroom of the medium where skills are honed, he possessed an innate talent, particularly comedic, which he put to good use in an array of classic programmes, including *The Frost Report*, *The Two Ronnies*, *Porridge* and *Open All Hours*.

Immaculate comic timing, an ability to embellish a laugh, always word-perfect, tremendous diction, verbal dexterity, extraordinary work ethic and an ability to inhabit a multitude of characters were some of his qualities as a performer. The last came to the fore while making *The Two Ronnies*, where a host of characterisations was required each week to populate the various sketches; in fact, it's just as well, because he hated facing cameras as himself. A diffident, self-effacing and intensely private man, he shunned the limelight and needed a mask, even if just a pair of glasses, to shield his true identity when in front of the camera or on stage.

Whichever character he chose to be for those few moments, he would always elicit a laugh from the audience. 'I've always said it's impossible to quantify or try to define that strange quality in someone that makes them funny. Of course, Ronnie had it, and importantly knew exactly how to use it,' said writer David Renwick, who I interviewed for the book. 'Comedy technique has to be mastered but never advertised. Ronnie's supreme skill was in controlling and manipulating his material via whatever character he was playing, in a way that made the whole thing seem effortless. If you study the actual mechanics of his performance in, say, a party sketch from *The Two Ronnies* you become aware of the way he deliberately directs a lot of his dialogue away from Ronnie Corbett, almost into mid-air, because there is something about that dismissive, non-directional treatment of the line that gives it an insouciant, "throw-away" quality. He also has a trick of widening his eyes at certain key points as a kind of punctuation device. Both of them were expert at controlling and absorbing an audience laugh by means of a sip, or an aborted sip, from a glass of wine.'

As well as acting, his writing talents were indubitable too. Although displaying a penchant for humour influenced by McGill's seaside postcards, which flavours much of his work, he didn't write exclusively in this manner; wordplay was not only his forte as a performer but as a writer, too.

Writing under numerous pseudonyms, most notably Gerald Wiley, his sketch contribution to *The Two Ronnies* was immense. Through his work, he didn't set out to be a harbinger of new-style comedy, simply to entertain the masses – and that is what he did so successfully. For an example of his prolificacy, let's visit two village idiots who have met at a stile.

RC: Morning.

RB: Afternoon.

RC: Nice evening, isn't it?

RB: It's not as nice an evening as it was yesterday morning.

RC: No. Yesterday morning was a lovely evening.

RB: I blame the weather, you know.

RC: You're the village idiot, aren't you?

RB: Yes.

RC: I'm the next village idiot.

RB: How do you know?

RC: I'm the idiot from the next village.

Let us leave the village idiots to their profound conversation and pop in to the Brooklea Hearing Aid Centre where Mr Crampton has an appointment with a specialist.

Rc: Is this the hearing aid centre?

RB: Pardon?

Rc: Is this the hearing aid centre?

RB: Yes, that's right, yes.

Rc: Ah. I've come to be fitted for a hearing aid.

RB: Pardon?

Rc: I said I've come for a hearing aid.

RB: Oh, yes, do sit down. I'll just take a few details. Name?

Rc: Pardon?

RB: Name?

Rc: Crampton.

RB: Pardon?

Rc: Crampton.

RB: Oh, Crampton.

Rc: Pardon?

RB: I said Crampton.

Rc: Crampton, yes.

Rb: Right, Mr Crampton. Now, I take it you are having difficulty with your hearing?

Rc: Pardon?

And so the sketch continues towards its wonderful pay-off line. But while Mr Crampton needs help with his hearing, Arnold Splint requires assistance of another kind, appealing for women only; his target audience, though, is men.

Rb: If you have an old woman you no longer need – send her to me. Simply tie her arms and legs together, wrap her in brown paper, and post her to me, care of the BBC, with your own name printed clearly on the bottom. Because that's the bit I shall undo first. Of course, I cannot guarantee to make use of all women sent to me. It depends on the condition, so make sure you enclose a self-addressed pair of knickers. Send as many women as you like, no matter how small. I assure you, all those accepted will be made good use of by me and my team of helpers – who, incidentally, carry on this work, many without any form of support.

   I do hope you can find time to send me something: we did originally start collecting with a van, from door-to-door, but this scheme was abandoned owing to the wear and tear on the knockers.

Mr Splint continues with his self-indulgent appeal, just one example – like the two previous sketches – of the creative talents of doughy-faced Ronnie Barker, whose splash of silvery wavy hair, dark-rimmed specs and often garishly-coloured jackets became the trademarks of this consummate professional. There was a sense of assurance in his mien: you knew you were in for a treat when sitting down to watch a Barker programme. Rarely were you disappointed.

   As well as natural talent, many of his fine performances were a result of hard graft, shaping the character and learning his lines; he expected the same level of dedication from everyone else working on any given programme. As Richard Briers told me, he didn't like amateurs, people who weren't dedicated to becoming First Eleven players. Here was a high octane talent who, naturally, wanted to plough his own furrow because he thought he knew what was right; he wouldn't have reached such stature without treading on a few toes here and there, but Ronnie's targets were always focused on improving the show – after all, it was his head on the block if a show bombed. Yes, like any human being he had his faults, but these were far outweighed by his many virtues.

But Ronnie was a generous performer, particularly when it came to fellow thespians. A sage actor, he was always willing to help less experienced colleagues; and he was never one to hog the spotlight: if he felt a line of script would help the end product if said by someone else, he'd willingly pass it on.

A life enhancer with his wit, warmth and ebullience, he earned respect from contemporaries and was regarded as a national treasure among the general public. It's not surprising several classic shows bear Ronnie Barker's hallmark, such were his abilities, many of which are examined in this book.

This volume attempts to complement rather than compete against any books previously written about Barker. Here, for the first time, is a biography of Ronnie's life and, predominantly, his work, told largely through the words of those who either worked with or knew him. I make no excuses for slanting more towards his long and varied career, much of which I've appreciated like the millions of others who delight in watching Barker don a prison outfit for another dollop of *Porridge* or slip on the brown overall to run his corner shop in *Open All Hours.*

So sit back, put your feet up and enjoy reading about a national icon.

Richard Webber
Minehead, May 2010

Chapter 1

Head sixty miles north of London and you arrive at the county town of Bedford, where agriculture, wool, lace and brewing have all played their part in the town's economic growth over the centuries. Leaf through the pages of its history some more and you discover that the seventeenth-century writer and preacher John Bunyan, author of the Christian allegory *The Pilgrim's Progress*, was imprisoned in the town's jail for twelve years.

Bedford also boasts a history when it comes to the world of entertainment. Not only were many scenes from the 1970s sitcom *Some Mothers Do 'Ave 'Em*, starring Michael Crawford as hapless twit Frank Spencer, filmed in and around the town, but chunks of the 2005 feature film *Batman Begins*, with Christian Bale playing the caped crusader, originated from the town, too. It's also the birthplace of a list of well-known people from all walks of life, including television presenter and maths genius Carol Vorderman and popular actor John Le Mesurier, who will forever be remembered as languid Sergeant Wilson in the classic sitcom *Dad's Army*.

Another native of this unassuming town, and among its most famous, made his first public appearance on 25 September 1929 – his name, Ronnie Barker. When his father registered the birth of his son at Bedford's register office on 2 November, five weeks later, his full name of Ronald William George was recorded; it would be some thirty years before the truncated version by which our subject is known would come into being, thanks to a radio producer who regarded 'Ronnie' as snappier than the more formal 'Ronald' when compiling the cast list for a radio show in which Barker was appearing – but more of that later.

Life for Ronald William George Barker began at 70 Garfield Street, Bedford, a red-brick nineteenth-century, two-bedroom terraced house around the corner from Bedford Park. It was home to Ronnie's maternal grandparents, the Carters; in those days it wasn't unusual for daughters to return to their parents' house during the latter stages of pregnancy.

The only son of Leonard William and Edith Eleanor Barker, who had married in 1925, Ronnie was their second child, three years behind sister Vera, born in 1926, and four ahead of sister Eileen, the baby of the family.

In the 1920s it was commonplace for mothers to stay at home, while the man of the house was the sole breadwinner, and in the Barker household Ronnie's mother, more commonly known as Cis (a nickname coined, it's believed, because she grew up as the youngest sister in her family), spent her years, save for a spell in munitions during the Great War, as a full-time housewife and mother.

His father Leonard – who for some unknown reason was usually called Tim – worked as an oil clerk with petroleum giant Shell-Mex. Moving back a generation, while Leonard's father earned his living as a master butcher, Edith's was a plumber; it seemed there wasn't a whiff of greasepaint in the Barker family tree: Ronnie would grow up and change all that by taking to the stage, initially as an amateur, before a glittering career spanning more than five decades saw him become one of the nation's most treasured comedy actors. Even though it seems there was a dearth of professional entertainers in the Barker lineage, it's clear from the myriad stories with which he regaled readers in his autobiography that Ronnie inherited his performing talents and quick wit from his father. One of Ronnie Barker's strengths was his adeptness at witty, sharp ripostes, a quality his father possessed. 'Father had an office job, but he wasn't your stereotype little clerk. He had a great sense of humour . . . he had a fund of funny remarks . . . "Any fear of lunch?" he would ask my mother, making me laugh and her annoyed.'[1] Another utterance regularly used by Leonard to bring a little mirth to the Barker household was, 'Money doesn't buy happiness, but it lets you be miserable in comfort.'[2]

An early friend of Ronnie's, Ivor Humphris, now in his eighties, is convinced that his pal had his father to thank for many of his personality traits. 'His father was an extrovert and I think Ronnie got his acting qualities from him; his father could be described as the life and soul of the party and always had a story to tell or something to contribute. His mum was very hospitable, but wasn't like Ronnie at all. She was quite different – shy and timid; I think Ronnie inherited his father's personality. Tim would take over things, such as conversations.'

It's clear that Barker Senior was a frustrated entertainer at heart, occasionally donning a straw boater to entertain his children, and making rare performances in local amateur events, with a repertoire normally consisting of the music-hall number, 'I'm Not All There'. Another sign of Leonard Barker's leaning towards the world of entertainment was tucked away in the back of his wardrobe in the shape of a Pierrot outfit; it interested his impressionable son, who, after checking no one was around, would creep into the bedroom and take a peek at the costume, hidden from inquisitive children. Ronnie reflected on whether such experiences could have been responsible for inspiring an interest in the world of performing, even at such a young age, but thought it was unlikely. 'We simply loved dressing-up games and the Pierrot suit was nice.'[3]

Leonard Barker's job with Shell-Mex took him from Bedford to Ilford for a brief period, before the crates were packed again as the family returned briefly to Bedford, before heading to Oxford, where Ronnie spent the remainder of his childhood and early part of his working life. Although it's unclear exactly when the family moved to the Essex town of Ilford – where John Logie Baird, the inventor of television, beavered away on his new invention during the 1920s – the Barkers were recorded on the electoral register from 1932–4, with Ronnie still being pushed around in a pram. Home was a flat at 87 York Road, a stone's throw from the main railway station and the A406, better known as the North Circular Road.

Work commitments meant the family were soon on the move again: after a brief spell back at 70 Garfield Street, they settled in Oxford, where Ronnie attended the newly built Donnington Infant and Junior School in Cornwallis Road. Local records in the city show that the family was first registered in the area in 1935 with home initially at 386 Cowley Road. The following year they moved to a recently constructed terraced brick property at 23 Church Cowley Road, built on farmland by a Welsh builder along with a host of other houses. The houses were originally intended for Welsh miners who had uprooted to the city to work in the Morris car plant in Cowley after losing their livelihoods down the pits back home.

Around five hundred yards away in Church Hill Road was Ronnie's school friend, Mike Olive. 'During the time we were at school, Ronnie would often call at my house after lessons to look at the rabbits and ducks I kept. We both left in 1939; I was eleven years old and Ronnie a year younger. We lost touch when he passed the eleven-plus and attended the City of Oxford High School and I went to the City of Oxford Technical School. I remember him being a quiet boy.'

Although in many respects Ronnie's childhood began in earnest in Oxford, he didn't lose touch with his birthplace, returning to Bedford during school holidays to visit his grandparents, who remained at Garfield Street, and other relatives in the district. While the adults caught up with the latest news, Ronnie found a route to escape grown-up chatter, befriending two older boys living nearby who introduced him to the schoolboy game of conkers and took him apple scrumping.

If he wasn't out with the boys, Ronnie often became part of the audience which gathered for the little concerts his sister Vera and her friend Barbara, whose family also lived in Garfield Street, staged in the garden during clement weather. For the price of a farthing the spectators were treated to a medley of singing and dancing. Although in later years Ronnie wondered whether these performances, staged in the afternoon sunshine, made any degree of impact, an impression was almost certainly indelibly printed in the depths of his subconscious: in later years he would create his own mini-shows with friends in Oxford; ultimately, performing was the path he trod with such aplomb.

It wasn't long, either, before Ronnie experienced what it was like to be the cause of ripples of laughter emanating from an audience – even if it was a classroom of nine year olds at Donnington Junior School. The class had been assigned a poem involving a windmill to learn. One morning, a pupil was struggling to remember a partic-ular line. While he uttered the same line repeatedly, hoping that the next would eventually surface in his mind, Ronnie grasped the opportunity. As he recalled, the boy, Thornton, kept saying, 'The swirling sails cut through the air – um, through the air, cut through the air . . .' '"He'll be bald," I predicted, "if he goes on like that, cutting through the 'air."'[4] The quip had everyone in the class in stitches – well, almost. The teacher was far from amused and with a face like thunder proceeded to reprimand the class's young comedian. Although a whack of the cane was inevitable for his impromptu actions, once the soreness had subsided Ronnie regarded the enduring of such pain as well worth it, purely to experience the gratification of hearing other people, albeit children, respond so uproariously to something he'd said in jest.

Another lasting memory of this period at Donnington Infant and Junior School involved an enforced absence of four months from his desk after Ronnie was hospitalised with nephritis, an inflammation of the kidneys. For a time his condition had his parents worried for their son's well-being. But thankfully, they saw him slowly recover strength and fitness – surprising, really, when his diet at Oxford's Radcliffe Hospital consisted largely of barley sugar sweets and rice pudding. He returned to junior school with no lasting ill-effects and, in 1939, aged ten, passed his eleven-plus, securing him a scholarship to the City of Oxford High School; it was a proud moment for the Barker family, whose meagre finances wouldn't have stretched to paying the school fees.

Just as Hitler was invading Poland in September 1939, Ronald Barker, wearing his brown uniform with blue trimmings and cap to match, started at his new school. It was the first day of a new school year. Founded in 1881 by English philosopher Thomas Hill Green to offer local boys an education that would prepare them for the rigours of university, the City of Oxford High School had its share of soon-to-be prominent individuals pass through the doors of the Victorian stone building. One pupil was Thomas Edward Lawrence, alias Lawrence of Arabia, whose boyish signature was scribbled across the flyleaf of the chemistry book given to Ronnie.

The usual first-day nerves were present as Ronald Barker joined Mr Soulsby's class, sharing a double desk with Brian Cobby, who recalls, 'We were very impressed with this grand building, in which our initial lesson was Latin, but were both shocked when our first day also included a sex education lesson. Ronnie and I giggled like mad because we had no idea school would be like that. We got on terribly well. He was slightly chubby and quiet; I was the noisy one because, wanting to be an actor, I was always showing off. I don't think Ronnie had any idea about what he wanted to do with his life.' Cobby did, in fact, realise his dream by becoming a professional actor and appearing in, among others, the television series *The Man Outside*, *Crane* and *The Detective*, as well as being the voice of the Speaking Clock from 1985 to 2007.

Another classmate, Bill Denton, concurs with Cobby concerning Ronnie's quietness. 'He was never outgoing and didn't seem to have any particularly close friends in those early days; he seemed very shy.' It was the vogue in the high-school classrooms for nicknames to be dished out, and Ronnie didn't escape. 'Everyone had nicknames: I was called Skinny Bill, even though my name was Clive. Ronnie's was Bumsy Barker, because he had a big bottom!' laughs Bill. 'He was continually being picked on – not bullied – just lighthearted banter. I don't think he liked it, but didn't get annoyed.'

Ernest Ames, who now lives in Australia, confirms that nicknames were used extensively throughout the school. 'I thought that even in those days it was unkind and inappropriate, but I think Ronnie had a thick skin and ignored it, from what I saw. I was given quite a few nicknames, too – and none of them complimentary. Ronnie wasn't fat as a schoolboy, just on the chubby side, which gave him a jolly look when he laughed at some prank. His facial expression was similar to that of Benny Hill at times, needing no words to elicit a laugh.'

Ernest, just a casual school friend, often met Ronnie while cycling to school, spotting him at the bottom of Church Hill Road. The conversations mainly consisted of mundane matters, but Ernest remembers a discussion concerning a prediction made by Mr Brodie, a physics master. Of all the subjects in the curriculum, the sciences weren't Ronnie's strongest, something Brodie hoped to rectify for the pupil's own good. 'Ronnie said sometimes that our esteemed Pongo [Mr Brodie's nickname] would tell him, in as many words, to get his act together or he wouldn't make anything of himself,' recalls Ernest, who has lived down under since 1957. 'As Ronnie was not inclined towards science – preferring the arts instead – it's not surprising that he received a comment or two, but as he eventually followed an artistic career and finished up laughing all the way to the bank, it proves that the education system at the time couldn't recognise talent when it saw it and should have nurtured it.'

The trouble was, the usual opportunities one associates with school weren't open to the young Ronald Barker, who never evinced any interest in considering acting as where his future lay. 'Because I was at school in the war years, a lot of masters had gone into the army and so the school was very short of staff,' he recalled, when I interviewed him in May 2000. 'As a result, they decided not to do many theatre productions or school plays.' However, one opportunity to taste a bit of classic literature arose when the English master introduced the class to Shakespeare's *The Merchant of Venice*, with Ronnie reading the part of Shylock, the Jewish moneylender. Uttering the words of the great bard, Ronnie enjoyed the experience – even if he still couldn't see beyond the four walls of the classroom. 'I was interested in it and thought it fun, but it was only in the class and I didn't do any more.'

Academically, Ronnie performed admirably and, although never top boy, found himself in the upper third of the class. Another of his strengths, understandably, was English and he began his writing career early with a poem which won him the school's Sir Oswyn Murray English Essay Prize; the poem was later published in the school magazine, circa 1943.

In the sweet, romantic spring time,
(It was May, I well remember.
When the trees were decked with blossom),
I was asked to write an essay. This was for a competition
Which is held once every twelve month
In the sweet, romantic springtime.
'Prizes both of books and money
To the value of two guineas
Given by Sir Oswyn Murray,'

Urged me to commence my travail.
I had but one day to do it;
So I set to work, that evening
Scribbled, swore, and sobbed and sweated;
And, by morning, got it finished.
Next day I took in my effort –
Waited for another fortnight –
Heard with glee the brief announcement,
'"Oswyn Murray" won by Barker.'

Then patiently I waited
All through the sweet, romantic springtime,
Watched the blossom fade and perish,
Watched the fruit spring from the blossom,
Ne'er heard mention of the Prize.
Now 'tis autumn, 'tis September,
Now the fruit is picked and eaten,
Now the trees their leaves are shedding,
Still no mention of the prizes.

Yet I will not give up hoping,
For I have my life before me,
Maybe in ten years (or twenty:
I must not be impatient)
I'll receive a printed letter
Typed out by the Secretary,
Short and simple, merely stating
That 'Your two and forty shillings
May be had on application.'
Until then I'll wait with patience,
Though my hair be turned to silver,
Though my bones be bent and weary,
Still I'll wait in passive patience
Since I would not dream of asking
For the cash I was awarded
In the flower of my childhood,
In the sweet, romantic spring time.

(When the poem was published, the magazine's editor included a line at the end confirming that Ronnie eventually received his prize.)

Analysing the poem, John Freeman, a published poet and teacher of creative writing at Cardiff University, states the work is written in a very distinctive rhythm made popular by H. W. Longfellow, in his poem *Hiawatha*. 'Not only the rhythm but the motif of repeated lines and phrases can be found in that poem. Ronnie Barker's work is, of course, intended to be funny, but all the funnier for keeping a fairly straight face. A sign of things to come in Barker's career?

'One thinks to begin with it is a straight but rather naïve and cliché-prone poem of romantic sentiment. As the image of the poet becoming improbably aged and still waiting for his cash becomes more exaggerated, the comic purpose becomes clear; one sees that this is where it has been heading all the time, and there is a hint of the poem's real stance in the interruption of the prevailing sweetness by the line about sweating over the essay. The comic tone allows the boy-poet to have his cake and eat it, enjoying the lush excess of language but assuring us that he sees its absurdity, at least as he has deployed it. The whole poem has a vigour and momentum and overall formal control which is impressive, in the way a bright teenager can impress. The language, judged by the highest standards, is hackneyed and undistinguished, though the comic tone turns this lack of distinction to advantage. It's an invigorating romp, and its playful energy is contagious – another sign of the mature Barker's hallmarks.'

Whereas Ronnie is remembered for his quietness and being rather reserved in the early years at the City of Oxford High School, it appears he came out of himself by the time he reached the fifth form, when he was something of a practical joker, as his school friends confirm. 'He was a good joker,' says Ivan Mason. 'In our classroom there were pictures on the wall and he used to hang little cartoons he'd drawn on bits of paper and place them behind the picture frame. He tied cotton to the paper and from his seat would pull the cotton when the teacher wasn't looking, causing the cartoon to pop up from behind the frame.'

Paul Jocelyn recalls an incident involving imitation ties and a new French master, Eddy Swire. 'Ronnie could be quiet, but was also a joker. I remember the new French master wore a different tie each day, so Ronnie made about twenty paper ties and we all wore them on our lapels. The master wore thick glasses and was unable to see the ties until one day Ronnie accidentally knocked them on to the floor – the teacher wasn't amused.'

Then there was the occasion with the buzzer, as Roy Beaumont – who also remembers playing in Florence Park with Ronnie, climbing trees, crossing the stream and trying desperately to dam its flow – recalls. 'He was good at practical jokes. At the front of the class there was usually a wooden platform on which a table stood so that the master was slightly above the level of the pupils. Ronnie managed to fix up a Morse buzzer underneath the platform and connected it to a wire. Occasionally, he'd buzz it and the teacher would hear this mysterious noise, but not know where it came from. That caused a lot of giggling and was probably the most outrageous thing he did. God knows where he got it; there was an ATC [Air Training Corp] at the school, so he might have borrowed it from someone,' says Roy, who remembers Ronnie as jolly, amiable and a lover of drawing.

Overall, Ronnie enjoyed his schooldays, although witnessed the usual shenanigans and acts of occasional cruelty handed out by prefects, who were free to issue detentions and administer punishments for what, at times, seemed like no apparent reason: a punishment detailed by Ronnie was standing on one leg while stretching one's arms out straight; if the poor victim happened to place the other foot down, even briefly, he was forced to stand on the other leg, this time for twenty minutes.

One pupil chosen as a prefect during Ronnie's time at the school was Denis Tomlin, who went on to teach English and Latin in Solihull. Denis, who is proud to have been associated with the City of Oxford High School, can't recall the aforementioned punishment being administered, and describes the use of prefects as 'generally a benign system'. He says, 'I can't remember anything of that nature, although physical jerks were dished out in the playground after school, as in most schools. Nothing barbaric went on; the prefects would just help the staff by getting boys from one place to another, keeping our eyes on behaviour. But if the treatment of the sort that Ronnie recalls was given out, it wasn't typical.'

Denis realises, though, that prefects weren't Ronnie's favourite people. 'When the headmaster of the school I taught at went along to a local bookstore in Solihull, where Ronnie was signing copies of his latest book, he happened to mention that a member of his staff – me – was a near contemporary of his. When he was told my name, Ronnie replied: "Yes, I remember, he was a prefect. I didn't like him much." I don't know why he didn't like me, because I have no recollection of coming across him in any disciplinary way. It sounds as though he thought it was a very repressive regime, but I regarded it as a happy period in my life. It was a wonderful school to attend.'

While friend, Roy Beaumont, who attended Donnington School with Ronnie before also winning a scholarship to the City of Oxford School, became a prefect, he doesn't remember any such punishments taking place, either. It was, however, common among those schools where prefects roamed the corridors for punishments to be dished out. But Ivan Mason, who was in Ronnie's class in the fifth form, does recall such occasions. 'I remember there were detentions organised by the prefects where we were made to lean against the wall with legs spread apart and arms above the head – it was uncomfortable.'

Each playtime everyone was required to leave the classrooms and go outside, although some boys chanced their luck by hiding behind their classroom's heavy curtains, risking the wrath of patrolling prefects if spotted. Although Ronnie wasn't a keen sportsman, he usually spent break times kicking a football around the playground or nipping behind the air-raid shelters for a quick game of pontoon with pals. Ivan Mason remembers Ronnie became an adept pontoon player. 'After he left school, we used to play pontoon in the garden of a friend called Charles Jefford, and Ronnie was very successful.'

But none of the games he played at school lent themselves to the world of performing, although he soon delighted in seeing his first professional production: Geoffrey Kerr's *Cottage to Let*, at the local New Theatre, starring Alastair Sim. With money tight in the Barker household, the expensive seats were out of reach on Leonard Barker's income; if on arriving at the theatre or cinema the cheaper tickets had already been snapped up, the family faced the disappointment of returning home. But despite having to count his pennies, Leonard tried his utmost to take his children to the theatre, cinema and pantomime.

Ronnie would grow to admire Sim as an actor, and his friend Ivan Mason remembers the day they tried inviting him over for tea. 'We were having a party at my house in Oliver Road. Knowing that Alastair Sim was performing at the theatre, we headed for a phone box to phone the Randolph Hotel, where we thought he'd probably be staying. We didn't have any success, of course.'

While Ronnie enjoyed every minute of pantos, he was equally enamoured of the big screen, with comic strip-turned-screen hero Flash Gordon in his 1938 adventure *Flash Gordon's Trip to Mars*, and 1940s *Bitter Sweet*, an adaptation of Noël Coward's operetta, among the first films he saw at the local Regal Cinema.

When, on that fateful night of Sunday, 3 September 1939, the sombre tones of Neville Chamberlain's voice boomed out of wireless sets around the British Isles declaring war on Germany, cinemas throughout the United Kingdom were immediately closed as a safety precaution. But the doors didn't stay shut for long, and within weeks many were trading again as it dawned on politicians that the public's immediate worries of war could be diminished, albeit temporarily, by patriotic, spirit-lifting films; it wasn't long, either, before the value of cinema screens was reinforced when newsreels came to the fore in helping keep audiences abreast of international developments; morale-boosting productions, propaganda offerings and instructional films all projected vital messages to audiences during the war-ravaged years.

Oxford, fortunately, was spared the destruction and casualties (save those who died on active duty) inflicted upon other cities by the Nazi war machine. It remained largely untouched, except for a handful of isolated incidents, like the time in 1941 when a stick bomb landed close to the Nuffield Works in Cowley – no casualties were reported.

For the younger generations, no obvious daily effects from the war on their own little worlds meant life ticked along pretty much as normal; in the Barker house, however, there were inevitable domestic changes: when presented with the choice of donning khaki and joining the army or learning to drive a petrol tanker, Leonard Barker, in his early thirties, opted for the latter. Although he wouldn't have to face the enemy on the front line, he was tasked nonetheless with a job possessing an element of danger: driving fully laden tankers to the south-coast city of Southampton, which had suffered badly under incessant Nazi bombing sorties.

Other alterations to the family's lifestyle which became part of everyday existence included retreating to the cold and damp metal Morrison shelter at the end of the back garden on hearing the plaintive wail of air-raid sirens. But even though airfields were sited in the locale, the German bombers droned across the sky intent on wreaking havoc on some other poor community – Oxford wasn't on their agenda.

The other main consequence of war was rationing, and every weekend Ronnie and his younger sister Eileen would hop on a bus and journey to the other side of Oxford, simply to buy half a dozen jam tarts from a bakery. But as the war showed little sign of relenting, Ronnie continued with his own particular pastimes, including playing near – and sometimes in – local rivers and streams, often feeling the sharp edge of his mother's tongue on the occasions he trudged into the house at Church Cowley Road dripping wet. Climbing trees, messing around at the water's edge and wandering in the countryside kept Ronnie, his friends and sister Eileen (who was often in tow) content. One of Eileen's most memorable jobs involved carrying a bag whenever Ronnie ventured out in search of grass snakes to add to his collection of mice and tadpoles. Shirley Day (née Noble), who lived nearby, remembers the time Ronnie returned with a surprise in a biscuit tin. 'It was a big grass snake and he asked me to feel it; I nearly died,' she says, shuddering.

With his friend Mike Ford, who went on to exploit his interest in sound and technology by becoming a radio producer at the BBC, Ronnie staged playlets. It was just lighthearted fun, of course, but hard toil and effort were invested to try and make each show as good as possible. Ronnie commented that he 'wanted it to be done right and go well'[5]. Even though, at that time, it never inspired him to pursue acting in any form, it's noticeable that he was not only taking the job very seriously, but establishing a philosophy that would remain with him. In later years, as a professional actor, his application and desire for perfection became traits deeply engrained in his psyche, always wanting the best for himself, his fellow colleagues and, ultimately, the show.

Back in Oxford during the 1940s, the one-act plays were performed in front of parents, with lemonade and Leonard's home-grown strawberries on offer. Those self-created adventures on a make-believe stage from the fertile imagination of a young Ronnie Barker were, arguably, the first signs of what was to come; meanwhile, the regular supply of American comics, spotlighting such colourful char-acters as Buck Rogers and Tarzan, passed on by a neighbour up the road, helped charge his imagination, with Ronnie regularly acting out the adventures with friend Ian Kempson. Pamela Jocelyn (née Cooper) also participated in the plays. 'Ronnie would write the scripts and I'll always remember he chose me for Cinderella while he played Buttons. It was sweet fun.' While costumes were designed out of crêpe paper and old clothes, a stage was erected from blan-kets thrown over a clothes line. 'We normally performed in Geoffrey Broadis's garden, because he had a raised section which was ideal. We always received a good reception from parents and refreshments were given out, including sandwiches, cake and pop,' says Pamela, whose parents adored Ronnie. 'He was nice-natured and not a bit quarrelsome. My mother thought the world of him, while my dad always said, "That boy is going to go a long way, but he'll have to be a comedian because of his figure." He was a chubby little boy.'

The seeds were being sown, but the influence of entertainment remained in the subconscious; he still didn't possess an inkling that he'd want to forge a career in front of the footlights – that wouldn't happen for a few years, not until the night he piled into a tiny car with friends and headed for a theatre outing in Aylesbury.

In 1944 the release of the Laurence Olivier-directed film *Henry V* – in which Olivier also played the title role – led to Ronnie playing truant from the City of Oxford High School. The movie spotlighted Shakespeare's play being staged at the Globe Theatre at the beginning of the seventeenth century, but as the production progressed the scenery became increasingly realistic. It was nominated for an academy award as 'Best Picture', while Olivier was put forward as 'Best Actor'. The High School took a group of pupils to watch the film. Such was its impact on Ronnie that he left the cinema desperate to see it again. Hatching a plan, the following Wednesday afternoon he didn't don his PE kit, but slunk off to join the queue gathering outside the cinema for a further glimpse of Olivier at work in the highly rated film.

Another medium was playing its part in developing Ronnie's latent talent in mimicry and comedy, too. Radio was the primary source of entertainment in most households during the 1940s, with families gathering around their wireless and listening to their favourite programmes. Comedy shows were particularly popular, especially during the dark days of war. There wasn't much to guffaw about, but the escapism of the airwaves afforded many the chance to forget the world's troubles momentarily. A favourite with Ronnie was *ITMA*, an acronym for *It's That Man Again*, a title coined from the increasingly frequent news stories in the pre-war press about Hitler laying claim to more territories, and a particular headline in the *Daily Express*. The show was written primarily by Tommy Handley, Ted Kavanagh and producer Francis Worsley, their lines brought to life by a succession of comedy performers during nearly ten years of broadcasting, including Molly Weir, Jack Train, Maurice Denham and Clarence Wright. After a trial, the first series aired in 1939 with Handley, star of the show, playing the Minister of Aggravation and Mysteries at the Office of Twerps. The show's premise underwent several makeovers during its lifetime, but the content remained largely unchanged, including a myriad of funny voices and comic situations. Ronnie recalled, 'I was twelve or thirteen. I think that's when I started to appreciate funny-line comedy. Radio was the thing and you never missed a minute of it.'[6] *ITMA* ran to over 300 episodes until its star's sudden death also sounded the death knell for the show.

The radio series ran beyond the cessation of hostilities which had engulfed the world, but as the final embers of battle were being extinguished in 1945 a sense of optimism – albeit muted by the longer-lasting effects of, among other things, rationing – coursed through the streets. Normality would be restored and futures unfettered by the threat of invasion could, once again, be considered. Ronnie was no exception, because the ending of World War Two coincided with the final days of his formal education. Having earned his School Certificate a year early, he faced the prospect of enduring a further two years' schooling to secure his Higher School Certificate. Unsure which direction to take, he enrolled in the school's sixth form and began studying Spanish. But, lacking guidance, he found himself drifting along in further education without a clear objective of what he wanted to achieve. Ronnie began questioning where his life was heading and concluded that he didn't possess any burning desire to earn his Higher School Certificate and couldn't bear to extend his schooling.

So he waved goodbye to the High School and considered his options: with drawing and mathematics among his best subjects academically, the thought of combining the two in a career appealed – temporarily. Wrongly believing that being an architect was all about drawing pictures of beautiful designs, he enrolled on an intensive five-year course at the Oxford School of Architecture, which had just relocated to a former girls' school, close to the city street called The Plain. Already studying at the establishment were twins Ian and Alistair Smith, who had been one year ahead of Ronnie at the City of Oxford High School. Their younger sister was Maggie, with whom Ronnie would later work at the Oxford Playhouse before she gained prominence as one of the industry's most respected and talented actresses – not bad for someone who Barker admitted he'd advised to give up the profession, one of the few judgements he got wrong in his lifetime.

Ian Smith, now living in America, remembers Ronnie at school. 'He was a round boy and very funny, even then. We'd see one another from time to time because our parents lived near each other.' Ian was in his first year of studying architecture when Ronnie suddenly turned up. 'I had no idea he was interested in architecture and, in fact, it proved that he had no ability whatsoever in the subject; he probably lasted a term, if that,' recalls Ian, smiling.

It didn't take long, either, before Ronnie realised that becoming an architect wasn't for him. Discovering the job was much more technical than simply drawing beautiful pictures, and finding that the subject involved physics and other topics in which he didn't have any interest, he knew his future belonged elsewhere. 'He didn't seem to get the knack of thinking in three dimensions and being able to get everything down on paper,' explains Ian. 'It became more and more obvious to him that architecture was something he couldn't handle and he'd be better suited doing something else.'

The amount of work overwhelmed Ronnie, too, with lectures extending into evenings and Saturday mornings; there wasn't a break at home, either, with burning the midnight oil essential simply to keep abreast of the relentless stream of assignments. It was inevitable something had to give and, six months into the course, Ronnie packed away his pens and pencils and quit. 'It was a seven-days-a-week business. As well as the assignments, we had lectures as well – it all got progressively more complicated as the course progressed. It was quite clear Ronnie's heart wasn't in it and he left.'

Despite Ronnie realising that joining the school had been the wrong decision, it didn't dampen his spirits and zest for life; he still found time to amuse his fellow students, as Ian recalls. 'We spent most of our time in the studio and, inevitably, there was a certain amount of gassing and fooling around. One day, he was sitting behind me and we got chatting; he continued to be a great source of humour. It wasn't a silly schoolboy humour; he was quite seriously funny, making interesting statements and observations which were humorous and particularly perceptive.'

Ian recalls one laughter-inducing moment in particular. 'He made an instrument he called the razor-bladerphone, as in gramophone. He found that by getting a razor blade, which we used to sharpen pencils, and embedding it into the edge of his drawing table, he could play quite a reasonable tune on it – he was always rather entertaining!'

Finally making the decision to throw away his drawing pencils was a great relief for Ronnie, removing a gigantic weight from his shoulders; trouble was, he had to decide what the next step would be in his attempts to not only make a living but establish a career. A fortnight later it seemed the next stage of his working life was underway when he joined the payroll of Westminster Bank's local branch. Ronnie's older sister Vera had always harboured dreams of becoming a nurse, but ended up a bank clerk at the Westminster Bank's Cowley Road branch. When she eventually managed to pursue her dream, she recommended her brother apply for her position. Before long, wearing his best jacket and trousers, Ronnie was walking to work as the branch's newly appointed junior bank clerk. But, once again, he was soon to realise his long-term future didn't belong among the dusty ledgers and well-thumbed bank notes. 'I didn't enjoy it at all. I found it very boring,' he told me. 'As a junior, everything was done by hand. The ledgers were terrifying and completed in pen; if you blotted them you were in terrible trouble.'

While researching this book, it was interesting how the number of people who, while trying to explain what Ronnie was like away from the rigours of work, described him as a pleasant chap, resembling a retired bank manager, with a name to match. But the thought of a long career in the banking sector, slowly progressing up the career ladder until reaching the pinnacle of branch manager, didn't appeal. Unlike architectural school, where he quit upon realising it wasn't for him, Ronnie didn't tender his resignation immediately. Although he found his duties vapid, he was earning a much-needed wage, so he decided to put up with the monotony for the time being, especially when a friend's suggestion provided him with a stimulating new interest.

Chapter 2

On a showery day in 1946 Ronnie Barker bumped into an old friend, Geoff Broadis, in the streets of Oxford. After exchanging the usual pleasantries, the conversation shifted to what Ronnie was up to. Telling his pal about the mundanities of his banking job, Broadis floated an idea which might bring a little excitement into his friend's life. 'He said, "Why don't you come and join us at our theatre group? It's something to do socially. There are a lot of girls there, and you don't even have to act – you can just help with the scenery, if you prefer."'

Broadis was a member of The Theatre Players, a dedicated and talented amateur acting group which performed a different play every three months or so at the St Mary and St John's Hall in Cowley Road. The idea of joining the group was made all the more inviting not only by the thought of socialising with new-found friends after rehearsals, but of meeting the opposite sex. Having attended a boys' school, Ronnie's experience with girls was limited and he was keen to remedy the situation sooner rather than later. As he noted in his autobiography, on attending his first session with the Players, he was soon chatting with a girl called Pauline, whom he'd later regard as his girlfriend. Meanwhile, the rest of his first evening in the presence of the Players involved sitting and watching, soon realising that he wanted to be part of the company.

The Players were the brainchild of Keith Andrews. At the local technical college he was involved in a dramatic society and on leaving decided to launch the Theatre Players. 'It was my baby,' he says, smiling. 'We enjoyed very good notices and audiences flocked to see the shows.' While the Theatre Players' productions were staged at the church hall, rehearsals and meetings took place further up the Cowley Road in a spartan room above a curtain and material workshop. 'A marvellous lady called Margaret Ray owned the building. She let us use this big room upstairs for rehearsing; in return, all she wanted was small parts in some of the plays,' explains Andrews, who rated the room ideal for their needs. 'Many professional companies up and down the country would have given their eye teeth for it.'

Ronnie's friend Ivor Humphris was already a member of the Players when Ronnie arrived on the scene, performing with him before departing for national service. Ronnie, who wasn't called up because of a combination of childhood and teenage illnesses, remained with the Players and was still performing when Humphris returned to civvy street. 'This is where Ronnie had an advantage over lots of people; for boys joining the Theatre Players, as soon as they reached about eighteen and began to mature, learn about acting and were able to play older parts, they were whisked away into the services.'

Although at school Ronnie was regarded as shy and relatively reserved by fellow pupils, his pal witnessed an extrovertish side developing in his personality. 'He didn't seem shy in my company, and was always sure of himself. He knew what he was going to do in any given situation, being a very forward young man,' says Ivor, who'll never forget the September afternoon they strolled through the main streets of Oxford. 'One moment we were walking along and the next he stopped in the street and launched into a rousing rendition of the "Once more unto the breach, dear friends, once more" speech to a crowd of people, some of whom must have thought him mad. Mind you, it was a good interpretation, delivered with a big, lusty, powerful voice, and he received a good response from the undergraduates wandering around – they were entranced.'

Ronnie and Ivor's friendship developed quickly, largely because they shared similar interests. 'After rehearsals we'd often go to a café along the Cowley Road and sit around for as long as they'd have us, then get on our bikes and cycle home; on reaching the point where we would head off in different directions, we'd stop and chat further – but it was theatre, theatre, theatre all the time.'

Keith Andrews remembers socialising in cafés with members of the Players, too. 'Opposite the church hall was a marvellous café-cum-restaurant called Fulbrook Farm and most of us almost lived in there, eating before the show. Ronnie liked his food and would often go in; and if we weren't rehearsing a play, we'd meet at the Cadena Café in the centre of Oxford, every Saturday morning, to socialise and talk about the business. Ronnie was very jolly and popular.'

Ronnie made his debut with the Players, albeit playing a musical director with his back to the audience, in Emlyn Williams' play *A Murder Has Been Arranged*, in which Sir Charles Jasper celebrates not only his birthday but a £2 million inheritance if he could survive a night inside a supposedly haunted theatre. Despite feeling incredibly nervous and spouting his lines like a Gatling gun, Ronnie enjoyed his first real taste of performing in front of a paying audience and soon secured the obesiance of fellow performers. Other performances followed, including *Blue Goose*, *Night Must Fall* and *The Shop at Sly Corner*, in which he played Corder Morris, a trilby-wearing spiv; it wasn't long before he'd established himself as a valuable member of the drama group. 'He had a very fertile imagination and could create so many characters,' recalls Ivor. 'I saw him in more serious parts, but it was comedy in which he excelled.'

As Ivor recalls, Ronnie didn't mind getting involved in some of the messy jobs, either. 'The scenery flats, which could be up to twelve feet tall, had to be carried almost the entire length of the Cowley Road, from where we'd prepared them in our rehearsal room to the church hall, ready for our performance; but being flimsy, they'd blow everywhere in the wind. Ronnie – who was good at painting the scenery – and I were so interested in the theatre that we found ourselves doing much of the unglamorous work, just to get the plays on.'

Keith Andrews' friend's father was a carpenter and made enough scenery for one room, providing the Players with sufficient flats to represent the walls, French windows and main door. When they weren't needed, they were stored at the back of a radio shop Andrews' father managed. 'We'd paint over them every time we had a new play. I remember them being pushed up the Cowley Road on a cart,' says Andrews, who agrees that Ronnie was skilled when it came to painting scenery. 'While people were wheeling the canvas flats along the road, Ronnie would occasionally be sketching a Mickey Mouse or something on the back of the canvases. He was a clever painter and good at sketching.'

Despite being an amateur group, an earnest approach was taken for each production. This attitude was engendered, initially, by director Keith Andrews, who became a highly respected casting director, and, subsequently, Margarethe Bayliss, who took over at the helm while Andrews completed his national service. 'I still kept in touch, though, and would often come back to watch,' he says. 'The Players were still running when I'd completed my service, with Ronnie, by then, a prominent member.'

Both Andrews and Bayliss exacted high standards from the band of actors, most of whom had no desire to take up the stage professionally – not that you would have known, considering the effort they invested. Ivor recalls, 'We took our acting seriously, thanks to Keith Andrews. He was very strict, knew his business and you didn't tangle with him. People realised that he understood a great deal about acting and respected him.'

Andrews, who worked in the local town hall by day, rated Ronnie 'extremely good, even in those early days'. He was well suited to character studies. 'He wasn't particularly tall and was a little tubby. You were aware there was an emerging talent there; he was also a very good team member.'

The city of Oxford boasted the Playhouse and New Theatre, the latter attracting all the latest hit musicals and plays; it was a welcome centre of drama for anyone interested in the world of entertainment. Productions in the city often sparked off ideas when Andrews sat down to consider what was next on the agenda for the Players. On one occasion, he saw an 'enchanting Aimee Stuart play' at the Playhouse titled *Jeannie*, which, in 1941, was made into a film starring Barbara Mullen, Albert Lieven and Michael Redgrave. The story of a hardy Scottish lass who spends her inheritance sightseeing around Europe, attracting the attention of a fortune-seeking count en route, before returning home to the Yorkshireman she'd left in the lurch before her travels was ideal material for the Players. Ronnie was cast as the man from Yorkshire and Keith Andrews couldn't have asked for a better performance. 'There was a lovely scene at the end. The way Ronnie delivered his lines was very gentle and truthful; he didn't try to turn the character into Ronnie Barker, he just played him truthfully and that impressed me.'

Considering Ronnie's initial motives for joining the drama group, Ivor Humphris is quick to point out that gathering each week in that bleak room above the shop wasn't just about enjoying a chit-chat, socialising and partaking in a little light-hearted acting. 'The Theatre Players tried to produce work of quality, which was acknowledged once by an Australian critic [Stanley Parker] in the *Oxford Mail*. He reviewed the play *Dangerous Corner* by J. B. Priestley in which one of the characters was homosexual – very daring in those days – and praised it, commenting that it was so carefully produced and on a theme about which Andrews, at his age, should know nothing. He [Andrews] wanted everything done properly, using all the semi-technical terms, like "stage right" and "stage left". You certainly didn't do things like gossip while people were rehearsing – it was probably stricter than some professional acting groups.'

Ronnie enjoyed the time spent with The Players. 'I was cast in a little part and then a few more roles and before long I knew that this was what I wanted to do.' Recognising Ronnie's talents, Margarethe Bayliss felt he possessed the qualities to progress beyond amateur dramatics, encouraging him to apply for the Old Vic Theatre School. Heeding Bayliss' advice, Ronnie's application was soon winging its way to the theatre school; it wasn't long before an invitation to audition arrived. Travelling to London in 1947 the seventeen-year-old bank clerk was intent on impressing the panel – which included a future employer, George Devine, the influential theatrical manager and director – with a speech from *Richard III*. Sadly, it didn't work out and Ronnie returned home, having failed his audition. Feeling despondent, he spent the evening with friends Michael Ford and Ivor Humphris, drowning his sorrows. 'We got drunk together,' recalls Ivor with a smile. 'We counted our pennies and bought a bottle of gin, which we consumed in Ronnie's bedroom.' The trouble was, Ivor had cycled to the Barkers' house and was determined to ride home, despite being the worse for wear. 'I kept falling off, so Ronnie's mother or father – I can't remember which – tried helping by lifting me up on one side of the bike, but I just fell off the other side; his parents were worried about whether I'd get home or not!'

Although Ronnie never attempted to join another professional drama school, being rejected by the Vic didn't dampen a growing desire to pursue acting full time; and if he retained any uncertainty that treading the boards was right for him, such feelings were quickly banished on travelling to Aylesbury one evening. After another mundane day at the bank, there was suddenly a spring in Ronnie's step as he walked briskly along the Cowley Road to meet colleagues from The Theatre Players. In their desire to study professional actors, members of the Players had already visited the local Playhouse Theatre, to watch the Oxford Rep in action; this time, though, Ronnie squeezed into Margaret Ray's car, the then manager of the drama group, with fellow actors and drove the twenty-eight miles to Aylesbury to watch a performance of *At The Villa Rose*, an adaptation of British author and politician A. E. W. Mason's early twentieth-century murder mystery in which his popular character Inspector Hanaud was introduced.

Performing the play at the County Theatre was the Manchester Repertory Company who, bizarrely, were based for a period at the town's theatre. The occasion would have a powerful impact on Barker. 'It was a very tatty rep, but as the curtain went up, I thought, I want to leave the bank and do this for a living.' For the first time in his young life he had a clear vision about his future: it wouldn't be behind a desk, recording figures in dusty ledgers; instead, he wanted the smell of greasepaint and the glare of the footlights and determined to turn his wish into reality.

After the show everyone strolled back to the car and returned to Oxford. The vehicle was full of excited chatter, everyone discussing the performance. For Ronnie, the evening excursion had shown him the way forward. But unlike today, where so-called stars are seemingly catapulted into the media spotlight without any substance or grounding, Ronnie's climb to the high peaks would be steady and assured, supported by foundations of solid, dependable repertory experience. Such a background would place him in good stead to refine what became one of his greatest attributes: the ability to inhabit innumerable characters.

The innocence of youth knows no boundaries and the following day, still inspired by what he'd seen on stage the previous evening, Ronnie wrote to the Manchester Repertory Company, enclosing a far from flattering photo, telling the unnamed recipient that he wanted to become an actor and would they employ him. As Ivor Humphris recalls, Ronnie wasn't backward in coming forward when it came to pursuing something he wanted to achieve.

Three weeks later, having heard nothing from Aylesbury, a vexed Ronnie decided it was time for further action. Reaching for his notepaper, he penned a brief, terse letter asking for the return of his photo if there weren't any jobs. Within days, a small white envelope dropped on the doormat; ripping it open, Ronnie read its contents and a smile steadily spread across his face: the missive was from Horace Wentworth, director of the Manchester Repertory Company, inviting Ronnie for an audition the following Monday. He couldn't believe his luck; this was the chance he'd been dreaming of.

Taking a day off work, he headed to the County Theatre, formerly known as the New Market Theatre, and was ushered through to meet Wentworth, who was dressed in a heavy overcoat and trilby hat. After admitting to the director that his theatrical experience was limited to amateur dramatics, Ronnie was handed a page of script and told to read the lines in six different accents. The ability to adopt accents and dialects is an essential tool for any actor and Ronnie's capacity in this respect shone through – he even surprised himself; he later put this adeptness down to huddling around the radio with his family during his childhood, where one could subliminally pick up regional accents, even from the outrageous characters regularly heard in *ITMA*.

Suitably impressed with Ronnie's efforts, Wentworth offered him a job earning two pounds, ten shillings a week – and he could start immediately. Astonished, Ronnie accepted the offer with alacrity, before pointing out that he needed to give notice at the bank and couldn't start that evening. The date was set for the following week, and an exalted Ronald Barker returned home to a mixed reaction from his parents: wanting to swap the relative security of the bank and a respectable career in the making for the insecurity of the theatre astounded his mother, while his father accepted it would be wrong to try and shatter his son's dream of becoming a professional actor. Clearly, though, he wanted Ronnie to stand on his own two feet at this crucial juncture in his life and wouldn't support him financially in his quest – he'd be on his own. Fortunately, Ronnie never had to turn to his father for financial support as he began to make headway, albeit slowly, in the adult world.

Once Ronnie had tendered his resignation at the bank, the manager of the Westminster Cowley Road branch, Mr Graham, did his utmost to persuade him to stay, believing he was making a rash decision. He knew, however, where his young employee's real interests lay: in the theatre, as Jim Tallett confirms. Tallett was a couple of forms below Ronnie at the City of Oxford High School and, on leaving, took up a post at the Cowley Road branch. Recalling his first day at the bank, he says, 'I started on a Monday, and having been introduced to the half a dozen staff, the manager – a man very much of the old school of bank managers – took me to one side and said, "Now then, Tallett, I hope you're going to prove a more reliable junior than your predecessor was; all he thought about was acting at the Playhouse." Ron had left on the previous Saturday.'

Leaving home for the first time, giving up the warmth and security of a close-knit family for unsalubrious digs in a strange environment wasn't too daunting for Ronnie, because he was moving to realise his new-found dream of becoming a professional actor. That goal would be achieved when on Monday, 8 November 1948 he began working as an assistant stage manager at the Manchester Repertory Company in Aylesbury. The company's programmes boasted, 'This is the oldest established repertory company in England, dating from 1908 when Sir Lewis Casson, Dame Sybil Thorndike and Basil Dean were young members. Since then it has produced many famous players, in recent times Miss Wendy Hillier who has been a screen and stage success in Bernard Shaw's plays, and during this recent war a popular member for three years was Noel Johnson, better known as Dick Barton on the radio. This is the famous company who are now making the County Theatre their headquarters. A fine company with a proud record.'[1]

Ronnie found digs in a small cottage, but a lack of heating, particularly with the onset of winter not far away, and no bath made it far from ideal. But beggars can't be choosers, and with little over a shilling from his weekly wage packet left after his rent and other expenses had swallowed up most of his earnings, he returned home regularly to enjoy the luxury of a bath and to wash his clothes. Fortunately, the dreariness of his lodgings was bearable because he was working flat out at the theatre. Being assistant stage manager meant involvement in virtually every aspect of preparation, and with the company being a weekly rep, with a different play being rehearsed and performed every seven days, everything was a mad rush.

With a meagre budget, many of the props had to be borrowed from all and sundry, including local shopkeepers. One of Ronnie's tasks was to collect props and he'd regularly be seen pushing a barrow around Aylesbury's streets seeking favours. Costumes, if period, would be hired; otherwise it was every actor's responsibility to supply their own clothes. Luckily, Ronnie owned a blue pin-striped suit, which was frequently seen during his time at the County Theatre. Operating on a shoestring meant everyone – and not just the assistant stage manager – had to pitch in and help get each play off the ground. Hanging posters around the town advertising the latest and upcoming productions was another task in an already crowded timetable, involving rehearsing for the following week's play in the mornings, prop-gathering in the afternoon and performing the current production in the evening.

Working in repertory theatres was extremely hard work, very tiring and poorly paid, but the chance to play a host of characters from all walks of life, even though the swift turnaround and shortage of rehearsal time meant errors on the stage were inevitable, was invaluable. For a green actor like Ronald Barker it was a sterling apprenticeship, affording him the chance to nurture his largely untapped talent for character portrayals and funny voices. Sadly, repertory theatre has largely disappeared from the theatrical map, resulting in today's actors losing out on the chance to learn the trade the old-fashioned way.

Ronnie enjoyed the medium from day one. He told me, 'Reps were wonderful because people came to see what actors and actresses were doing that week; often, they were more interested in the performers than the plays. It was before television, really, and audiences were much less sophisticated then, very naïve. So I got into rep and really started to enjoy it.'

Although arduous at the time, Ronnie acknowledged the value of the effort and commitment expended during his repertory days – even if, financially, the rewards were a pittance.

'Fortunately, study was never difficult for me, so when I worked on television it wasn't hard focusing on a thirty-minute script, because I'd had so much experience in rep. I did two hundred plays in rep: one hundred in two years at Aylesbury and Bramhall, which was one a week; and with a play being two and a quarter hours, which you have to study in a week, that's forty minutes of script a night to learn. Then I got into Oxford Rep, which I'd always wanted to do, and stayed four years. They were doing plays fortnightly so that's twenty-five a year, so another hundred plays over the four years.'

Ronnie's professional stage debut was in J. M. Barrie's *Quality Street*, a four-act comedy featuring two sisters who not only open a school for blue-blooded children but face the arrival of love in their lives. In the play, first staged in the UK at London's Vaudeville Theatre in September 1902, Ronnie was given a small part of a young officer, Lieutenant Spicer. Sadly, the local papers didn't carry reviews for the Manchester Repertory Company's stint at Aylesbury, but Ronnie was full of nerves before his first appearance, even though his time on stage was brief. With an aptitude for learning lines, he was soon word-perfect and quickly settled in with the other performers in the company, including Alan Jones, Edwin Morton and Lucy Craig.

Leading up to Christmas 1948 Ronnie appeared on the cast list of J. B. Priestley's farce *When We Are Married*, playing Gerald Forbes; although he was busy with his assistant stage manager duties for subsequent productions, copies of the theatre's programmes indicate that Ronnie didn't make it on to the stage until that year's pantomime, *Red Riding Hood*, playing Trunch, a village policeman, alongside Patrick Fegan's Punch. No performance was staged the previous week to allow for extensive rehearsals for the panto which began on Monday 27 December and included a performance for around five hundred Aylesbury children on New Year's Eve, guests of the Aylesbury Children's Santa Claus Fund; each child received a shilling and ice cream on departing the theatre.

With the usual Christmas festivities to consider in addition to rehearsing and performing the panto, it was a struggle for the cast to contemplate *Treasure Island*, which kicked off on Monday, 1 January 1949; adding to the strain was Ronnie having to play three roles, including Ben Gunn in the latter stages of the play. The sheer lack of time prevented him learning the part adequately and he 'went to pieces'[2], staggering to the end of the scene by ad-libbing. Such problems happened in the high-pressure environment of weekly rep.

Some discrepancies appear regarding dates and timings leading up to the repertory company's closure at the County Theatre. Precise details such as dates can obviously be remembered incorrectly. In Ronnie's autobiography *It's Hello – from him!* he recalls dates or periods of time which don't tally with the theatre programmes and the company's regularly placed newspaper adverts plugging upcoming plays, held in the archives of the Centre for Buckinghamshire Studies, based in Aylesbury. Any differences are understandable because, as Ronnie acknowledged in his 1993 book *Dancing in the Moonlight*, he retained few records from this period of his career. In an interview with Bob McCabe for his splendid authorised biography, Ronnie said it was in the fourth week of his professional career that he played a chauffeur in *Miranda*, a role in which he discovered his metier: making people laugh. But delivering those few comedic lines – if the repertory company's adverts in the local rag, the *Buckinghamshire Advertiser*, were correct – didn't happen until the production week beginning Monday, 7 February 1949. The amusing story concerning a young man who brings home a mermaid had fascinated London audiences for months and went on to entertain Buckinghamshire audiences, too, with Diana Granville playing Miranda Trewella, the mermaid, and Ronnie as Charles, the chauffeur. Such was the significance of the response elicited from the audience, the memories would remain with him until the day he died. He once told me, 'I can remember that first laugh now. I can hear it.'

Another play of significance during his Aylesbury days was *The Guinea Pig*, in which he played the lead role, Jack Read, a tobacconist's son who wins a scholarship to a prestigious public school. Warren Chetham-Strode's successful 1946 play was adapted for the big screen by Roy Boulting, who also directed the picture with Richard Attenborough cast in the lead role. Playing the fourteen-year-old schoolboy on the Aylesbury stage, nearly a year after its cinematic release, was Ronnie. The play was performed at the County Theatre from the 17 January 1949, with Ronnie reprising his role at the seaside for a week in the spring.

Dodging the April showers, he pulled his raincoat tight as he confronted the bracing wind for his five-minute stroll from his digs at 75 West Parade to the Pavilion Theatre, Rhyl, on the north-east coast of Wales. Such was the success of *The Guinea Pig* in Aylesbury that W. Armitage Owen, the repertory company's director, who also had a branch of his rep performing at the Pavilion, wanted to stage the absorbing play in Wales. Once again, Barker played the lead role, now earning the ample sum of around six pounds. The show began on Monday, 4 April, finishing the following weekend, with Ronnie reporting that he never returned to Aylesbury. Among the archives at the Centre for Buckinghamshire Studies, however, theatre programmes reveal *Just William*, a three-act play based around Richmal Crompton's schoolboy character, being performed at Aylesbury from the 18 April 1949, with Ronnie not only back as stage manager but playing Egbert Huggins, too. The following week, though, turned out to be the company's last. In Norman Cannon's play *He Walked in Her Sleep*, Ronnie's role was a character called Geoffrey Deacon. The programme carried a message from W. Armitage Owen. Titled 'Farewell to Manchester Repertory Company', it read:

'Dear Theatre Patrons,

It is with sadness that I have to tell you that my Company will be moving from this theatre at the end of this week. This decision has been caused by my business interests in the North, which make it essential that our activities in future be confined to that region. After all, it must be remembered that we are a Manchester organisation and our return to Manchester is only a matter of time.

During the year we have been in your charming town we have made numerous friends and have been supported loyally by the theatre lovers of this district. In return I hope my

Company have given the pleasure and entertainment we all require as a relaxation from the cares of modern life. If they have succeeded in doing so I shall feel that our long run in Aylesbury has been worthwhile and we shall leave, with great reluctance, yet happy in having done something worthwhile.'[3]

The tradition of weekly repertory at the County Theatre continued when Tom Wright's company The County Players performed *The Rose Without A Thorn* from 9 May. It's unclear what precipitated the decision to move, but rumours were rife that the company had struggled financially for some time; in fact, it's equally unclear why the disparity between Ronnie's accounts of this period contradict what the Aylesbury programmes show; perhaps through the mists of time the precise details were a little hazy or could it be that the programmes were printed in advance, assuming Ronnie would have been back from his Welsh jaunt? Ultimately, it is just fine details in the emerging career of a young repertory actor who was approaching his twentieth birthday. What is certain is that as holidaymakers headed for the deckchairs and beaches of the seaside town of Rhyl, Ronnie and the rest of the Manchester Repertory Company found themselves unemployed.

Everyone bade farewell to each other, in most cases never to work together again. Ronnie's only contact was with a girl named Juliet, who'd moved from Aylesbury to become assistant stage manager with the Rhyl company. Ronnie writes at length about their relationship in *Dancing in the Moonlight*. In some cases, he used fictitious names in the book. As there is no reference to a Juliet in any of the programmes, it can only be surmised that he adopted a different name for her in his writing. Romance had already blossomed by the time they were reunited in Rhyl. After the company's closure, they kept in touch, with Juliet spending several days at Ronnie's home in Oxford before their paths headed in different directions. By the time Ronnie next saw her, she was performing in repertory at a West Country theatre and dating another young actor; it was clear Ronnie's time was over. He commented, 'She had been much too young and so I suppose was I. It was a wild and immature liaison, but never to be forgotten.'[4]

After leaving his seaside digs at West Parade, with no sign of work on the immediate horizon, he returned to the comfort of his home in Oxford, which by then was 4 Oliver Road, with the family having moved from 23 Church Cowley Road. Six months' unemployment followed, the longest period he'd spend 'resting' in his career. But Ronnie wasn't one to sit around twiddling his thumbs. After rushing to the local newsagent each week to buy *The Stage*, the industry newspaper, he scoured the 'situations vacant', applying for any suitable positions; time and again he was rejected for jobs, including entertaining at Butlin's. With nothing in his pocket, he was desperate to earn a wage and eventually found employment not as an actor but an orderly at Wingfield Hospital, Oxford. Working alongside him was old friend Ivor Humphris, who also secured work at the hospital when not acting. He recalls, 'We'd push trolleys around and clear up in the operating theatre.'

Ronnie's duties also took him to Wingfield's swimming pool, helping patients receiving polio remedial therapy. The number of polio cases in Britain reached epidemic levels during the 1940s; in one particularly bad year, 1947, nearly eight thousand cases were confirmed, ten times more than the previous yearly average; instances remained in the thousands into the next decade, leading to widespread panic. Iron lungs, used to assist patients with breathing difficulties, were a feature of many hospital wards. Initially, Ronnie found the work distressing, but learned to cope with the upsetting scenes encountered daily. His blossoming comedic talent helped to inject a touch of humour into the desperate lives of the polio sufferers. When Sister wasn't prowling the ward, Ronnie and a colleague entertained in a variety of ways, including picking up empty bed pans and pretending to strum banjos as they strolled up and down the ward, bringing a welcome smile to the patients' faces.

Despite gaining satisfaction from punctuating the grim atmosphere inside the Wingfield ward with moments of light relief, much to the patients' obvious delight and appreciation, Ronnie was desperate to return to the theatre. But it would be six months before he walked on to the stage in May 1950, as a new recruit of Frank H. Fortescue's Famous Players, a repertory company based at the Tudor Theatre in Bramhall, Cheshire – now a suburb of Stockport but, back then, a village. In the meantime, his resilience and tenacity in the job market paid off when, upon applying to an advert in *The Stage*, he was invited to an interview with Cardiff-born Clifford Williams at a location in London's Haverstock Hill.

The following Thursday, Ronnie strode along the wet pavements of north-west London to be greeted by Williams, who later became a director at Stratford's Royal Shakespeare Company. Williams told Ronnie about his latest project: the launch of the Mime Theatre Company, which he planned to take out on the road. Experience in mime wasn't a prerequisite, much to Ronnie's relief, and before long a job offer was on the table, paying £6 a week. The news made Ronnie exultant; he could, at last, return to what he enjoyed best – even if it was breaking new ground, having never mimed before in front of an audience. Handing in his notice at the hospital, Ronnie enjoyed the Christmas festivities at Church Cowley Road before packing his suitcase once again.

As 1950 dawned he set off for digs in London, anxious to begin the intensive three-week training period before the six members of the company set out on tour. The weather was bleak and from an early stage it was clear the company's future was, too. The prospects of a long assignment weren't good as a brief and scattered tour of Wales began in the north, focusing on schools and towns that didn't possess their own theatre. The small team lugged the scenery with them from town to town, but as bookings tailed off and wages were slashed, Ronnie knew it was only a matter of time before the Mime Theatre Company would be read its last rites. To make matters worse, Ronnie was struck down with a severe bout of flu while in Cardiff, confining him to his fridge-like digs at 22 Clare Street with little to eat.

Eventually rejoining the company, everyone travelled south to Cornwall, where the inevitable finally happened: the company folded after performing at Penzance. Stranded over two hundred and fifty miles from home, Ronnie faced the prospect of making his own way back to Oxford: with the company coffers empty, save enough cash to buy five of the six performers a ticket home, Ronnie drew the short straw. With hardly a penny to his name, he had no alternative but to hitch a lift, all the way back. Fortunately, being April, the nights were getting longer, but it still took nearly three days to get home, between catching lifts and walking, reaching the door of his parents' house in time to attend his elder sister Vera's wedding.

Just when it seemed like his stop-start acting career had reached another hiatus, he was en route to Bramhall, Cheshire, marking the advent of a fruitful and portentous period.

Chapter 3

Three weeks after arriving back in Oxford, to the familiar task of browsing *The Stage* newspaper's 'situations vacant' column, Ronnie was on his way to the Tudor Theatre in Bramhall, Cheshire, where he remained for the next fifteen months; it was a period during which, in Ronnie's opinion, he began learning his craft in earnest.

In the 1940s and '50s repertory theatre in Britain, particularly the north, was dominated by two impresarios: Harry Hanson and Frank H. Fortescue. While Hanson had his Court Players, Fortescue ran his Famous Players, both operating tough schedules which, at some venues, involved twice-nightly shows. Like Hanson, Fortescue controlled several acting companies within the 'Famous Players' umbrella, one based at the Tudor Theatre, Bramhall. A former cinema, this impressive building dressed in the period's distinctive black-and-white design stood on a street corner and had been converted into a repertory just after the war. Sadly, it was demolished in February 1961 and the site, situated on the corner of Woodford Road, Birch Road and Maple Road, has since been occupied by various retail outlets, including Superdrug.

Joining the company as stage manager and junior character actor, Ronnie stepped into the shoes of Roy Dotrice, who was on his way to becoming an award-winning actor of stage and screen; Dotrice was a hard act to follow. Also in the company, as leading lady, was Patricia Pilkington, who'd later make her name as fiery-tempered, woman of the world Elsie Tanner in *Coronation Street*. Someone who'd play a pivotal role in the shaping and direction of Ronnie Barker's career was leading man Glenn Melvyn, whom Ronnie, in his autobiography *It's Hello – from him!*, credited with teaching him almost everything he knew about comedy – a rich accolade, indeed. One thing Melvyn taught him, which he put to good use over two decades later in Roy Clarke's hilarious sitcom *Open All Hours*, was the trademark stutter utilised so beautifully whilst playing miserly shopkeeper, Arkwright. Melvyn used the stutter when playing a character called Wally Binns, who appeared in various Melvyn-penned productions, including the 1955 film *The Love Match*, alongside Arthur Askey's Bill Brown. The comedy concerned two football-mad engine drivers who got into hot water after tearing home in their train to avoid missing a match. Binns then featured in two sitcoms, both Jack Hylton productions for Associated-Rediffusion, beginning with *Love and Kisses*, a spin-off penned by Melvyn. The five-part series, which aired between 4 November and 2 December 1955, was based on a summer stage show with Askey's Bill Brown quitting the footplate to run a pub. Among his customers was Alf Hall, a milkman played by Danny Ross, and, again, Wally as his stuttering assistant. Then, in March 1959, Alf and Wally were back for a further twenty-six episodes in *I'm Not Bothered*, in which Melvyn later offered Ronnie Barker a small role.

Ronnie learnt much during his fifteen months at the Tudor Theatre, sensing, too, that he was making headway, albeit slowly, as an actor – again, thanks in part to Glenn Melvyn, with whom Ronnie would socialise occasionally. 'We were friends, he was fun to work for and with, but Glenn wasn't easy on me,'[1] recalled Ronnie. As stage manager, Ronnie was, again, responsible for securing props for the various plays; at times it was a difficult task cajoling people into lending the company everything from table and chairs to vases and glasses. Occasionally, Ronnie would struggle back to the theatre with a plethora of props, only for Melvyn to admonish him for bringing unsuitable items.

Like most repertory work during this period it was a hard slog for little financial reward. But by now Ronnie had learnt all about frugality, the ways to survive as an aspiring actor just beginning his career. With money tight, he'd often pop to the Tudor Café, hoping to pick up a bit of food on the cheap. Ronnie and his fellow performers were regular visitors to the café, situated above the theatre's entrance hall. Frequented by locals, too, it was a busy little tea room, run by the Davidsons. Their daughter, Betty, was in her twenties and remembers those days well, especially with Ronnie regularly turning up eager to source props. 'He'd frequently come in to borrow items, perhaps a standard lamp, vase or coffee table. Also, round the side of the theatre was a small antiques shop and he'd often pop there to get items, too.' That wasn't the only thing the penurious actors asked for, as she recalls. 'Ronnie and his colleagues would come in, asking for scraps of food or old bread that we'd be throwing away, but which they could toast; they would often cadge free leftover food.' They would also try and save a few pennies, now and again, in other ways. 'Occasionally, they'd sleep in their dressing rooms,' says Betty. 'They had digs in Bramhall, but when they couldn't afford to pay the landlady they would sleep in the theatre.' Reflecting on her time at the café, she remembers Ronnie as 'dark haired and chubby' and, in her company, never giving a 'hint of his comic potential'. She adds, 'He was quite a serious young man.' Betty recognised the amount of hard work which went into producing a different play each week. 'On Saturday night, when the final performance of the current play had finished, they had to change the scenery for the next production, so everyone would be busy clearing the old and putting up the new – it seemed to go on all night. It was a hard life.'

Plays usually ran from Monday to Saturday, with two performances on the final day. Although no programmes or documentation exist at the Stockport Local Heritage Library, it would appear that Ronnie made his debut in either the crime thriller *The Shop at Sly Corner*, written by the then MP Edward Percy, or *The First Mrs Fraser*, a comedy written by St John Ervine. But it wasn't long before his name – still Ronald, of course – began popping up in reviews published by the local paper, the *Stockport Express*. At the end of October 1950 the company performed *Secret Lives*, a thriller written by Zelda Davees, the then leading lady and wife of the company's leading man and producer John Pickering-Cail. The critic complimented the Fortescue Players for their 'excellent performance'.[2] The play was described as a fascinating story of a father's domination over his family, oozing mystery, suspense and natural domestic comedy. The reviewer noted Hilary Dean, as the rebellious daughter, gave one of her best performances, and Ronald Barker and Eric Howard were very likeable as their sons.

As the curtain rose to greet the beginning of a new year, the Players began rehearsing Ronald Wilkinson's comedy drama

Mountain Air. Wilkinson, a practising doctor, novelist and play-wright, wrote the play, set in Switzerland, in 1948. Spotlighting a Swiss doctor – played by Barker – desperate to speak fluent English, he's aided by his wife, who invites four British strangers to their home. Unfortunately, each possesses their own personal problems. By now, rather than simply seeing his name mentioned in the local rag's review, Ronnie's contribution to the production was singled out for particular praise, highlighting his growing prowess in the comedy field. 'John Pickering-Cail's production makes the tale skip light-heartedly along, while Ronald Barker's impersonation of the doctor provides some of the funniest moments.'[3]

Six weeks later and Ronnie was the only actor whose perform-ance was mentioned in a positive light – it's sad, however, that the critic couldn't get his name right. Regarding the Fortescue Players' version of Terence Rattigan's 1944 play *Love in Idleness*, which was first staged at the Lyric Theatre, London, he wrote, 'Robin Barker, as the returning son, gives a very creditable performance and makes full use of expression acting.'[4] Ronnie's laudable performances over the coming months, until his departure in August 1951, were recog-nised increasingly by the anonymous theatre critic. In Lionel Brown's *There's Always Tomorrow* he was 'particularly good as the tactless priest'.[5]

Many of the qualities that would, in time, shape Ronnie Barker, the performer, were beginning to reveal themselves, such as his talent for characterisations. Special praise was, again, bestowed upon him for his performance in the three-act comedy, *What Anne Brought Home*, with the critic writing, 'Acting honours, however, go to Ronald Barker for his performance as Sam Bennett. This young actor took this character part in his stride.'[6] Shortly after, the *Stockport Express* carried a short potted biography of Ronnie, the fourth in a series titled 'Tudor Personality', offering to his growing band of followers in the locale an insight into the 21-year-old's life and career. The journalist wrote, 'In addition to being a very capable actor, Ronald Barker is also responsible for some very fine contributions to the décor, being of more than average talent as a painter. He is held in affection by audiences for his effective performances, and by fellow artists for his cheerfulness behind the scenes, where some of his best work must remain unknown to those "out front".[7] A string of glowing notices followed, culminating in a farewell notice in the *Express* on 2 September 1951. After taking his final curtain in Martin Flavin's comedy *Too Young to Marry*, the local critic, classing Ronnie as one of the most popular members of the company, informed readers that he was moving on; revealing that he'd become a dab hand when it came to the baize, the journalist wrote, 'During his stay in Bramhall he has made quite a name for himself at billiards, and at the conclusion of last Saturday's performance of *Too Young to Marry* he was presented with a billiard cue by an admirer.'[8] It seems it was a leaving present from the company, including the backstage crew, who, despite being close to the breadline, pooled any available cash they could spare to bid farewell to their friend.

Ronnie's spell at Bramhall had been an important learning curve, affording vital experience on the stage and allowing him a glimpse into the future, realising that goals he may have regarded as unreach-able in the past were, in fact, attainable, if he got the breaks, enjoyed the luck and continued to progress professionally. At this stage, not a man to map out his career or set strict objectives way into the distance, Ronnie's aspirations were rather more modest, inasmuch as he wanted to progress steadily, becoming adroit in whatever he was working on at the time before moving on; like any thespian he had dreams, one being to work at the Oxford Playhouse at some point, but he grew quietly determined; an assuredness in his own capabilities and skills would develop over the coming years. But the way he realised his dreams would always be carried out quietly, respectfully and with dignity.

It's clear Ronnie's contribution during his Bramhall days was appreciated by critics, fellow actors and local audiences at the Tudor Theatre, but a letter from his old Oxford chum Ivor Humphris heralded the next phase in a blossoming career. Ivor and their mutual friend Michael Ford were working at the Oxford Playhouse – Ivor dividing his time between assisting in the publicity department, where duties included cycling around the city pinning up publicity posters, and playing small roles in the occasional stage production. His friend's letter was full of news and started Ronnie ruminating about what life must be like, working back in the city where he not only grew up but began his theatrical journey with the Theatre Players. Whereas he was currently in weekly rep, the company based at the Oxford Playhouse was performing fortnightly rep. To actors in weekly rep it must have seemed a luxury having so much more time to rehearse and polish roles, rather than the helter-skelter schedules associated with a weekly turnaround.

On one of Ronnie's fleeting visits to Oxford from Bramhall, he met Ivor and Michael Ford, the latter suggesting that if he wanted to try his luck at Oxford, he should drop a line to the director, Frank Shelley. In the meantime, Ford would put in a good word, in the hope it would encourage Shelley – real name Mario Francelli – to offer Ronnie a chance: the plan worked. Frank Shelley, who directed the repertory company between 1946 and 1954, was in his early thirties when he took on the role; one of the changes he oversaw was turning the company into a fortnightly rep, a move he undertook with severe reservations, as he explained in March 1951 at the end of the first year of the new practice. 'When the council decided to go over to fortnightly production I had serious misgivings. All repertory theatres stand or fall – in the long run – according to the number of their regular supporters, people who make a habit of attending every, or nearly every, show. It seemed that to double the run of each production would halve the number of regular supporters expected in any particular week. Nevertheless, since going over to fortnightly we have made not an enormous but a respectable profit.'[9] Actor Donald Hewlett, a leading man at the Playhouse during this period, says, 'Frank was very eccentric, but a good director and organiser. He didn't act a lot, but when he did he'd occasionally let himself go – it was a bit over the top.'

That same year, 1951, Frank Shelley also opened the Playhouse Theatre School. He enjoyed nurturing growing talent and another young performer he'd help organised time off from the Tudor Theatre to return to Oxford for the interview. Unfortunately, it didn't go entirely as Ronnie had hoped. Although Shelley was able to offer a job, it was in the Playhouse's publicity department and he'd have to suffer a 50 per cent pay cut: £3 a week was the offer on the table. Having been informed there were no vacancies for actors, Ronnie faced a dilemma: he'd just managed to get his foot on the first rung of the acting ladder, receiving worthy praise from various quarters at Bramhall in the process. Accepting Shelley's offer could, of course, eventually lead to an acting debut at the Oxford Playhouse, but nothing was certain; to top it all, his already miserly wage would reduce significantly. Before making a decision he had to consider whether staying at the Tudor Theatre would outweigh any benefits reaped from returning to Oxford. After much musing Ronnie was disappointed about the lack of an acting job but knew he'd at least be able to enjoy the benefits of living back at home – with all its comforts, such as home-cooked food – and would be in the company of his long-time chums. Coupled with a long-held wish to one day work at the Playhouse, the draw became too strong and in August 1951 he left Cheshire behind and returned to his home town.

Ronnie regarded the Oxford Playhouse as the mecca of all theatres. 'It played a very important part in my life from the time when, at the tender age of sixteen, I had my very first date with a girl. I took June Bowles to see a play there,'[10] he told writer and historian Don Chapman, who has penned an authoritative history of the Oxford Playhouse. 'We sat in the back row of the stalls, and I remember having just enough money to pay for the two seats, two ice creams, a small presentation box of Milk Tray chocolates for me to give to June, and subsequently help her to demolish, and the bus fares home.'[11]

During his days as an amateur actor he would occasionally frequent the Playhouse, sometimes with Ivor Humphris. At one point, Ronnie was drawn to the talents of actor John Moffatt and actress Patricia Gilder, who were performing at the venue. One September afternoon, while wandering through Oxford's traditional St Giles' Fair, which runs for two days every September, he spotted the performers enjoying themselves on the merry-go-round horses, a regular feature of the annual fair. 'I begged them for their autographs, without offering either pen or paper. I finished up with their names scrawled upon a scrap of paper picked up from the floor; in the absence of anything better, Patricia Gilder provided an eyebrow pencil.'[12]

It wasn't the only time he came face to face with actor John Moffatt. One evening, not long before launching his own professional career at Aylesbury, Ronnie and Michael Ford were in the audience on the last night of Frank Shelley's production of *Cinderella*. He recalled 'clambering on stage to present the ugly sisters with a bottle of brown ale each!'[13] In hindsight, Ronnie realised it was an embarrassing and 'ill-judged'[14] act, made worse by Ford putting his foot 'through the wire mesh covering part of the orchestra pit, destroying a large section of it. The two ugly sisters took it in good part – John Moffatt, splendid as always, and his rather more subdued partner, a very young and very slim Tony Hancock.'[15]

Ronnie, who was to spend the next four years at the Oxford Playhouse, started with his new company in September 1951, distributing posters, handing out 'throwaways' plugging the next production and even employing his own artistic talents to design posters. 'The publicity department was housed in a little office left of the front of the building, overlooking Beaumont Street, on the opposite side to where Frank Shelley's office, the Holy of Holies, was situated. Between these two rooms was the celebrated coffee bar, which at the time seemed to be the hub of amateur theatre in Oxford. It was a constant attraction. Kenneth Tynan would be there, with his strange clothes and yellow hair, and future theatrical and TV moguls Brian Tesler, Ned Sherrin and Michael Codron.'[16] Ronnie saw plenty of the Playhouse, supplementing his wages earned assisting in the publicity office by working as a stagehand, helping dismantle sets at the end of a production – usually on Saturdays – and replacing them in time for the next show. Such work happened at night, leaving Ronnie exhausted by the time dress rehearsals started on Sunday morning.

Fortunately for Ronnie his spell in the publicity department was shortlived and within weeks he was applying the greasepaint again, initially for a walk-on role in *The Sport of Kings*, which ran for twelve nights from 1 October. His first real speaking role was a small part in *Pick-Up Girl*, a courtroom-based drama set in New York, staged a fortnight later. The play, written by Elsa Shelley, who'd become worried about juvenile delinquency among young girls, necessitated the recruitment of extra performers. With Frank Shelley needing to assemble additional personnel for the 1944 drama, set in a juvenile court on a late June afternoon, he was more than happy to listen when leading man Donald Hewlett made a suggestion. 'I met Ronnie one day when he was putting advertising posters in windows around Oxford,' says Hewlett, who has worked extensively on screen and stage, but is best known as Colonel Reynolds in Jimmy Perry and David Croft's popular 1970s sitcom *It Ain't Half Hot, Mum*. 'I had a word with Frank, the manager, and he put him in the plays and Ronnie never looked back.'

Although he had made a walk-on appearance, the chance of his first speaking part came out of the blue. Ronnie was just preparing to leave the publicity office to press more flyers upon the Oxford public, when Shelley entered with the kind of offer he had hoped to hear. He jumped at the chance to play musician Peter Marti, who is smitten with the accused and comes to the defence of fifteen-year-old Elizabeth Collins, who is charged with being a prostitute. Grabbing the script Shelley asked him to read, Ronnie studied his part intently before heading to the director's office; realising this was a golden opportunity to show his boss what he could do, he read his lines with gusto, every syllable clearly pronounced. Investing such effort into the reading did the trick and Ronnie found his name pencilled in to the cast list – it was a start, at least.

On Monday, 15 October 1951 Ronald Barker made his professional debut in a speaking role at his beloved Playhouse; it was the start of many such appearances at the venue, where he soon appreciated the benefits of fortnightly rep, a format more conducive to turning out quality productions. 'The vibes were excellent; and the luxury of having a fortnight rather than a week in which to rehearse and prepare a play was extremely comforting. Above all, the thing that made it work for me, the one single factor more important than all the rest, was being able to work week in, week out with the same actors, the same directors, the same staff. This is what brought the audiences in. Show after show, seeing their favourites giving a hundred different performances as a hundred different characters in a hundred different plays. Performances as characters that this week made them laugh, next week brought a tear to their eye or a chill to their marrow; and as they streamed from the theatre into the night air, with saddened heart or aching ribs, they already eagerly awaited the delights in store for them next week. Those days were without question my happiest times on stage – the Playhouse my theatre of all.'[17]

Just as his performances at the Tudor Theatre, Bramhall, had started to regularly catch the local theatre critics' eyes, his performance in *Pick-Up Girl* didn't go unnoticed, either. Although the time spent on stage was brief, he executed the role so adeptly that his colleagues complimented him, as did the *Oxford Mail*'s critic, S. P. B. Mais, who wrote: 'Among the minor characters, I was particularly impressed by the quiet, earnest manner of Ronald Barker.'[18]

Ronnie, meanwhile, was impressed by the strikingly attractive actress playing the lead role of Elizabeth Collins. Her name was Christine Pollon and she was the wife of the company's leading man, Donald Hewlett. Although, as Ronnie admitted, 'Being married to Donald she behaved very properly,'[19] it didn't stop him falling in love with her. He enjoyed being in her company and grasped every opportunity possible, even when out and about around the streets of Oxford. Of Ronnie's feelings towards Pollon, pal Ivor Humphris says, 'Really, I think he was just infatuated with her; after all, from what I recall, he got over her quickly.'

Until that point, though, his feelings grew stronger, not helped by being cast together in *Point of Departure*, playing two people in love. The play was staged in May 1952, some seven months after he'd first glanced across at Pollon in that mock courtroom in *Pick-Up Girl*. One afternoon in his dressing room the tears began rolling down his cheeks as he realised that his adoration of the actress would lead nowhere. He felt compelled, however, to inform Hewlett of his feelings. 'Ronnie knocked on my dressing-room door and said he was very sorry because he'd fallen in love with my wife. I replied, "Don't worry, you'll get over it." I wasn't offended, I was too busy learning my lines,' chuckles Donald. 'Ronnie was serious, though, but the play came to an end soon after, so I wasn't unduly worried.'

Despite the obvious advantages of fortnightly rep in terms of preparation time, it was still a busy timetable, leaving little opportunity for socialising. But when the chance arose, fellow actor Francis Matthews – who later found fame playing Francis Durbridge's amateur detective Paul Temple, making over fifty appearances as the BBC sleuth between 1969 and 1971 – would often eat in the evenings at the nearby café, The Lantern, in High Street, accompanied by Ronnie, Donald Hewlett and Christine Pollon, after which they wandered down the road for a drink at the Randolph Hotel. Regarding Ronnie's feelings towards Christine, he says, 'It was obvious to all of us in the company that he was very fond of her.'

Soon, though, Ronnie's attentions were drawn to another actress, this time called Jean, although dates of when they first met are uncertain. During the early 1950s Frank Shelley launched the Playhouse Theatre School, indicative of his predilection for nurturing young talent aiming to make the grade in the world of acting. More experienced members of the regular cast were required to run training classes occasionally, which is how Ronnie first met Jean, then a part-time student. According to Ronnie, their romance blossomed and they became engaged, although their relationship fizzled out when, eventually, their careers took them in different directions. But it wasn't his only connection with a student from the theatre school: there's the oft-told story involving one Margaret Smith, sister of the Smith twins with whom Ronnie had studied during his brief spell at architectural college. Margaret – the award-winning actress we all know as Dame Maggie Smith – would eventually reach the highest echelons of the acting profession. It's remarkable, therefore, to think that Ronnie once tried persuading the then rather green Margaret Smith to consider quitting acting for another career.

Francis Matthews, like Ronnie, would help the aspiring students. He didn't, however, share Ronnie's views on Maggie Smith's acting prospects. 'She was about seventeen when I met her with Ronnie and I thought she was brilliant, even then. Ronnie and I were roped in to teach the students for nothing as part of our acting contract.' Francis is surprised, however, to hear about the misguided advice Ronnie offered Smith. 'It's odd because I remember us all saying what an extraordinary girl she was at the time. The drama school was set up to make money for the theatre by attracting young local people wanting to enter the profession.'

Francis joined the rep in 1952 and enjoyed having Frank Shelley at the helm, whom he regarded as a 'vibrant and quite brilliant director'. Ronnie was already an established member of the cast by now. 'Being a university city, the repertory company at Oxford had more claim to intellectual pretensions than some theatres. When we were there, though, the regime was not too intellectual. Although we did classic plays, we also did commercially successful plays and comedies.' Ronnie was recognised as the company's primary character man. 'He was playing strong character roles, even though he was a young man. He did a lot of accents, too; his talents for voices and different characterisations were obvious, even then.' That wasn't the only quality Francis noticed in Ronnie. 'He was fabulous at learning his lines and one knew he was going to make it big – he was too good not to. He was always promising to be an important actor – he certainly had all the makings of one, including a hugely wide talent.'

The aforementioned play, *Point of Departure*, is one that will always stick in Francis Matthews' mind – purely because he was convinced the role of Orphée, played by Ronnie, should have been given to him. 'I was furious when he was cast in the only role, in all the time I was at Oxford, that didn't need a character actor,' recalls Francis. 'It was a love story about two lovelorn youngsters, with the male role having been played by Dirk Bogarde in London. I thought that part should have gone to me and remember having a little contretemps about it – nothing serious. Ronnie had been playing all these funny character roles and the one leading role that I thought was bound to be mine was given to him. I was a juvenile actor, playing the young romantic role, and this was the best romantic role of the season – and I didn't get it. Ronnie wasn't a juvenile romantic actor at all. He couldn't understand why they'd given it to him, either, and we both eventually had a laugh about it. That apart, he was quite extraordinary in everything he did.'

With his medical record, which included having contracted nephritis in childhood and surgery to resolve a problem with a tubercular gland during his teenage years, preventing his call-up for national service, Ronnie could focus his efforts on improving as an actor, showing Frank Shelley that he was right not to send him back to publicity duties after making his company debut.

Chapter 4

Reflecting on a long career, Ronnie Barker identified particular milestones which he regarded as major advances towards the success that followed. These crucial moments helped lift him to the next level of performance and the furthering of his theatrical and televisual career. 'The first was getting in to the little tatty rep at Aylesbury, and getting into Oxford was another. That's where I met Peter Hall, who took me into the West End, which is another milestone.' Others included meeting David Frost and becoming part of *The Frost Report* team. 'He signed us up for Paradine Productions, his own production company, which led to us joining the BBC and doing sitcoms and *The Two Ronnies* – we were under his contract for five years doing that. *The Two Ronnies* brought us into the limelight with the Beeb, bringing fame and fortune, and that was the last milestone.'

The four years – or thereabouts – Ronnie spent at Oxford Rep, his longest spell at one venue, was, therefore, fundamental in his development; it was here that he matured as a stage actor: at Aylesbury he was starting out on his professional career and his performances were raw; at Bramhall he began to shape and structure his work, but during the Oxford years, as he moved towards his mid-twenties, his performances began to show growing maturity and greater promise. His confidence was such that he'd occasionally partake in a little fun with Frank Shelley, on the odd occasion they appeared in the same play. Actress Caroline Turner, née Barrington-Ward, has fond memories of working with Ronnie early in her stage career at Oxford. 'A wonderful actor and a very sincere, kind and considerate person, Ronnie was a delight to work with, and very good at telling funny stories – in fact, he was as much fun off stage as on.' She may not have been thinking that, though, the evening Frank Shelley and Ronnie decided to play a little game. Now, able to recall the story with a smile, she says, 'They kept feeding each other pretend lines that were nothing to do with the script – it was terrible. They'd cut out great chunks during the performance, in which I was playing a small part. Sometimes, Frank would do it out of sheer devilment. The poor prompter was all over the place. Not knowing where to prompt, she just shut up. Ronnie was quick enough to know what Frank was up to and would sometimes go along with it.'

Before 1951 drew to a close, Ronnie's performance as Hendricks, a minor role in John Willard's black comedy *The Cat and the Canary*, was singled out for praise, despite his efforts being handicapped by a badly fitted wig. Meanwhile, the Christmas production, Brandon Thomas' farce *Charley's Aunt*, which was first performed in the late nineteenth century, attracted glowing reviews and went down a storm with the punters. Originally intended to run from 26 December until 12 January, the play had the theatre packed to the rafters each night, resulting in its run being extended twice, finally closing on 2 February 1952. A local critic classed the show as 'good holiday fare',[1] adding, 'One of the best bits of characterisation was that of Ronald Barker, who gave a very satisfying and faithful picture of the old type of college scout who was accustomed to being tipped with money borrowed from himself'.[2] A critic in *The Stage*, meanwhile, described Ronnie's performance as Brassett as well-observed and immaculate.

The play's success was aided by a clutch of actors, including Ronnie and Donald Hewlett, actively promoting it around the area. 'Ronnie and I, in costume, journeyed in a pony and trap around Oxfordshire, signing autographs and generally promoting the play – we even went to the Witney blanket factory,' recalls Hewlett, who visited local villages donning the Aunt's costume, while Ronnie, as the college scout, wore trousers, blazer and gown.

As the months rolled by, Ronnie's personal life reflected his stage performances, everything running smoothly with his girlfriend Jean, other than a brief fling with a mysterious woman who remained anonymous in Ronnie's memoirs, *Dancing in the Moonlight*. Jean's father, however, had no reason to think that his daughter's relationship was anything other than serious, so floated the idea of Ronnie quitting acting and working in the family business, a gentlemen's outfitters. But Ronnie didn't give it a moment's thought: never in his wildest dreams would he contemplate packing in acting, especially with such positive notices continuing to flow in. His performance in Christopher Fry's 1948 three-act play *The Lady's Not for Burning* drew a round of applause from the audience, while his portrayal of a dim-witted schoolboy in Ian Hay's comedy *Housemaster* was deemed a 'small triumph of make-up and acute observation',[3] by a critic in *The Oxford Magazine*, a well-respected varsity publication founded in 1882 and issued weekly during term time.

For the traditional Christmas offering in 1952, Frank Shelley wrote and staged *The Cinderella Story*, his own musical fantasy based on the classic fairy story. Running until 24 January 1953 it received mixed reviews, one critic believing it had virtues and faults in equal measure. Another left space in his review to laud Ronnie's perform-ance, writing, 'The comic honours of the evening, however, undoubt-edly go to Ronald Barker . . . his portrayal of a lascivious but mentally defective Spaniard is an exquisite cameo and brought the house down. The young actor is a great asset to the Playhouse.'[4]

During the three years they worked together, Ronnie forged a friendship and successful professional relationship with the eccentric but astute director Frank Shelley. Therefore, it's no surprise that the announcement of the director's impending departure in 1954 left a sense of melancholy among the company. As everyone assembled to begin rehearsals for A. A. Milne's *The Dover Road*, which ran for twelve nights from 8 March, Shelley broke the news. It was thought that the present theatre incumbents were suffering financial difficul-ties, so new owners – in the shape of The London Mask Theatre Limited, run by Thane Parker – were taking over the reins at the Playhouse. The change was explained to patrons in the programme for *Don't Listen, Ladies!*: 'An association has been formed with the London Mask Theatre, which, like the Oxford Repertory Players, is a non-profit-distributing organisation . . . by this association the Playhouse will have the advantage of additional financial backing, but will not lose any of its present powers in the direction of policy.'[5]

Thane Parker was bringing with him his own director, Hugh Goldie, resulting in Shelley's departure in April 1954. But he wasn't the only casualty: the incoming regime instigated major restruc-turing among management and performers alike. Sweeping changes on the acting front brought a completely new set of faces, with only two performers – Ronnie Barker and Derek Francis – retained from Shelley's era. Thane Parker ran The Young Elizabethan Theatre Company, an acting company whose personnel made up the lion's share of the newly formed Oxford Playhouse Company. The new arrivals were under the artistic direction of several directors: Colin George, Toby Robertson, Hugh Goldie and a young, enthusiastic Peter Hall, who would subsequently play a crucial role in Ronnie's stage career.

One of the early plays the new company tackled was *Carrington VC*, the first time it had been staged outside London. Written by husband and wife playwrights Campbell and Dorothy Christie, the play had been an instant hit on opening at London's Westminster Theatre in 1953; within a year, not only would it be regularly performed outside the capital to appreciative audiences, but a big screen adaptation was in the making with David Niven playing the leading role, Major Carrington, in the tense military drama where a distinguished and decorated major is arrested for embezzling £125 of his unit's funds.

Hugh Goldie directed the Oxford production, which opened on 17 April 1954 for thirteen nights with Michael Bates in the lead role. Despite a long stage and film career, Bates would always be remembered for his roles in two long-running sitcoms: Blamire in *Last of the Summer Wine* and Rangi Ram in *It Ain't Half Hot, Mum*. Ronnie, meanwhile, played Sergeant Crane, a supporting role, while a new face at the Playhouse, Frank Windsor, a member of The Young Elizabethan Theatre Company, was cast as Bombadier Owen; however, that was only after their roles were switched, as Windsor, who became a regular in police drama *Z Cars* as Detective Sergeant Watt, recalls: 'Sergeant Crane was the army sergeant who came in and out, carrying coffee, all with rigid military precision. Bombardier Owen, meanwhile, was the lowest of the low, but he was the sympathetic guy who thought the world of Carrington.'

When the scripts were handed out, Hugh Goldie had cast Ronnie as Owen and Frank as Crane. Later that afternoon, Ronnie sidled up to Frank, saying, 'Look, I don't know how to put this, but I don't want to play Bombadier Owen. I hate those boring, sympathetic, tearful characters. I want to play Sergeant Crane because I think I could get a lot of fun out of him.' That comment surprised Frank. 'After all, it wasn't really a funny play. He asked if I'd be prepared to swap, which I didn't mind doing because I thought Bombadier Owen was a lovely part and didn't see much in Sergeant Crane, walking backwards and forwards with a tea tray – it didn't appeal to me. But Ronnie was different: he spotted things that lowlier people, like me, didn't,' says Frank, smiling. 'He had a much clearer idea, even at this early stage, of where he wanted to be. If the roles had been reversed and I'd thought that I wanted to play Owen, I couldn't have gone to another actor and asked if they minded swapping – I wouldn't be that confident about what I could do with the part. But Ronnie didn't have any qualms about it. He knew he could get something out of it.' Ronnie was always examining roles, dissecting them in his mind to see if an extra ounce of comedy or drama could be found. Such a degree of intense study set him apart from many contemporaries. 'He could have got something from Crane that others wouldn't have even bothered to think about,' says Windsor. 'He was much more aware of where his talents lay and directed himself in that line. To recognise that side of your abilities at that age is talent in itself.'

Before swapping roles in *Carrington VC* they had to broach the subject with Hugh Goldie, but that didn't daunt Ronnie, who'd become increasingly self-assured in knowing what would work best for him and the team, and whose steely determination came to the fore inside Goldie's office. 'Ronnie went to Hugh, dragging me along, and asked him. Hugh replied: "No, no, I've done the casting." Ronnie was adamant, though, and, I think, became rather heavy, saying he wouldn't play the character. In the end, Hugh gave in and I played Owen, which I thoroughly enjoyed, especially as I received favourable reaction.' Ronnie's performance, however, evoked an even better response from the audience and critics. 'Ronnie stole the show every time he came on,' recalls Frank. 'How he managed to extract humour from the character, I'll never know, but he made it an absolutely hysterical performance.'

One might question whether Ronnie Barker was right trying to eke out comedy from the character, considering the play's serious theme. Surely, an actor playing for laughs in a tense military court-room drama would have been incongruous and frowned upon by some, particularly the director. That wasn't the case, as Frank Windsor confirms. 'From the very first entrance it established that Sergeant Crane was the light relief and Ronnie continued like that all the way through, doing all the music-hall gags, such as making the tea cups rattle on the saucers as he walked across the stage. Every time he came on he was an absolute hoot and got applause on each exit.' As for Hugh Goldie's view on Ronnie's display, Windsor says, 'When Hugh realised what was happening, he made the rest of the cast play to it.'

Infusing the performance with touches of comedy wasn't univer-sally appreciated by the critics. Reporting in *The Oxford Magazine*, a reviewer reminded readers that the majority of the cast were new to the Playhouse, save 'those two favourites from the recent company, Ronald Barker and Derek Francis'[6]; he thought that the company carried the show without any signs of weakness. Across at the *Cambridge Daily News*, the critic enjoyed how Ronnie executed his role in a production regarded as 'superb theatre'[7], believing Ronnie's portrayal of Sergeant Crane supplied 'a good deal of comic relief'[8]. But while Montague Haltrecht at the *North Berkshire Herald* remarked that the new Playhouse company was brimming over with enthusiasm and acknowledged what Barker was trying to achieve, he didn't feel it worked, noting that 'the inevitable low comedy part gives Ronald Barker a chance to be very funny, but he is a thought too conscious of his own powers to amuse'.[9]

Although Ronnie could turn his hand to dramatic roles just as easily as comedic interpretations – proven by the variety of parts he'd already performed in repertory theatres – it was clear he had an innate talent in the field of comedy. He admitted, however, that at this stage of his career he didn't see himself as a comedy specialist. Frank Windsor recalls their time in Nikolai Gogol's *The Government Inspector*, a satirical play penned by the Ukrainian playwright and novelist, and adapted by Peter Hall. 'It was a very loose translation and we had a very makeshift set. I remember Ronnie walked on the set and went to sit down, only to bang his hand on the side of the set. He remarked, "Bed and board, you see!" He was always coming out with comments like that, it was constantly gag, gag, gag – anything to get a laugh.' It didn't take long for Windsor to realise that here was a man suitably confident in his own abilities. 'It proved to me that there were actors who knew what they could do much better than others – and Ronnie was one of the lucky few. He understood comedy and could do things that were different and special; he knew how to make things work on several levels.'

A critic at the *Cambridge Daily News* was equally enamoured of Ronnie's playing of the servant, Yosif, writing, 'Deliciously comic was the pleasant guile of Ronald Barker . . . who entertained with a rich rustic characterisation which never over-played, and a competent music-hall manner groomed for scene-stealing.'[10]

But it wasn't all work and no play. The close-knit group of performers often socialised and, in September 1954, Ronnie had a wedding to attend – and it wasn't his own. A new arrival at the Playhouse was Ann Elsdon, whose whirlwind romance with company member Derek Francis, who became one of the industry's busiest character actors, led to them tying the knot after just three months. Ronnie was asked to be best man and duly obliged: he was an obvious choice, says Ann. 'Derek and Ronnie had worked together some time. My husband had very little in the way of family and his friendships were all in the theatre.' Whether the best man experienced more butterflies in the stomach than either the bride or groom will never be known, but years later, while being interviewed on Michael Parkinson's chat show, Ronnie said he couldn't ever be a best man because he wasn't any good at making speeches. Although she can't remember, Ann is convinced Ronnie's best man speech would have hit all the right notes. 'He would have given a wonderful speech, but I don't remember a thing because I was in a complete cocoon of excitement.'

On the eve of the wedding, Ann's family saw her performing in Barré Lyndon's *The Amazing Doctor Clitterhouse*, a crime story which played for three months on Broadway. Her relatives, however, were in for a shock as they took their seats at the Playhouse. While Ann was playing Daisy, a prostitute, Derek was Benny Kellerman, a heavily made-up pimp. 'They were absolutely horrified and extremely relieved to see Derek the next day not looking anything like the character he was playing.' That morning, as Ronnie made his way to the Church of St Mary Magdalene, just a few yards from the Playhouse, he gathered his thoughts, ready for his speech in front of the guests at the reception party being held at the Playhouse. After the celebrations were over, the newly-weds were chauffeur-driven by Ronnie's father, now running his own taxi in the area, to their honeymoon cottage in Witney, owned by ex-Playhouse stalwart Donald Hewlett.

Ann's spell at the Oxford Playhouse lasted just under a year and she soon slotted in to the routine of fortnightly rep. Arriving for rehearsals at ten each morning, the company worked through until around 4 p.m., giving everyone a couple of hours before the evening performance. While one play was running, rehearsals began on the following week's production. It was frenetic at times, but Ann still relished her days at Oxford and enjoyed being in the company of Ronnie Barker. 'Wherever Ronnie was during his life, he created a friendly, jokey atmosphere – he was a really lovely man.'

Unlike some actors who can be single-mindedly protective of their own little patch within a play, selfishly looking out for what's best for them, Ronnie was always willing to help others reach their highest level of performance. For Dame Eileen Atkins, Ronnie was her 'favourite actor in the company'. Eileen, who in addition to a successful acting career co-wrote the period dramas *Upstairs, Downstairs* and *The House of Eliott* with Jean Marsh, was just twenty and fresh from drama school on joining the repertory company; her time at Oxford was brief, though. 'I was cast by Hugh Goldie, but Peter Hall came in and sacked me; he was quite right to do it, because I was very rude and didn't want to be an ASM [assistant stage manager]. I was very resentful of people who'd been to university [like Peter Hall], because I'd wanted to go myself.'

Eileen, who would work with Ronnie again in a BBC production of *A Midsummer Night's Dream*, screened in 1971 as a *Play of the Month*, remembers him offering advice about how she could add a touch of realism to her waitress role. 'I came on stage with my tray high in the air, thinking it would attract attention. Ronnie turned to me, saying, "Look at waitresses, they couldn't hold the tray like that all day." He showed me how to hold it and was very nice. It was Ronnie and another actor, Tony Church, who made life bearable for me while I was at Oxford.'

After rehearsals, Tony and Ronnie would occasionally nip off to the local café, inviting Eileen along. 'Now, as an older woman looking back, it vaguely entered my head that they might have asked me out for sausage and chips sometimes because they had an eye on me, but I was too dim and innocent to have known if there was anything behind it,' laughs Eileen, who'll never forget a sketch Ronnie drew for her. 'He used to do little drawings and, knowing I was bored stiff because all I seemed to be doing was prompting, he did this sweet little drawing of me on a stool, asleep, with my finger falling off the end of the book. Ronnie was terribly nice.' Eileen is equally complimentary of his acting abilities. 'I knew immediately that he was a good actor. He was often quiet, never actorish: if you met him in the street you'd think he was a bank manager.'

Another actress who remembers sharing a snack with Ronnie and other members of the company was Christie Humphrey. She enjoyed being in his company, too. 'He was well-covered rather than thin – not fat, just stocky. He wasn't good looking, but there was something attractive about him – attractive about his personality. He had an awfully nice face and was amusing most of the time. I'm sure he had his serious side as well, but was always extremely pleasant.' During the occasions they frequented the local eatery, Christie witnessed how Ronnie's engaging personality won him an admirer. 'All of us would have supper at a little restaurant in the centre of Oxford. The lady who ran it, a nice woman probably in her fifties, absolutely fell for Ronnie – she couldn't do enough for him. It was perfectly obvious she adored him, but he was worth adoring because he was so lovely.'

So many of his Oxford contemporaries speak highly of Ronnie and his performances, which were always embellished with fine details other performers may not have considered or worried about. Ronnie was always intent on producing the best possible performance, going the extra mile to turn a decent showing into a top-rated offering. Being inquisitive and observant helped in this respect. 'On one occasion, Ronnie, myself and others were sitting around. In those days, women had loose powder in their compact and we'd often have a discreet look to see if we appeared as lovely as we thought we were,' says Christie. 'I remember putting the puff on my face. Because the powder was loose, you always held it away while snapping it shut. When I closed my compact, Ronnie saw me do it and turned to the man beside him, saying, "See, that's another thing they do." Meaning, I'm going to keep that in my mind, just in case the little detail is useful sometime. Of course, he would go on to impersonate women so beautifully in shows like *The Two Ronnies* and noticing such things helped.'

Christie was impressed by Ronnie's performances, particularly when she appeared alongside him in *Theatre 1900* in November 1954, a production containing Victorian songs and based around the Player's Theatre's *Late Joys*, which had become part of our theatrical history with Don Gemmel controlling the gavel and making a commentary – the role handed to Ronnie. The production was a cornucopia of music-hall numbers, which Ronnie enjoyed, once he'd overcome his nerves; over two decades later, song-and-dance routines were to play a fundamental part in *The Two Ronnies*. As chairman, Ronnie talked to the audience, introducing the various songs and acts and coming up with the linking material, of which the lion's share was ad-libbed. Christie enthuses, 'He was first class and marvellous with the gavel. Even though he'd said similar things on previous nights, his performances were always exemplary.'

Trawling through the archives and old newspaper cuttings, it is striking just how many times local critics pinpointed Ronnie's performances. Examining these reviews, a common theme is his versatility in turning his hand to any type of character. A review published in the *Oxford Mail* in 1954 was typical of those printed. The play was Frank Harvey's *Saloon Bar*, which ran for eleven nights during October 1954. The *Mail*'s critic, acknowledging the building tension as the play progressed, wrote of Ronnie's portrayal of Joe Harris, 'Particularly well cast was Ronald Barker. He not only consumed his beer with gusto but gave a first-rate performance as the loud, vulgar, know-all salesman with an unfailing supply of quick repartee and boisterous geniality.'[11]

Over the years, Ronnie created a large gallery of characters from which he could pick when appearing in a play, television series or sketch show; when he found the one he wanted he could simply pluck it from the shelf. Take *The Two Ronnies*, where around seventy hours of mainly sketches demanded a plethora of characters from both Ronnies. Ronnie B., however, was a master craftsman in this department and equally adept at transforming himself into a yokel, tramp, government spokesman, partygoer, vicar or doctor. Interviewed by Terry Wogan on 15 January 1983 for his popular BBC1 chat show, Ronnie explained that when he developed a character he began with the voice, from which the face emerged. During an interview clip on the 1997 documentary *Ronnie Barker – A Life in Comedy* he acknowledged that many contemporaries believe one should begin from inside the character. That wasn't Ronnie's way, and it certainly didn't weaken the quality of his characterisations. As he pointed out, 'If it was good enough for Laurence Olivier, it's good enough for me. That's how he used to do it, he started with the make-up.'[12]

Considering the positive press coverage he enjoyed during nearly four years at the Playhouse, it's no wonder his departure in January 1955 was celebrated with glowing tributes from local reviewers. The *Oxford Mail*'s Laurence Marks wrote, 'Many people will be sad to hear that Ronald Barker, one of the most popular actors of the last few years in Oxford, has to go further afield.'[13] And days after he'd left, *The Oxford Magazine*'s critic stated, 'Ronald Barker, whose progressive development as an actor of considerable versatility has been one of the outstanding features of Oxford Playhouse productions, recently left to tour in *Hot Water*, a new comedy by Glenn Melvyn.'[14]

The door closed on his Oxford days with a musical play for children and adults alike. In Angela Ainley Jeans' *Listen to the Wind*, directed by Peter Hall, he played two roles: a character called Popple and a gypsy. Leaving the Playhouse, which he'd regarded as the mecca of all theatres, wasn't a decision Ronnie took lightly – after all, he'd appeared in around one hundred plays, covering all genres, and had honed his skills as a performer during this time. But he was becoming restless. It was time for a new challenge and as events unfolded he wasn't short of offers, either, with one originating from an unexpected source.

Towards the end of *Listen to the Wind* Ronnie was sitting in his dressing room when there was a knock on the door. A backstage employee informed him that Alastair Sim – one of Ronnie's idols – was at the theatre, asking to meet him. Believing the man had got his wires crossed, Ronnie was stunned to discover that it was, in fact, the veteran actor of stage and screen, famous for, among other titles, the *St Trinian* films, who was waiting to see him. The esteemed actor was impressed with Ronnie's work and wanted to offer him a part in his upcoming London play. Under normal circumstances Ronnie would have delighted in accepting the chance to appear alongside one of his all-time heroes, but he'd already agreed to join his friend Glenn Melvyn on a pre-London tour and wouldn't go back on his decision, even for Sim's exciting opportunity.

Within five months of leaving Oxford, and swapping home life for digs, Ronnie would be making his West End debut. It was another major step in the advancement of his career, and it was Peter Hall, with whom Ronnie had worked so successfully at Oxford, who'd bring him into the capital of theatreland. Before then, however, he toured between January and May 1955 with Glenn Melvyn. His early mentor had penned *Hot Water* – a sequel to his earlier production *The Love Match* – for Arthur Askey and himself. To test it out before Askey stepped into the lead role, Melvyn took the show out on the road, asking Ronnie to join the cast, offering him the role of Mr Seymour, a referee.

Ronnie recalls being asked to play sidekick Wally Binns, the stutterer, in the pre-London tour, but when during the third week of its tour the comedy arrived at the Palace Theatre, Westcliff, Southend, in February, the theatre's programme shows Harry Littlewood playing Binns. Of course, it may be that Ronnie swapped roles before the play entered London or had appeared as the character at the start of the tour.

Actor Ian Gardiner, who became something of a cult figure playing Reginald Molehusband, dubbed Britain's worst driver in a public information film from the 1960s and 70s, played Percy Brown in the farce. Recalling Ronnie as the referee, he says, 'Ronnie was fine because he was such a good actor, but I didn't think he had the maturity to play the referee.'

Arthur Askey, who'd step in to the lead role when the play, renamed *Love and Kisses*, later arrived in the capital, turned up at a Southend performance and was mobbed by autograph hunters. He'd have been pleased with the reception the play received from the local audience, with a critic reporting that it had them 'rocking in their seats with laughter'[15]. Over at the *Southend Times and Recorder* the reviewer felt the play was well cast, particularly Littlewood as Wally, 'stuttering through life'[16].

Times were changing for the 25-year-old actor. Having clocked up nearly four years at Oxford, Ronnie left the 'city of dreaming spires', a phrase coined by nineteenth-century poet Matthew Arnold. Although the period had been immeasurably enjoyable and professionally rewarding, Ronnie had achieved just about everything possible during his time at the Playhouse. He'd begun hankering after a new challenge, one which would help propel his acting career forward. Although *Hot Water* wouldn't necessarily provide that, it did offer him a few months' work before the West End beckoned.

Chapter 5

On a late spring morning in 1955, Ronnie Barker hurried along London's Great Newport Street. On his agenda was the inaugural rehearsal of Eugene O'Neill's monumental trilogy *Mourning Becomes Electra*, which was being staged at the Arts Theatre Club. Ronnie had recently completed the short pre-London tour of Glenn Melvyn's northern farce *Hot Water*, which had provided much-needed income, but he regarded his new engagement in the O'Neill play as a big break, and he had Peter Hall to thank for offering him his London debut.

Hall was impressed with Ronnie the first time he set eyes on him at the Oxford Playhouse. 'My initial impressions were that he was a natural clown, but one who, in many respects, was an actor rather than a clown, so the paradox was there from the beginning. He was a wonderful straight actor, but also had the ability to make audiences laugh by doing almost nothing. That was evident, even in those early days.'

When Hall became resident director at Oxford, he swiftly regarded Ronnie as a 'valuable member' of the repertory company. 'When we did *Listen to the Wind*, a musical for children, at Oxford, Ronnie played a wicked gypsy and did a tango – it was a fantastic dance number. He was a man of great prowess, even though still in his twenties, and his ability for character studies and voices was clearly evident.'

Peter Hall left the Oxford Playhouse to help run the Arts Theatre and when he considered the casting for his first play, one person he wanted was Ronnie. 'When I moved to London I always knew I wanted to work with Ronnie Barker again, because he was a fabulous talent, although nobody really knew him at that point.' It didn't take Ronnie long to adjust to the London stage. 'Had events been slightly different in their synchronisation, he might still have been at the Arts when *Waiting for Godot* arrived – he would have been wonderful in that,' says Peter Hall. 'He had a very natural talent as an actor, his timing was there – even in the 1950s.'

Mourning Becomes Electra premièred on Broadway in 1931. Set at the house of a Puritan family in New England in April 1865, the production is split into three plays: *The Homecoming, The Hunted* and *The Haunted*. Totalling around thirteen acts, it's renowned as a lengthy production. This, combined with the fact that it normally demands a large cast, means that over the years it hasn't been staged as frequently as the playwright's other work.

The play opened on 9 June with a cast containing, among others, Beckett Bould, Mary Ellis and Mary Morris, bringing to life a production based on the trilogy of Agamemnon plays by Greek playwright Aeschylus. Its duration – a staggering four and a half hours – didn't seem to deter the opening-night audience from enjoying the show, which *The Times*' critic classed as 'well acted and directed remarkably well'[1], although he regarded the third play, *The Haunted*, as the most successful. The length of the play was also mentioned in the *Observer*'s review, but the critic noted 'a sort of war-time camaraderie pervades the audience, as if they were sharing a shelter during a prolonged air raid'[2]. Of course, it wasn't just the watching audience enduring an unusually long show, it was draining on the actors, particularly those seen regularly throughout the three parts, like Mary Morris. Ronnie, however, only appeared in parts two and three, but would bump in to people heading home while he was only just arriving for work.

While the jury was out in terms of the merits of O'Neill's story, the majority of journalists praised Hall's style of direction, particularly considering the limitations of the small stage on which he delivered the product. Although Ronnie's contribution in two small parts – the Chantyman and bystander Joe Silva – wasn't singled out for particular praise (something he'd become accustomed to in repertory), the thumbs-up were given by most in terms of the cast's collective performance, which included Welsh actor Ronald Lewis playing a lead role, who would die so tragically in his early fifties.

Before the end of December Ronnie would add two further Peter Hall shows to his growing list of credits, appearing – for a time – simultaneously in *Summertime* at the Apollo Theatre and *Listen to the Wind*, back at the Arts Theatre. Ronnie played a farmer in Italian playwright Ugo Betti's comedy *Summertime*, which was adapted for the British stage by Henry Reed. Set in an Italian village and the surrounding mountains during a warm summer's day, the play opened at the theatre on Shaftesbury Avenue on 9 November, with Dirk Bogarde and Geraldine McEwan in the leading roles, although when Bogarde became ill three weeks into the run, Nigel Stock stepped in to take over as Alberto.

The play's opening night was met by a lukewarm reaction from the following day's newspapers. Most acknowledged that *Summertime* was arguably the lightest of the playwright's works, with Milton Shulman in the *Evening Standard* rating it as a 'fluff of a comedy almost aggressive in its search for innocent charm. Unfortunately, it has tired us out long before it eventually finds it.'[3] Over at the *Daily Express* John Barber felt it was a comedy 'spun out of treacle and thin air'[4]; he did, however, believe the result – a gentle tale of love – was favourable, stating, 'they combine most of the time into the prettiest of candy-floss'[5].

Again, Ronnie's role was minor and, understandably, his contribution wasn't acknowledged in any of the nationals. Whereas he'd become a big fish in a relatively small pond at Oxford and preceding repertory theatres, he was now a small fish in a big pond: the London stage, where performances were analysed by a host of national theatre critics. But Ronnie was patient, because his qualities as a stage actor were apparent to all those around him; his enthusiasm and energy couldn't be questioned, either, as the unfolding weeks proved.

On 16 December Peter Hall was back at the Arts Theatre for the opening night of their Christmas offering, *Listen to the Wind*. After being loaned out to work on *Summertime* until the show was up and running in the West End, Hall was able to concentrate entirely on a play he'd directed at the Oxford Playhouse, in which Ronnie played two roles, including the dancing gypsy, his last outing for the repertory company. When, one afternoon, Hall remarked, jokingly, that it was a shame Ronnie couldn't play the role again, this time at the Arts Theatre, Ronnie didn't see any reason why not. Hall reminded him that he was already committed to *Summertime*, but Ronnie had a solution. As his appearance at the Arts Theatre only involved him in the first act, he had just enough time to change and nip round to the Apollo Theatre on Shaftesbury Avenue, to dress and make-up, ready to perform in the third act of *Summertime*. 'So he ran between the theatres and appeared in two plays at once,' says Peter Hall. He maintained this hectic schedule for six tiring weeks, buoyed by the thought that not only was it extra experience but more money, too, bringing in a combined weekly wage of nearly £30.

Although Ronnie had only played small parts since arriving in London, Peter Hall had no doubt he was heading for the big time. 'If you met Ronnie in the bar of a pub behind the Oxford Playhouse you would have thought he was a trainee estate agent or bank manager, but after two minutes' conversation you knew you were in touch with a very anarchic spirit who'd be making you laugh.'[6]

Someone who found Ronnie making her laugh frequently during rehearsals was Miriam Karlin, who played Miranda, a mermaid, in the play, before going on to establish herself as one of the industry's busiest stage and screen actresses. She, like Hall, also recognised Ronnie's obvious talents. 'It was 1955, prior to anyone having heard of him, but I knew from that performance that he was going to be a big star. He just had star quality about him.'

Miriam regarded *Listen to the Wind*, which played to packed houses, as a 'bloody good show', although she'll never forget one incident which, thankfully, Ronnie didn't experience. The play, which premièred to notable success at the Oxford Playhouse before entering the West End, was a children's musical and, therefore, several children were among the cast. During one matinée, in a scene where Miranda the Mermaid was fished up by two children, Miriam noticed in her peripheral vision that one of them had her hands over her mouth. 'I thought, I'll kill that child afterwards, because she's laughing and shouldn't be.' However, it wasn't laughter she was desperately trying to keep in. 'She took her hands away and threw up over the stage – there was a mass of diced carrots and other vegetables all over the place!' Soon, Miriam found herself alone on stage. 'Nora Nicholson, who played the grandmother, pulled up her crinoline and ran offstage, together with everyone else, leaving me to sing a number while walking up and down the stage, trying to make the audience believe that the pile of vegetables wasn't there.' When the number finally finished and Miriam could head backstage, she was met by a mystified chaperone asking what had happened. 'I showed her my messy fish tail and screamed, "This is what's happened!" She replied, "That will be her lunch, dear. She's such a pro she wanted to go on." I told her it wasn't professional to throw up on the stage.'

The play concerns a group of children kidnapped by gypsies from their grandmother's house in the late nineteenth century. The kids use a spell to summon the winds to rescue them and are carried away to the King of the Winds' palace. The play received healthy notices after its opening night, with Ronnie collecting, arguably, his first mention since moving to the capital. Writing in the *Daily Telegraph*, W. A. Darlington noted that Gillian Webb and Clive Revill formed the spine of the grown-up cast, but added that Ronnie 'scores heavily with an enchanting, unethical song in dispraise of bread and butter'[7]. While the reviewer in *Punch* felt the play deserved to join the 'regulars in London'[8] after its success at Oxford, the *Daily Mail*'s critic, who admitted that halfway through he 'gave up trying to cope with all the plot'[9], still rated the production as a welcome entry in London's Christmas shows.

Listen to the Wind closed on 21 January 1956 and the new year ahead proved to be eventful and memorable on both professional and personal fronts. From a working perspective, not only did Ronnie appear on stage in two productions during the following months but he experienced the media of radio and television for the first time, too; even though his appearances in both were fleeting, it was a start.

His small-screen debut saw him in an uncredited role as a waiter caught up in crossfire during an episode of the adventure drama *Sailor of Fortune*. His screen time may have been brief – most of it spent hiding behind a table – and earnt him less than a tenner, but it was another entry on his CV. The role came his way after he was spotted in the Arts Theatre snack bar. Having worked at the venue in two productions, *Mourning Becomes Electra* and the recently completed *Listen to the Wind*, he'd started to frequent the snack bar, like many other thespians, in the hope he would pick up work or news of upcoming projects. But it wasn't just actors visiting. Silent movie actor-turned-casting director Ronald Curtis, whose office was a stone's throw away, would often find just the person he was looking for at the snack bar when casting a television series or film, such as horror pictures *Tales from the Crypt* and *The Vault of Horror*. On this occasion, he was looking for someone to play the waiter in an episode of *Sailor of Fortune*, a series made for ITV by Mid Ocean Productions, with Canadian actor Lorne Greene, whose greatest successes saw him play Ben Cartwright in the long-running cowboy series *Bonanza*, and Commander Adama in the sci-fi series *Battlestar Galactica*, in the lead role, Grant Mitchell, captain of the freighter, *The Shipwreck*. Although playing the waiter introduced Ronnie to the world of television, it couldn't have made a very strong impression, because in time he forgot much about the series.

By the summer of 1956 Ronnie had made his second television appearance, playing Monsieur Fleury in 'Child of Her Time', the fourth episode of the series *Nom de Plume*. Broadcast on 8 June 1956 it was a run of half-hour plays spotlighting famous individuals known to the world by names other than their own. The instalment in which Ronnie featured focused on George Sand, played by Mary Morris.

While the summer holidays began in earnest and people flocked to the seaside for a well-earned break, Ronnie tried his luck in another area of the profession new to him: radio. During his formative years, the wireless had played a key role in his life, so he was excited as he arrived at the BBC to record *The Floggits*, a comedy series based in a general store and aired on the Light Programme between 1956 and 1958. Its stars were sisters Elsie and Doris Waters, who had become one of Britain's best-loved radio acts. Recruited to supply character voices were Joan Sims, Anthony Newley and, of course, Ronnie. He would also appear in the second series, which hit the airwaves during 1957, but the first season was notable because it is when the shortened Christian name, Ronnie, was used in a cast list for the first time – and director Alastair Scott-Johnson was to blame. Unbeknown to Ronnie, while Scott-Johnson prepared the cast list for publication in the *Radio Times* he abbreviated the name, thinking it sounded friendlier and more inviting than 'Ronald'. Ronnie didn't mind, but a memo at the BBC Written Archives at Caversham, Berkshire, reveals that Ronnie didn't formally request the BBC to use the shortened version in future shows until 5 January 1962.

If the first half of 1956 had been about expanding horizons and experiencing new media, the second was chock-a-block with stage work, beginning with a week in Cambridge – and what a week it turned out to be. Making sure you're seen and being in the right place at the right time are adages which, in Ronnie's case, rang true. Where he'd been hired for a day's television work after being spotted at the Arts Theatre Club, visiting the Buckstone Club, opposite the stage door of the Haymarket Theatre in London, had its benefits, too. Not only did he meet Ronnie Corbett for the first time (more of which later), but it led to him being hired for two plays at the Cambridge Arts Theatre, where he would meet a certain Joy Tubb.

The basement club was a well-known spot amongst the acting fraternity, with people from all corners of the entertainment world dropping in – often into the early hours – for a drink and chat. At this time the club was run by Anthony Knowles, who periodically organised short theatre tours under the company name Buckstone Productions. In September 1956 he took his production company to the Cambridge Arts Theatre with a double bill, kicking off with Wolf Mankowitz's *The Bespoke Overcoat*, an adaptation of Gogol's short story 'The Overcoat', with the action relocated from Russia to the East End of London. After a ten-minute interval, the audience was treated to Somerset Maugham's *The Letter*, set on a plantation in the Malay Peninsula and Singapore, shortly before the war; being such a short play, *The Bespoke Overcoat* was added as a curtain-raiser.

Ronnie's spell in Cambridge was enjoyable for another reason. As he mentions in his autobiography, it afforded him the chance to catch up with his mother, who had moved to Cambridge after separating from her husband. Being a private man, this was something Ronnie chose not to discuss further in his life story.

At the theatre in Cambridge Ronnie played Ranting, an employer, in the opening play and Chung Hi in the second. Also appearing in both productions was Martin Friend, who has since appeared in a host of stage and screen productions, including *The Avengers*, *The Prince and the Pauper* and *Only Fools and Horses*. Martin was a friend of Joy's, who within a year would become Ronnie's wife. 'Believe it or not, I was the person who said before first rehearsal, "Oh, Ronnie, this is Joy Tubb, and, Joy, this is Ronnie Barker." I introduced them in that sense.' Joy was stage director and had a small part playing Mrs Parker, a wardress, in *The Letter*. 'In that one I played Ong Chi Seng and Ronnie played Chung Hi, general dealer,' says Martin. 'We were Chinese and had a wonderful conversation in Chinese, which we invented. How brave it was in Cambridge, where people actually spoke Chinese, to speak gobbledygook to each other and hope it sounded authentic.

'Joy was hearty, fun and a very strong woman – we were quite friendly,' says Martin, who remembers punting on the Cam with Ronnie, Joy and the rest of the company. 'It was hysterical, but a great occupation in the afternoon. I remember on one occasion, Anthony Knowles, who directed the plays, was canoeing, while one of the ladies in the company was standing on the bank, saying, "Oh, let me have a ride." There was a classic moment when he paddled into the bank and she put one leg into the canoe, which immediately began to leave the bank. We could all see what was going to happen, but no one could help.'

Martin has happy memories of his time at Cambridge with Ronnie. 'He was up for fun, a delightful person. Even when he was immensely successful, there wasn't any coldness or big-headedness; he was still warm and bubbly. And his work was such a high standard. He was very good in *The Bespoke Overcoat*. His performances were much bolder. He was never reticent. He always had that brilliant comic actor's ability to engage an audience.'

Ronnie and Joy's friendship developed during the three-week period they rehearsed and performed at the theatre, and it wasn't long before Ronnie was smitten with Joy, who had grown up in a family full of theatrical influences, including an aunt who became a Tiller Girl before joining the Folies Bergère in Paris. Joy began her working life in a secretarial position at the Rank Organisation, indulging her passion for performing with the firm's acting club during the evenings. In 1953, when she heard about a vacancy for assistant stage manager at the New Theatre, Bromley, she applied and was offered the position. Quitting Rank, she trekked across London to begin her job at the New Theatre, only to be informed that the management company couldn't afford to pay her initially. Determined to prove her worth, she worked hard and, before long, had shown she was indispensable and, thankfully, a wage was soon forthcoming.

Joy worked for Buckstone Productions at Cambridge as stage director and actress and hit it off with Ronnie from the first day they met. 'Joy and I were on the same wavelength from the start, though she was seeing another actor at Cambridge called Martin. I set about altering that! She'd be sitting by the prompt book at rehearsals and the more I saw of her, the more I liked her.'[10] The only Martin in the company was Martin Friend, who insists he wasn't dating Joy. 'It could be that Ronnie always had the wrong idea. I'm not so old that I can't remember the young ladies I knew,' laughs Martin. 'Ronnie obviously thought we were closer than we were; we were matey, but weren't involved in any way. I think I fancied a mutual friend who wasn't in the company.' If there had been a misunderstanding it didn't matter in the long run, because it was only a short time before Ronnie and Joy fell in love.

They shared similar interests and laughed at the same things, even when that involved isolated incidents in the play, like the time one of the leads in *The Letter* was nowhere to be seen when the curtain went up one evening. Momentarily, he must have been distracted, perhaps by the numerous phone calls he'd been involved in regarding an offer of work in New York. Neither Ronnie nor Joy was on stage; they were waiting in the wings wondering, like everyone else, when he'd finally appear. Moments later, they were trying their hardest to hold back the laughter, while Martin Friend desperately tried not to give in to the almost overwhelming desire to laugh, too, being one of the unfortunate cast members on the stage at that time. The cause of the hilarity was James Ottaway, playing the solicitor, Howard Joyce, who, on making his entrance, standing with his hand on his hip, announced, 'I'm Joyce!' The audience reacted accordingly and, flustered, Ottaway messed up his next line. 'Instead of telling the leading lady to pull herself together, he demanded, "Pull yourself to pieces!"' laughs Martin Friend, remembering the incident some fifty-four years later.

All too soon, the two plays Buckstone Productions had staged at the Cambridge Arts Theatre came to an end. For Ronnie and Joy it meant a temporary separation, with Joy due to tour as stage manager on two productions, *The Trial of Mary Duggan* and *The Caine Mutiny*, while Ronnie headed back to the West End to play Mr Thwaites in *Double Image* at the Savoy Theatre, after a short pre-London tour. But it wasn't long before they could resume their courtship and while dining at the Royal Court Theatre's restaurant in Sloane Square, Ronnie proposed. Joy accepted and they tied the knot at the All Saints Church in the parish of Harrow Weald, Middlesex on 8 July 1957 – Ronnie was twenty-seven, Joy twenty-four. At the time, Joy, whose full name was Beryl Joy Tubb, was living at 19 Sitwell Grove, Stanmore, Middlesex, but the newly-weds began their married lives in Ronnie's flat at 12 Hampstead Hill Gardens.

Ronnie became a devoted husband and, in due course, father; to him, his wife and family became the most important elements of his life. During his married years he was never the gregarious, party-going type of actor, who enjoyed socialising on the town with a wide circle of contemporaries, preferring, instead, to finish work and rush back to the privacy of his home and comfort of his wife and family. Joy became more than his best friend and wife; she was someone who understood the acting profession inside out and had an ingrained understanding of comedy, just like her husband. She was a staunch supporter and critic of Ronnie's work, as Ronnie once informed me. 'My wife was always at my shows and if you heard only one person laughing in the audience it was her; she was most loyal and has a great sense of humour and would tell me if scripts I was writing weren't working. She was a great, constructive critic.'

Joy's involvement in her husband's developing career was crucial, so it's an apposite moment to reflect on how their solid relationship was seen by those who knew Ronnie, professionally or socially. Richard Briers, who became a friend of the Barkers and worked with Ronnie on television and stage, acknowledges what strength and confidence Joy, who gave up the profession to raise their family, brought to the relationship. While he regarded Ronnie as 'shy' and, at times, 'uncertain', he says, 'Joy is an amazingly strong woman. She was incredible, the power behind the throne. She came to every single television performance he did, and he really couldn't go on without her there. It was obvious that Joy was an immense strength and must have encouraged him – she's no fool. So, from contracts and fees to building his confidence and having complete and utter faith in his talent, she was what they call a bastion – an amazing woman. I don't know if he'd have got so far without her.'

Barry Cryer, who wrote for *The Frost Report* and *The Two Ronnies*, could see what marriage and family meant to Ronnie. 'His family was everything to him and he had a solid marriage: he had a real bedrock of home life. Ronnie wasn't a showbizzy man, but he did throw lovely garden parties at his home in Chipping Norton, Oxfordshire; amazing people used to turn up and he was a great host: the perfect avuncular, beaming host.'

But as Richard Briers points out, Ronnie was always 'very guarded' and protected his privacy intently. Francis Matthews, one of Ronnie's contemporaries at the Oxford Playhouse, adds, 'We knew each other for years, but he never allowed me to have his phone number – and that was common among his friends, only his address was given; he couldn't bear people ringing him up all the time.'

Sometimes he wouldn't even disclose his address. In an interview shown in Channel 4's hour-long documentary *Heroes of Comedy*, transmitted in December 2000, Ronnie's daughter Charlotte talked about her father's wish for privacy. She said, 'It's always been very important to my father that his private life is private, which is why he never gives his telephone number or address out – and we never gave the telephone number or address out as children. We knew that when he was home that was his private time.'[11] Charlotte acknowledged the importance of Ronnie being able to separate Ronnie Barker, the actor, from Ronnie Barker, the private individual. 'I think it's what kept him sane, the ability to say, "This is the performing and this is me, and when I'm me I want to be away from the public eye."'[12]

As he once said, 'Of course – and this is corny but true – I should start to worry if people didn't recognise me. But it would be nice to be anonymous.'[13] The media spotlight wouldn't be shining on Ronnie for a few years yet, so he could enjoy the anonymity for a little while longer. But his life was getting busier and on 13 November 1956, after a few weeks' rehearsal, he stepped on to the Savoy Theatre's stage in the Strand as Mr Thwaites, alongside a host of talented performers, including the much-respected character actors Raymond Huntley and Ernest Clark, actresses Sheila Sim and Zena Dare and, at the head of the cast list, Richard Attenborough, playing twin brothers Julian and David Fanshaw.

Laurence Olivier, Ronnie's idol, presented the show in association with Marjan Productions. Roger MacDougall and Ted Allan's script, based on a story by Roy Vickers, was a clever thriller centred around the brothers whose uncle is murdered for his money. The audience was kept guessing throughout about whether it was just one brother all the time, pretending to have a long-lost twin. The majority of the reviews focused on Attenborough's performance or performances – one critic even suggesting he should be paid two salaries. The show itself was complimented in varying degrees. The *Daily Mail*'s Cecil Wilson felt it 'compromises uncomfortably by being not quite funny enough for a really good comedy, not tense enough for a really good thriller. But at least it kept me curious, if hardly in a fever of suspense.'[14] Someone who would have experienced a 'fever of suspense' was the *Daily Telegraph*'s Patrick Gibbs, who summarised that 'thanks largely to Mr Attenborough's minutely but cleverly contrasted performances and to Murray Macdonald's smooth staging, the essential tension was preserved – and with it our curiosity until the end'.[15]

Chapter 6

Ronnie saw in the New Year still a member of the *Double Image* cast, but by the time it transferred to the St James's Theatre on 4 March 1957 he'd already been released from his contract to appear, once again, for Peter Hall. This time the venue was the Phoenix Theatre on the Charing Cross Road. The play, Tennessee Williams' *Camino Real*, would run for two months from 8 April and it was an ambitious project for Hall. A huge cast of thirty-nine played out Williams' 1953 story, set in a poor Spanish-speaking region with many famous literary characters popping up in dream sequences. Hall had launched his own production company – the International Playwrights' Theatre Company – and assembled some star names for his first show. 'I had a wonderful group of people – Harry Andrews, Diana Wynyard, Denholm Elliott, John Wood and Robert Hardy. It was a very big cast for this showy, epic play. Ronnie had a good part in it.' In fact, he had three roles: Sancho Panza, servant to John Wood's Don Quixote; Nursie, a transvestite working in a brothel; and a tramp called Bum.

Playing Lord Mulligan, a wealthy industrialist, was John Nettleton, who had worked with Ronnie in his Oxford Playhouse days. John, in his twenties, was heavily made-up to play the elderly role, and remembers Tennessee Williams flying over from America during final rehearsal week to meet the cast and watch the play. 'Peter Hall said he was coming along to the dress rehearsal, which put us all on tenterhooks.'

Star of the show was Denholm Elliott, playing Kilroy, the all-American southern boy, but Elliott's confidence was severely dented by a comment from the playwright, as John recalls. 'For an English actor, American accents are hard to do well: southern American accents are particularly difficult. Denholm worked terribly hard for many weeks trying to perfect his southern accent and we thought he did it well.' So did Denholm until Tennessee Williams arrived.

'He saw the dress rehearsal and came on stage to greet everyone. He was very pleasant and said he enjoyed the performance very much. Then he went off to Denholm Elliott's dressing room, obviously to talk to him as leading actor.'

Next day, John Nettleton remembers Denholm arriving at the theatre, looking pallid and unwell. 'We were opening that evening and met up beforehand for notes and a quick discussion. Apparently, the previous night, Tennessee had congratulated Denholm, saying: "I thought it was a very good idea for you to play the part of Kilroy as an Australian." That was a devastating thing to say to poor Denholm, because he was trying so hard to do a southern accent – I don't think he ever got over it.'

John was pleased to be working with Ronnie again. 'Appearing in three parts meant he had a very busy evening, including going into drag to play Nursie – I still remember him coming on in this long, black dress and black wig.' One critic described his role as a 'beskirted bouncer'[1] and donning women's clothes for the sake of his art was something he had become accustomed to in repertory theatre, where actors were frequently asked to play characters of the opposite sex. Appearing in drag also became an integral element in *The Two Ronnies*' success, with Ronnie occasionally dressing up extravagantly for a musical number, sketch or even the popular 1980 serial *The Worm That Turned*. Shown during the eighth series, the two Ronnies found themselves wearing frocks and carrying handbags when women rose to power, forcing men into subservient roles – an obvious dig at the feminist movement.

Ronnie knew, of course, that appearing in women's clothes occasionally was part of his job and that it was a popular segment of *The Two Ronnies*. Nonetheless, it was something he increasingly disliked. Terry Hughes, the original and longest-serving director/producer on the show, remarks, 'He felt uncomfortable doing it, but knew he could do it well, could write it well and understood the value of it within the show; he just didn't like the execution of it.'

In 1983, prior to a new series of the show, he told a journalist that he intended ditching dresses for the upcoming season or, at least, reducing the number of appearances in drag. 'I've grown to hate seeing myself playing a woman, it makes me ill . . . I don't know why, I just feel that it's faintly obscene. But that's just because of my straight background.'[2] It was something he'd felt uncomfortable about for some time, because he had discussed the subject eight years earlier. 'In fact, the only thing I absolutely detest doing professionally is playing in drag . . . it's agony. My wife says it makes her feel sick to see me – although she finds other drag artists hilarious – and Ronnie Corbett says that in a frock I'm positively intimidating. What troubles me, I suppose, is that in drag I'm not myself. To make it work I have to immerse myself in the role, so I'm always glad it's over.'[3]

Ronnie had to put aside his dislikes for the sake of the show when appearing in drag for *Camino Real* until the show ended prematurely on 1 June, not dissimilar to its earlier fate on Broadway, where the production closed after just three months.

After its American failure, Tennessee Williams returned to the drawing board and revised the play, stripping out the 'original nonsense . . . the whole treatment was too crazy'[4], while retaining its theme of fantasy, which still left many people, including critics, struggling to come to terms with the play's basic premise. Regarding its early demise in London, Toby Rowland, a director of the International Playwrights' Theatre Company, blamed high running costs. 'Audiences have been most enthusiastic,' he said, 'and any normal straight play would be happily making a profit on the money we are taking at the box office. We need to play to near capacity to pay the cast of thirty-nine. The technicians and stage staff are legion.'[5]

The play received a mixed bag of reviews. W. A. Darlington, writing in the *Daily Telegraph*, commended the acting and directing, but stated, 'These characters and a score of others are woven into a design which has no settled pattern, but every now and then gives you moments of delight.'[6] At the *Daily Sketch* the critic believed the play contained passion and imagination, but 'There is also much tedium that even the director, Peter Hall, cannot erase. Nevertheless, he has done wonders with a piece that, textually, gropes in the dark.'[7] In fact, it was Hall's directing that occupied most of the lineage in the reviews, with critics interested to see how he coped with Williams' fantastical play; one reviewer wrote that his directing wasn't only ingenious and restrained, but gave the play 'which appears flabby in thought at least a striking physical vitality'[8]. Not only was it, arguably, the playwright's most unorthodox play, but an ambitious project to stage, leaving many theatregoers and critics rather bemused.

Ronnie would be back on the West End stage during the autumn, after another stint on radio, this time his vocal capabilities being utilised in a further six instalments of *The Floggits* and, in August, *The Trouble With Toby*, a product of the Variety Department for the Light Programme. He was heard in two episodes, aired on the 1st and 8th of the month, of a radio vehicle for Richard Lyon – of *Life With The Lyons* fame, the domestic sitcom in which he appeared with his real-life family. In his own series, Richard played Tobias T. Todd, a likeable character who struggled not only to retain a job but pay the rent.

Before the summer was out Ronnie began rehearsals for Jean-Paul Sartre's political farce *Nekrassov*, which was performed at the Edinburgh Festival and on tour before reaching the Royal Court Theatre for its opening night on 17 September. Playing a waitress in the show was Ann Davies, wife of Richard Briers. 'My first job on moving to London was as assistant stage manager, understudy and walk-on in *Nekrassov*. Richard and I got to know Ronnie and Joy, because they'd only been married a few months, like us.' Ronnie was playing Perigord, a newspaperman, and Ann remembers his performance as 'very good'. She adds, 'He was always keen and worked hard – a very kind and lovely man.'

Unfortunately, the critics weren't overly impressed with the French writer's satire on politics and popular journalism – and it wasn't spite behind the frank criticisms filling the newspaper columns. One critic in the *Evening Standard* thought that while the idea was interesting, the playwright's treatment didn't do the play any favours, commenting that 'if the politician in him had not gained the upper hand of the artist, *Nekrassov* could have been extremely funny'[9]. Cecil Wilson of the *Daily Mail* acknowledged improvements had been made to its earlier showing in Edinburgh, but that the play finally collapses in a 'shambles of satire and sermon'[10]. Only *The Times*' scribe filed upbeat copy about the play.

Two months after *Nekrassov* closed at the Royal Court Theatre, Ronnie was opening on the same stage in *Lysistrata*, although this time playing two parts: Drakes, True Leader and Old Man. He remained with the play for its six-week run, and unlike his previous play at the theatre this received favourable comments in the newspapers. The production, regarded by some as the first anti-war play, was based on an ancient Greek tale about Lysistrata, the leader of women.

Played by Joan Greenwood, Lysistrata incites her followers to reject their husbands' advances until the men cease fighting the Peloponnesian wars. A lascivious script with plenty of sexual references, it shocked some theatregoers, and although praised by the Press, it took some effort from Ronnie and fellow cast members to knock it into shape. At first, Ronnie didn't find it an easy play to learn. Not only was it a lengthy script with segments sung to Greek folk songs, but Ronnie worried about how the play would come together. With hours to go before the dress rehearsal, many scenes still hadn't been linked; the smooth transition between the fourteen scenes wasn't to the level he expected and the actors grew increasingly concerned.

Directing was Minos Volanakis, a Greek director who specialised in ancient Greek plays; his pedigree was outstanding but, as Ronnie recalled, 'scenes he didn't like, he would not rehearse'[11]. Ronnie, along with James Grout and others instigated their own rehearsal to sort things out; thankfully, by the time the play opened everything worked like clockwork. Investing extra time and effort to ensure the scenes flowed seamlessly paid dividends with the *Observer*'s critic expressing his pleasure at watching 'the smoothness and ease with which the cast move from speech to song and back again'[12].

One performance, however, was momentarily interrupted when a cloud of leaflets, claiming the play was disgusting, fell from the circle. The protestors were few in number, but made a significant racket. James Grout, however, killed the protest dead and received a round of applause with his appropriately timed line: 'The gods are angry.'

Ronnie didn't agree with the protestors' claims, although he would have had to acknowledge that the play's content did shock some.

Critic John Barber reported that several people had already left the theatre by the second half, because they were so shocked. He wasn't surprised. 'Aristophane's jokes are hair-raising, they are so bawdy. The Lord Chamberlain had stretched a point to pass this version with few cuts – because the play is a classic.'[13] Although he didn't believe Joan Greenwood, in the lead role, lived up to expectations – not that his contemporaries agreed – and admitted the play was raunchy, he rated it a 'superb comedy'[14]. After being staged at the Royal Court until 8 February, it transferred to the Duke of York's Theatre, running from 18 February until 10 May.

Ronnie's diary was reasonably full for the rest of 1958. By the end of the year, he'd recorded his final episodes for *The Floggits* after, allegedly, being dropped from the series when its stars felt Ronnie and Anthony Newley were getting too many laughs. He also worked on radio with Frankie Howerd, not only heard in his Christmas Day show *Pantomania*, but in seven episodes of the comedian's series *Fine Goings On*, which struggled to find its true identity.

After having worked in every other medium, this was the year cinemagoers caught sight – briefly – of Ronnie on the big screen. *Wonderful Things!* was made by Everest Pictures and directed by Herbert Wilcox. Ronnie was cast as an uncredited head waiter. The star of the film, Frankie Vaughan, played a Portuguese fisherman with a complicated love life, but the comedy drama did little for Ronnie's career, save introduce him to the world of celluloid – a world he'd never visit on a regular basis. Except for his performances in the big screen adaptation of *Porridge* in 1979 and *Futtocks End* nine years earlier, Ronnie's film work was restricted to relatively small or supporting roles, mostly inconsequential; in many respects, we never had the chance to see the best of his talents on the cinema screens. He wasn't entirely at home making films, either. Filming is often a drawn-out affair involving being away from home for lengthy periods, the idea of which didn't appeal to Ronnie. Reflecting on the medium, he said, 'Filming is disjointed. It's always a mess with any film. Sometimes you're completing a scene for the end of the movie before you've even filmed the opening scenes.'

In July 1958 Ronnie was onstage at the Lyric Theatre in what would become one of the worst experiences of his professional life. The play, *Irma La Douce*, was first produced in Paris two years earlier. It premiered at the Theatre Gramont and ran for four years. In London, the play was a huge success, too, notching up more than 1,500 performances in nearly four years. A long run, of course, is what every playwright and theatre production company longs for, because it signifies a successful play bringing in the money. Nowadays, during long runs the cast changes from time to time, even though some actors are content to remain with the show, relishing the security.

Ronnie writes at length in his autobiography about his time in the production, acknowledging, rightly, the merits of the play, which became a huge hit this side of the English Channel. In fact, *Irma La Douce*, directed by Peter Brook, received rave notices from the start. The musical comedy concerns a law student who rescues the heroine, a woman of the night, from her unfortunate occupation; to prevent her returning to the streets he impersonates a rich client whose money will be sufficient to keep her, but jealousy creeps in, with dire consequences.

Patrick Gibbs in the *Daily Telegraph* gave it a warm welcome, listing some of its merits as 'originality of subject, gentle humour and great gaiety'[15]. *The Times*, meanwhile, felt that although the first half of the production was stronger than the second, the play kept a 'perpetual tipple of open and more or less sunny laughter'[16]. Praise wasn't universal, however, with T. C. Worsley in the *Financial Times* unimpressed: 'There is no more brilliant raconteur of his day than Mr Brook; and people around me were – to be perfectly fair – slapping their knees and guffawing away, while my head sank lower and lower with aching boredom at this musical tale of a Paris tart . . . You must either be very simple or very sophisticated to be tickled by it. Woe betide you, if, like me, you fall between the two.'[17]

Ronnie played Roberto-les-Diams, a Paris gangster who becomes a friend of Irma. The thought of regular work earning £30 a week appealed, especially as he was a recently married man and felt lucky to have landed the job. He recalled, 'Joy and I danced round the kitchen of our little North London flat.'[18] Although nothing was written into his contract, Ronnie thought he had agreed with the management that, although a get-out clause couldn't be included in the contract, no one would stand in his way if after a year another decent job opportunity came his way. An offer did, in fact, materialise, in the shape of the lead role in a musical version of *Sweeney Todd*; to his surprise, though, he couldn't secure the release he was expecting. Ronnie soon realised that being part of a long run wasn't for him, but ended up spending two years in the play: he found the experience tortuous, admitting, 'Towards the end . . . I used to be physically sick at home before I set off for the theatre. I wouldn't have believed it could happen, but it did.'[19]

Friend Richard Briers sympathises with how Ronnie felt being trapped in a long-running show. 'Stage acting is terribly hard work. Ronnie was a natural, wonderful actor, a first-eleven stage actor, but he didn't want to do the repetition – it's that which kills you in terms of retaining interest and freshness each performance.'

The experience of *Irma La Douce*, which Ronnie described as like a 'sentence'[20] taught him two harsh lessons: first, he hated long runs and would never put himself in the position again of having to endure the monotony of delivering the same lines day in, day out for what seemed an eternity. The second lesson was to ensure that anything he agreed with management, whatever the medium, should be confirmed within the contract, otherwise misunderstandings can happen, as he discovered, again, later on the big screen.

Ronnie was able to finally rid himself of *Irma La Douce* after reaching an agreement with Peter Brook. The director wanted him to step into Clive Revill's shoes as Bob-le-Hotu – something he'd already done for a fortnight when the actor took a holiday. The role, securing him an additional £15 a week, needed to be filled because Revill had been asked to open *Irma* in New York. Ronnie realised that already knowing the role made him the ideal candidate, so struck a deal with management that he'd cover for a few weeks until a replacement was found in return for his release. Ronnie breathed a huge sigh of relief when he walked away from the Lyric Theatre for the final time in May 1960. Spring was giving way to summer, but the warmth and brightness in the air seemed magnified, the birds singing in the trees were in fine voice and a smile was back on Ronnie's face; it was as if all the world's troubles had been lifted from his shoulders as he strolled along, a free man.

Whilst it felt like he'd endured purgatory on stage for the past two years, it hadn't been all doom and gloom in other areas of his professional and personal life. Personally, he had the great pleasure of becoming a father when the first of his three children – Laurence, named after Ronnie's great hero, Laurence Olivier – was born on 23 October 1959.

On the work front, Ronnie popped up on television in two programmes during the year. *The State of the Prisons* was a BBC production for its schools programming broadcast on 23 June – one of several schools' programmes Ronnie would appear in at the beginning of his television career, another being a project based on Shakespeare's *Macbeth*. In *The State of the Prisons* Ronnie played Bob the Turnkey in a story written by Rosemary Hill and produced by Ronald Eyre. It was billed as the state of prisons as seen by Charles Dickens and John Howard, with Robert Gillespie – another jobbing actor – appearing with Ronnie in the production. He recalls striking up a conversation about a shared interest – stamp collecting. Robert enjoyed being in Ronnie's company, fleetingly in this production and, later, as a vicar in an episode of *Porridge*. 'He was a lovely man to be with. He was never funny in the exhibitionist way, as in being the life and soul of the party, but was very witty and amusing in a quiet, downbeat way. He was modest and discreet and never took over in a way that other actors did.'

Despite the world of television being new to everyone, including Ronnie, Robert says it was still 'strikingly obvious' that here was a medium in which Ronnie would quickly feel at home. 'He was a noticeably talented actor and had tremendous depth. There was intensity in what he did. He could concentrate effortlessly and shut everything and everyone out and just be the person he was playing.' According to Robert, this ability was one of Ronnie's greatest assets. 'For any character he undertook, you wouldn't notice he was performing; his performances were well crafted. I wouldn't have been surprised if he hadn't spent hours and hours working on the rhythms at home, because his portrayals were beautifully shaped, modulated and punctuated. He knew how to deliver text and get it to look as if he was making it up in front of you.'

Ronnie's other forays into television had included a reunion with his friend Glenn Melvyn, who created, co-wrote and appeared in *I'm Not Bothered*, a comedy for Associated-Rediffusion. Once again, Melvyn dusted off his popular stutterer Wally Binns, ably supported by Danny Ross as his sidekick Alf Hall, and Betty Marsden as Dolly Binns. Carrying on from Melvyn's 1955 series *Love and Kisses* the programme failed to hit the heights, but nonetheless supplied Ronnie with two brief roles, including that of a patient in a hospital bed, and his first real opportunity to write comedy scripts, ghostwriting for fifty pounds a time – a most welcome fee for an impoverished young actor. Ronnie supplied three scripts for the 26-part series, although it was Melvyn's name attributed to the programmes. Ronnie didn't get the credit, just a token payment, but it was the start of his professional writing career – it's just a shame he didn't get the chance to shout it from the rooftops, or simply inform director Henry Kendall, who directed one of Ronnie's scripts, that it was him and not Melvyn who had slaved away in creating this particular script, especially when the director proceeded to compliment the writing.

Ronnie told writer Bob McCabe for his biography how it pained him not to be able to tell Kendall the real identity of the scriptwriter. 'In the bar afterwards I said, "That went very well, Mr Kendall, didn't it?" And he said, "Bit of quality in the writing, old boy." I still couldn't tell him, but I was very delighted with that. That was my first praise for my writing. Amazing.'[21]

Radio remained a powerful medium in the late 1950s and while Ronnie's list of professional credits across all media – not just radio – was, to date, nothing more than minor roles, that changed when a radio series titled *The Navy Lark* sailed on to the airwaves on 29 March 1959. Little did anyone realise that it marked the start of fifteen series and numerous specials which would become inordinately popular, attracting avid listeners in their millions. Ultimately, the series earnt cult status and, seemingly, never-ending appeal thanks to subsequent CD releases and welcomed repeats on BBC radio, meaning new audiences were continually being introduced to Laurie Wyman's comedy series about antics aboard the Royal Navy frigate HMS *Troutbridge*, based in HMNB Portsmouth.

The idea was conceived in early 1958 when Wyman was chatting to radio director Alastair Scott-Johnston. The extreme success of ITV's military sitcom *The Army Game* had led the writer and director to consider using a similar format, comedy based around military life, for radio rather than television. When, on 2 May 1958 a buff-coloured envelope containing Wyman's synopsis arrived on Scott-Johnston's desk at the BBC's Aeolian Hall, he swiftly referred it to the Head of Light Entertainment (Sound). In his original synopsis, Wyman envisaged not only Leslie Phillips and Jon Pertwee being in the show, but Thora Hird and film actor Michael Denison, too. It was also hoped that notable names from the profession might drop in for the occasional guest role, such as Jack Hawkins arriving to inspect the detachment in real stiff-upper-lip manner.

Suitably impressed by the idea, the Head of Light Entertainment (Sound) sanctioned a trial script. By the beginning of October it had arrived and was circulated by Scott-Johnston with a covering note informing the Head of Light Entertainment (Sound) and Assistant Head J. H. Davidson that he regarded the script 'promising'[22], even if it was too long and would 'benefit from some judicious pruning early on'[23]. Scott-Johnston still saw Denison or Dennis Price, Phillips and Pertwee in the frame for central parts, and when the green light was given to make a trial programme, arrangements began in earnest to sort out the casting.

With Denison unavailable, Dennis Price was signed up to play Number One, a role taken over by Stephen Murray from Series Two, when Price headed across the Atlantic to work in a play. With Leslie Phillips playing Sub-Lieutenant Phillips and Jon Pertwee Chief Petty Officer Pertwee, among other characters, the reaction from the pilot programme was sufficient for a full series to be commissioned, running from March to July 1959. Ronnie, who was still appearing in *Irma La Douce* when the radio series began, was originally heard providing voices to 'Fatso' Johnson and Lieutenant Commander Stanton, but whenever scripts demanded more characters, his abilities were tapped further. Over the years, characters he played became so popular they were adopted as semi-regulars, such as 'Dumbo' from Intelligence, Mr Merrivale of Naval Expenditure, 'Snogger' Pettigreaves, Commander Bell and Lieutenant Queeg, the engineering officer. Leslie Phillips was impressed with Ronnie, with whom he'd strike up a long-lasting friendship from day one. He stated later that he realised 'from the off that Ronnie was a character actor of mind-boggling versatility'[24].

Although comedy was clearly the primary ingredient in the radio programme, Wyman originally intended injecting realism into his scripts. He wanted to make the plots 'plausible and the characters real. The listener should believe that this detachment could, and maybe even does, exist. To this end, an element of suspense and thrill will be introduced from time to time . . . these authentic happenings will assist the credibility of the characters in the more hilarious moments.'[25] In short, he saw the show as a comedy about naval life, 'rather than a wild variety show which is using the navy as a peg to hang a string of gags on and failing miserably!'[26]

The naval detachment was stationed on a fictitious island off Portsmouth, although this setting was ditched by the beginning of the third season and the unit returned to the mainland, and the battles they regularly fought were those threatening their cosy lives in which they avoided work and wangled as many comforts as possible.

It had been Wyman's intention not to overload the scripts with quips and comic lines, but an appraisal of the series shows little in the way of pathos or seriousness. It appears, however, the show wasn't funny enough for one BBC executive and it could have been this realisation which triggered the comments from R. E. Gregson, Head of General Overseas Service, when supplying the Head of Light Entertainment (Sound) with his views on the potential for selling the programme overseas. In a memo dated 6 May 1959 he pointed out that the show's slower pace would be advantageous when considering short-wave broadcasting; he did, however, have several concerns about the show. While impressed with Pertwee himself, Gregson was worried about how the two resident officers were realised, believing that in their accents they portrayed 'lack of intelligence and general absence of toughness, the stereotype of a certain category of Englishman that we are not anxious to cultivate in overseas broadcasts.'[27] As a result Gregson felt the standard of humour frequently became 'footling and puerile'[28], while he regarded regular references to petty fiddling as an 'unhappy projection of Britain'[29]. Summarising, Gregson didn't believe the show contained enough jokes and wished the situations were more fantastic, quoting *The Phil Silvers Show* as an example. If this were the case, the show might have been more suitable for overseas sales. Regardless of its level of success abroad, and it did eventually sell to overseas territories, the show's popularity grew steadily initially, but by the time the last of fifteen series was broadcast in 1976, followed the next year by a special, the comedy's premise had seemingly metamorphosed several times before returning to its familiar guise.

Ronnie left at the end of the 1967 series, when it became clear that the next season's recordings would clash with his commitments on *Frost on Sunday*. He enjoyed his eight years on the radio show and was well-liked by fellow artists and the loyal audience. Three years into the show's life, actress Judy Cornwell joined the Troutbridge gang as WREN Cornwell; she would go on to work with Ronnie twice more: in *Mr Whatnot* at the Arts Theatre in 1964 and, two years later, in *Sweet Fanny Adams* at Stratford East. Judy, then in her early twenties, admits she was 'a bit in awe' of the other cast members as she arrived at the Paris Studios, a converted cinema in London's Lower Regent Street, for her first recording. 'When we got our scripts on a Sunday, we'd read through them twice before recording in front of a live audience, which could be quite hairy.' There was much camaraderie and jollity within the team. 'Heather [Chasen] showed me how to push the men out of the way, because they would grab the microphones and not let us in, so we had to kick them in the shins and get to the microphones that way,' laughs Judy, who enjoyed working with Ronnie. 'He was witty, friendly and marvellous at doing all those voices. I admired him enormously, thought he was terribly talented and learnt a lot from him.'

The Navy Lark supplied Ronnie with much-welcomed steady work, with an average of seventeen episodes a series being recorded, for which he collected around £20 an instalment. Just as important, it provided a major step forward in his developing career, affording him a level of national exposure not experienced before, as millions tuned in each week to listen to the Light Programme's long-running comedy show.

Chapter 7

The Swinging Sixties was a liberating period in more ways than one. Leaving behind the shackles associated with post-war Britain, it was a time of freedom, adventure, hope, growing prosperity and increasing technological ingenuity. There was a deluge of major achievements, from the introduction of the contraceptive pill to arguably the decade's single greatest feat: the Moon landing in 1969. It was good riddance to rationing and rebuilding following World War Two, and a warm welcome to an air of sunny optimism and expectation, and this uplifting sense of well-being was reflected in Ronnie's professional and personal life. The Sixties heralded an important stage in his career. As the decade progressed, his diary became increasingly busy, with offers of radio, stage and screen work flowing his way.

It's often said that the decade was to become the most exciting and innovative of the twentieth century, and this is undoubtedly true of the world of television. In 1951 there were fewer than one million television licences in Britain; by 1961 there were almost twelve million and sales of sets were booming. Television became the prime medium, a dominant force in popular entertainment, and increasingly important in Ronnie's life. Gradually it would occupy the lion's share of his time, to the point that it became the only area of the industry in which he worked. His big break in this field happened mid-decade when David Frost and BBC producer/director Jimmy Gilbert invited him to join a team being assembled for a new satirical show. This will be covered in more detail later, of course, but it's apposite at this point to note that not only did *The Frost Report* introduce his face and comedic brilliance to the living rooms of millions, it brought together two up-and-coming performers who would subsequently forge one of the industry's most successful partnerships: Ronnie Barker and Ronnie Corbett. But that wasn't all that the Sixties had to offer for our subject: before the calendar clicked over to 1 January 1970 Ronnie would be appearing in his own sitcoms for commercial television; inevitably, such a busy television career meant anonymity – which he missed so much in later life – would become a thing of the past. No longer could he stride down the road unnoticed, just one of the prices actors pay upon achieving success.

Rewinding to the beginning of the decade, though, and months after his long-awaited departure from the cast of *Irma La Douce*, Ronnie returned to the stage, this time back at the Royal Court. Rehearsals for Chekhov's *Platonov* began in September in plenty of time for the first night on Thursday, 13 October. Ronnie played Nikolai Triletski, joining a cast including Frank Finlay, James Bolam, Peter Bowles, Rosalind Knight and star names Rex Harrison and his wife-to-be Rachel Roberts, as Platonov and Anna Petrovna respectively.

The script represented Chekhov's first attempts at writing a play and was only unearthed after the writer's death in 1904. The original manuscript – found among documents – for his melodrama was rather unwieldy and underwent surgery to not only reduce its size but translate it into English. Its opening night was followed next morning by the usual mixed bag of reviews. The *Sunday Times* reported that Chekhov used to be outraged and disappointed whenever he heard that his plays moved people to tears, so the critic felt the Royal Court Theatre had been right to present *Platonov* as a farce, before remarking that 'it is a pity that it does not make this clear until more than halfway through the second act . . . that the whole thing is intended to be laughed at. Even then we do not laugh very much.'[1] Meanwhile, Anthony Cookman, writing in *The Tatler*, thought earnest theatregoers excited about seeing a performance of Chekhov's first long play 'should have been warned that they would be considerably disconcerted. They will have found out by this time that they must make do with an evening of amusing period burlesque.'[2]

Like many actors Ronnie would often be busy earning a living on stage and radio simultaneously. With radio shows usually rehearsed and recorded the same day, it was possible for thespians to combine both in their schedules. On the wireless, Ronnie was not just dipping into his extensive library of character voices for *The Navy Lark*, but *Variety Playhouse* as well. The Home Service had assigned a regular Saturday evening slot for variety programmes since the 1920s. Various shows had run their course before *Variety Playhouse* came along in 1953. It occupied the weekend slot for ten years, with the likes of Arthur Askey, Ted Ray, Leslie Crowther and June Whitfield regularly heard. As the title suggests, it was a real variety of acts, including singing and comedy strands supplied by the likes of Ronnie, June and Leslie, who would become good friends and, later, form a trio in *Crowther's Crowd*. Ronnie remained with *Variety Playhouse*, which he had first worked on in the 1950s, until its demise and quickly became popular with listeners; his contributions, however, didn't strike a chord with everyone, as surveys conducted by the BBC revealed.

One method the Beeb employed to gauge public opinion towards its shows was to conduct an audience survey after every episode or selected episodes. Those taking part became known as members of the BBC viewing panel and, after watching or listening to all or part of the episode, expressed their views via a questionnaire. The sample audience was small compared to the number of people tuning in, but it provided management at the Corporation with an almost instantaneous snapshot of how a programme was received; while there is no doubting the popularity of *Variety Playhouse* and those who brought the show to life each week, it wasn't all plain sailing. Although criticism was rarely aimed at the performers themselves, the material they had to deliver was, occasionally, criticised. In response to the episode aired on Saturday, 12 November 1960 a report was completed detailing the survey's findings. Its author noted that comedy sketches delivered by Leslie Crowther and Ronnie, who were paid around £18 per show, were 'less enthusiastically received'[3], although no one faulted the artists. More detailed opinions were expressed a few months later regarding the episode transmitted on Saturday, 21 January 1961; this time, the artists came in for some criticism. The report's author stated, 'Leslie Crowther and Ronnie Barker's comedy sketches were not, as a rule, much enjoyed by listeners reporting. A minority, it is true, marked them very highly, finding their material witty and amusing and agreeing that they were both talented and versatile artists. More generally, however, listeners considered them very mediocre, particularly as "Edie" and "Hazel", when they were said to sound like a very inferior copy of Gert and Daisy.'[4]

Overall, however, the hour-long show was extremely popular with the public. 'It was a great show and well received,' says June Whitfield, who first met Ronnie on the programme. 'Leslie, Ronnie and myself were the regular comedy trio amongst all the musicians, singers and others. The sketches required us to use lots of different voices and we'd meet before the show with the writers George Evans and Derek Collyer to read through the sketches and ask each other what voices we should use for the characters.'

On the recording day everyone gathered at the Sherlock Holmes pub, a stone's throw from the Playhouse Theatre in Northumberland Avenue, where the show was recorded. June remembers the day Ronnie turned up looking somewhat the worse for wear. The trio was an established team by this point in 1964, and as radio programmes were usually rehearsed and recorded at weekends, the artists were free to undertake other projects. Ronnie, at the time, was making one of his rare film appearances, playing a bargee alongside Harry H. Corbett in the Galton and Simpson scripted film *The Bargee*. June takes up the story. 'Ronnie was superb, but one day arrived looking a bit fragile. When we reached the pub he quailed slightly at the suggestion of a drink, explaining that the previous day he'd been scheduled to do some filming for *The Bargee*, but the weather had been awful and he couldn't do it. While they were waiting for a break in the weather, Ronnie and one or two of the cast decided to spend their time in the local pub, toasting the Queen Mother, whose portrait hung in virtually every pub at that time. He was eventually poured into a taxi and sent home. When we heard the story, we told him he must have a hair of the dog and managed to give him a small port and brandy to settle the stomach. He winced a bit, drinking it, but then a warm smile spread over his face and after another little dose he was back on peak form and gave his usual wonderful performance.'

Leslie, June and Ronnie – and their respective partners – became good friends and regularly socialised. The occasional summer break was spent together, too. Sometimes the Crowthers rented a house at Middleton-on-Sea, close to where June and her husband were living in West Sussex. One year, the Barkers met up with them as well, booking in at the Beach Hotel in Littlehampton, just along the coast. June remembers a particular occasion when after an enjoyable dinner the six of them decided on a game of bar billiards, not that June was on top form. 'A most frustrating game, particularly if one's concentration is not as clearly focused after dinner as before. Grandad would have been ashamed of me. Not only did I forget the skills he'd so carefully taught me, but each miscue was accompanied by a ripe expletive, causing Ronnie and Joy to wince – not out of prudishness, but from a growing awareness that they would have to face the eyes of their fellow guests in the dining room at breakfast the following morning.'[5]

The late Leslie Crowther's wife Jean remembers the times spent socialising with Ronnie and Joy, who remained friends beyond the period Leslie worked with Ronnie on *Variety Playhouse* and, later, *Crowther's Crowd*. 'Ronnie was ebullient, very witty and gentle. He loved playing games, as we all did.' One of his favourites was always first on the agenda whenever the Barkers dined at the Crowthers' house. 'My sister had visited Belgium and brought back a game called Yahtzee, which wasn't so well known in the UK then. Ronnie used to arrive at our house rattling the dice in his pocket; he loved it. Most of our social evenings were spent having a meal and then playing games – all sorts, including poker.'

As well as popping up from time to time in Michael Bentine's madcap television series *It's A Square World*, which kicked off in 1960, Ronnie was also contracted for another run of *The Navy Lark*. Unbeknown to him, sitting in the audience one day watching an episode being recorded was a BBC producer/director, who would go on to play a crucial role in his television career. James Gilbert, later to become the BBC's head of comedy, had nipped along to the Playhouse Theatre on London's Embankment specifically to watch Ronnie's performance. Jimmy had been producing and directing *On the Bright Side*, a television revue starring Stanley Baxter, with Betty Marsden, Pip Hinton, David Kernan and Richard Waring providing valuable support; the show had won many plaudits and earnt Stanley

Baxter and Jimmy Gilbert BAFTAs – or SFTAs as they were then known – in the process. 'It must have been the first revue on television,' says Jimmy, who had been asked by Eric Maschwitz, the then Head of Light Entertainment, to find a revue which would work on the small screen. Maschwitz was a well-known lyricist, having penned such classic songs as *These Foolish Things*, but had little experience in television. Soon after taking over at the helm, he invited Jimmy Gilbert to his office. 'Eric, who was a delightful character, said, "Jim, do a revue." I asked him who with and he said that was up to me. I'd worked with Stanley Baxter at Glasgow's Citizens' Theatre, so made contact and invited him down to London. We ended up making *On the Bright Side*, which ran for two years.'

Its televisual success didn't go unnoticed and before long West End theatre producers Peter Bridge and John Gale announced their interest in transferring the show to the stage. Their plan was to embark on a three-month tour before entering the West End. Just when it seemed like the entire cast from the television show would be free for the theatre production, Richard Waring announced his unavailability, meaning Jimmy Gilbert had to recast the role. 'Richard was playing second lead to Stanley and I started to think about who could replace him. Then Betty Marsden said, "There's a very funny man I know who's in *The Navy Lark*. Why don't you go along and see a recording of it?"' So he did, and was suitably impressed. 'I thought Ronnie was funny, too, so met him afterwards – that was our first meeting. I told him about *On the Brighter Side* and he seemed very keen, although no offer was made at that point; that was done through his agent later.' Reflecting on his initial impressions of Ronnie as a performer, Jimmy says his timing was 'absolutely first class'. Here was someone he wanted to work with. 'When you're casting a show like I was, you often have a gut feeling about whether someone is right or not, and I just felt, "Yes, you'll work."'

James Gilbert's background was in theatre. After leaving the Royal Academy of Dramatic Art he joined Glasgow's Citizens' Theatre in the late 1940s, where he not only acted but wrote. He later appeared in films before returning to his typewriter, co-writing the long-running musical *Grab Me A Gondola*, set against the colourful backdrop of the Venice Film Festival. Opening in late-1956 it ran to nearly 700 performances at London's Lyric Theatre and was staged in Australia, South Africa and across Europe. On joining the BBC Jimmy remained deeply passionate about the theatre and didn't let his commitment with the Corporation prevent him from indulging his passion further. 'I had what I call an "elastic contract" with the BBC,' explains Jimmy. 'The experience of *Grab Me A Gondola* made me want a flexible contract, so that when offered the chance to direct a show in, say, Johannesburg, I could go along to my bosses and tell them I wanted to do a play for three months. They would grant a three-month period without pay on the understanding that it would be added to the end of my contract – the arrangement worked very well.'

On the Brighter Side headed out on tour, visiting the likes of Glasgow, Manchester and Leeds, where Barry Cryer caught the show at the Grand Theatre and was impressed with the thirty-year-old performing alongside Stanley Baxter. Standing next to the bar at The Swan, Barry recalls Stanley lauding Ronnie. 'He was saying to people, "Watch out for this one, he's stealing the show!"' Barry agreed with his friend's assessment. 'Stanley was superb, obviously, but there was this portly young man, playing an Indian guru and all sorts of characters. You couldn't take your eyes off him, he was that good. He didn't look as if he was trying to steal the show from the start, he just couldn't help it and Stanley spotted this, thinking, "He's good. He's going to make it."' Barry admits he didn't possess Baxter's prescience to that extent, but knew he was watching a promising talent.

Stanley Baxter regarded Ronnie as 'a talented, creative man' who was very funny off-screen. 'Any witticism or put-down someone said, he could top it. He was so quick-witted. But a lot of the time, if somebody said something and he thought of a funny rejoinder, he'd quietly tell me, and when I said it I'd get a huge laugh. I'd ask him why he didn't say it, and he'd reply, "I just like to hear you say it." That's how generous he was.' Generosity with lines became something of a trademark of Ronnie's, but it was surprising to find such a young, up-and-coming actor willing to sacrifice the chance of a laugh; many in his position, wanting to show their worth and make their presence felt, would never dream of passing such an opportunity to a fellow actor. But that wasn't Ronnie's style.

Even in *Porridge*, his own comedy vehicle, where a less proficient actor could have hogged the limelight and wanted to grab as many lines as possible, particularly those likely to elicit a laugh from the audience. But not Ronnie, as Tony Osoba, who played fellow inmate McLaren, confirms. 'He was the leading man, but if he saw moments where another character was doing something and it was funny, he'd be the first to suggest dropping some of his own lines in order to incorporate it; obviously he was comfortable in his own abilities.'

Touring a show before entering the West End is all about testing out the material, identifying weaknesses requiring attention before settling in to its London run. While out on the road, alterations and tinkering were commonplace and the excessive number of scene changes meant the production struggled to settle into a fixed rhythm. 'It was a tremendously onerous project for the stage staff to cope with,' admits Stanley. 'There was something like twenty-two changes of scene, it was incredible. The only place they got it right, from the dress rehearsal onwards, was in Glasgow. Anything we thought wasn't going too well, perhaps because it was too sophisticated for the provinces, we'd change.'

Feeling the brunt of any alterations to the sketches or running order was Douglas Cornelissen, company and stage manager for Bridge and Gale. 'From the first rehearsal right through to the time it closed, it was never-ending change, including change of minds,' he says. 'While on tour, five weeks prior to the West End, we didn't do the same bill twice in one week in terms of running order or content – it was always changing. I was rushing about and on the phone during the day, desperately getting new bits of scenery made and sent to us for that night or the next day – and we were endlessly rehearsing. It was hell on wheels, frankly, but I still enjoyed it, because I loved my job and the responsibility.' If a number or sketch didn't work while out on the road, it was pulled. Douglas says, 'That's why the running order kept changing, practically nightly. Also, you can never find a pattern that works, because the show doesn't settle. It's a shame it didn't work better, because it was a very talented company.'

Production designer Clifford Hatts was the man who took the calls from Jimmy Gilbert or Douglas Cornelissen. 'I'd suddenly get a call to be told Stanley wanted to do a submarine sketch or something. Then it would be described to me on the phone and I'd design it. The contractors were marvellous and would build things overnight, then we'd rush it down to wherever they were performing; we were doing this all the time.'

Eventually arriving in London, the show's life remained equally unsettled, opening at the Phoenix Theatre in April 1961 before shifting to the Comedy Theatre in August. Douglas Cornelissen remembers being told about the switch in theatres. 'The show fitted the Phoenix, but wasn't taking the money needed, so one Saturday I was called out of the theatre by Bridge and Gale to be informed they'd decided to transfer to a smaller theatre, where the level of money coming in would just about keep the show going. They told me they were thinking of the Comedy and I said I'd go over on Monday and see if I thought it was possible and practical, because, frankly, it's a very small theatre by comparison, but they said: "Oh, we've signed the contract." At which point, I foolishly didn't resign my job; I should have done, because I knew it wasn't going to work and it didn't.'

Douglas feels the excessive number of scene changes hastened the show's demise. 'In a revue of that sort there would be blackouts allowing you thirty seconds to change the scene before the curtain went up and you'd be ready to start the next. It worked all right at the Phoenix and the other theatres, but the show didn't fit the Comedy Theatre in Panton Street and we had to cut and reduce things. When we got to the end of a sketch or number, we had to get all the cast off before we could bring the next lot of people and props on, because there was no wing space; it was so cramped it was frightening. Scene changes were taking up to a minute. You can't sustain a revue like that. Word of mouth became appalling and we closed.'

John Gale, who produced the show with Peter Bridge, acknowledges there were many changes during the run. 'One kept tinkering with it, trying to bring things up to date. If there was some new scandal that you could comment on, then a sketch would go in, changing the running order.' John, however, feels the production was hit by various bouts of bad luck. Timing in the theatre is paramount and he believes that, in hindsight, *On the Brighter Side* was conceived at just the wrong time. 'Peter and I had watched *On the Bright Side* and decided we'd love to do a stage show. Revue had fallen out of favour in the West End, television had taken over, so we thought that this could be the last of the great revues. But we were defeated, in terms of commercial success, by *Beyond the Fringe* coming down from the Edinburgh Festival.' The show, written and performed by Peter Cook, Dudley Moore, Alan Bennett and Jonathan Miller, became a sensation at the Fortune Theatre; it was also seminal to the new wave of satirical, biting humour marking the end for the intimate revue format typified by *On the Brighter Side*. 'It knocked the old-fashioned revue, which is what we were doing, for six,' admits John Gale. 'We staggered along. Although we weren't losing money, we weren't getting any back against the large production cost. But as we were nearly breaking even on the running costs each week, Peter and I wanted to keep going, so moved to the Comedy.'

Douglas Cornelissen concurs with John that the end was nigh for intimate revue when the sharper style of *Beyond the Fringe* arrived on the scene, heralding a new era. 'In parallel, satire also arrived in a very big way in the form of *That Was The Week That Was* [first transmitted in November 1962], so it was a whole melting-pot period, out of which the old-style revue simply disappeared.'

When *On the Brighter Side* opened, most critics in their notices acknowledged there were good and bad bits. A reviewer in *The Times* stated that out of around fifty items in the revue, '10 hit their not very difficult targets bang in the middle. This proportion is high enough by present-day standards for us to hail the revue as a success.'[6] And considering the laughter and applause at the Phoenix on the opening night, the *Daily Telegraph*'s W. A. Darlington thought 'its future is assured'[7]. How wrong he was. The *Daily Mail*'s reviewer, however, wasn't so generous, stating, 'What is right with this show will take few lines to say, what is wrong with it could fill a volume entitled, "What to avoid when writing a revue."'[8]

Despite the obvious frustrations and challenges faced on *On the Brighter Side*, Douglas Cornelissen has nothing but happy memories of working with Ronnie, whom he describes as a 'rock'. He explains, 'There are two kinds of performer in live theatre: the good company people and those who are not. Good company people are like Ronnie Barker, who were the bedrock of talent, but whose generosity as performers towards fellow actors was legend – and Ronnie was one of those.'

He remembers how Ronnie took every opportunity to indulge his passion for collecting and antiques. Recalling the time he bumped in to him one lunchtime, he says, 'Ronnie particularly liked prints, and when we were on tour I saw him outside the theatre, just after we'd done yet another rehearsal. He said, "Oh, I'm dying for a snack, let's go and have a quick drink and sandwich." So we did. While we were enjoying the snack, he said, "I've just got time before we're called back at three o'clock to pop round to a nearby road where I'm meeting a bloke who's selling me some suit fabric." So we trawled round to this place, which was like a bomb site, and spotted a parked car. This chap opened the boot and it was full of suit lengths. Both Ronnie and I bought one each.' That wasn't the only place Ronnie intended visiting en route to the theatre. 'We passed a junk shop and he said, "Oh, I must go in there." And he came out with three prints that he'd bought on spec.'

Ronnie's insatiable appetite for memorabilia, antiques and collectibles, which later saw him open an antiques shop in the Oxfordshire village of Chipping Norton, influenced another member of the company – Amanda Barrie, who later played Alma Sedgewick in *Coronation Street*. Amanda credits Ronnie for introducing her to antiques, one of her great loves. 'We used to go snooping around antiques and junk shops together, and he taught me all about Victorian postcards.'[9]

One of Ronnie's qualities Amanda noticed straight away was his quick-wittedness. She recalls burning the midnight oil with him while on tour, writing one-liners. 'We used to sit up at night for hours writing "quickies". "Quickies" fascinated Ronnie and me, and we used to spend for ever trying to make them up.'[10] In between their moments of inspiration, they would idle away the time playing cards and sipping wine, 'very avant-garde at the time'[11].

On the Brighter Side may have failed to live up to expectations on the stage compared to its screen success, but it proved to be a springboard for Ronnie's career. His indubitable talent didn't go unnoticed by anyone linked to the show, with John Gale classing him as an 'astonishing performer' and Jimmy Gilbert pleased he'd invited him to join the cast. In fact, he liked his work so much Ronnie's name was quickly brought into the frame when directing his next television series *Seven Faces of Jim*, starring Jimmy Edwards. Seven episodes were transmitted between 16 November and 28 December, each an individual comedy in its own right. Edwards had become a well-loved face on television, thanks largely to the success of the sitcom *Whack-O!*, which began in 1956 with him playing headmaster of Chiselbury, a public school which had seen better days.

This was Jimmy Gilbert's first taste of directing television comedy, having been hired by the BBC as a music producer, given his track record writing lyrics and music for several theatre shows. When Frank Muir and Denis Norden were looking for a director to take on their series, they gave a script to Jimmy Gilbert. 'We got on well together, and they knew I had been involved in writing musical comedy,' says Jimmy. 'They drove me down to meet Jimmy Edwards at his farm in Sussex. I think they thought the two of us would hit it off because we'd both been bomber pilots in the war. They were right. We got on like a house on fire and became friends as well as colleagues.'

After Ronnie Barker's cameo appearance in *Seven Faces of Jim* it didn't take long for writers Denis Norden and Frank Muir, who was comedy advisor for Light Entertainment at the time, to spot the new face when he popped up for his one line. 'I cast Ronnie in this tiny part and Frank spotted him immediately, saying, "He's good!"' With the remainder of the series still being scripted, Norden and Muir wrote in parts for Ronnie, including characters called Sid Figgins, Inigo Pengallon and Ronnie Green, a recording manager. 'They knew they'd get good value from him. He fitted in perfectly, as did Richard Briers, another new face. They were both sheer gold.'

Denis Norden didn't take any persuading to write bigger roles for Ronnie's consumption. 'Most of the television comedy in those days was live, so one of the first qualifications required of an actor was that he knew his lines. The star of the show was Jimmy and we were white-knuckled all the way through the show and we could tell if he was looking for his lines. But Ronnie was always comfortable, he was rock solid – such a valuable quality. When he came to rehearsals you knew he was prepared.'

By now, although still relatively unknown, particularly in television, Ronnie's confidence in his own abilities was growing and he was beginning to make suggestions or offer self-penned jokes and one-liners. While some writers wouldn't entertain the thought of performers offering material for use in a show, Norden and Muir were always open to ideas. 'Any suggestions Ronnie had were always right on the button. They were not only original but in exactly the right context. Sometimes he'd suggest a line or bit of business, but it would always carry the story forward – everything you want as a writer.' Denis rates Ronnie as one of the best comedy actors he worked with. 'As writers, you felt absolutely secure and comfortable with him, because you recognised that he was a kind of male June Whitfield; he could be relied on to give all the rather facetious and frivolous stuff we wrote a core of reality.'

Although it was an era boasting a plethora of sterling character and comedy actors, Denis Norden was adept at spotting top talent. 'Ronnie was absolutely copper-bound quality. You could recognise it from the start. He wasn't a star at that time, but we knew we wanted to do something with him and had an idea for a legal series; sadly, it never came to anything,' admits Denis, who'll never forget Ronnie telling him his so-called favourite joke. 'He always quoted this as his favourite, with one man saying to another, "I have four hundred more bones in my body than you." The other man said, "Why?" He replied, "Because I had a kipper for tea."'

Normally, Jimmy Gilbert would inform Norden and Muir of the people he intended casting, just in case the person in mind was a bête noire. In Ronnie's case, though, he didn't feel the need to involve them, deeming the tiny part of a newsreader in the episode 'The Face of Genius' unimportant. Ronnie fitted into the team perfectly and found himself invited along to a party for 'stars', as Jimmy recalls: 'There was a party where producers were meant to bring their stars. I asked Jimmy [Edwards], but he couldn't make it, so I invited Ronnie instead. I remember telling everyone, "All of you are bringing your stars, but I'm inviting a star of the future

– Ronnie Barker." The only person who knew of him and, incidentally, spoke most highly of him was Dennis Main Wilson who, I think, was a fan of *The Navy Lark*.'

The Jimmy Edwards' series received favourable comments from the television critics, with Peter Black in the *Daily Mail* classing it a 'skilful example which never fails to sustain the right proportions of under-writing and over-playing'[12]. Philip Purser, meanwhile, in the *Sunday Telegraph* thought the omens for the series were good, stating that the team 'can knock out a brand of hearty, allusive comedy which makes a nice change from the cosier behaviour stuff'[13].

When the team returned to the screen for a second run, this time in the imaginatively titled *Six More Faces of Jim*, during the closing weeks of 1962, Ronnie was regarded a regular and one of his performances was highlighted by Peter Black in the *Daily Mail*. In the episode 'The Face of Fatherhood', transmitted on 15 November, the writers introduced the Glums to the screen, a misfit family created by Muir and Norden, which became an integral part of their popular radio series *Take It From Here*. While Jimmy Edwards and June Whitfield reprised their radio roles, Ronnie was allocated the Ron Glum role, formerly played by Dick Bentley. Journalist Black was pleasantly surprised, feeling the comic family transferred from radio better than he'd anticipated. Acknowledging the welcome return of the team, he took time to make a special mention of Ronnie's performance. He wrote, 'It is by no means easy to put your own face to a radio character that millions have imagined for themselves. But Barker did it with complete success.'[14] Not everyone thought it worked so well, though. June Whitfield says, 'Transferring that sort of thing to television is difficult and much of the humour is often lost. The imagination on the radio conjures up all kinds of wonderful pictures; there aren't many radio shows which transfer successfully to television.'

Chapter 8

By the time 1961 drew to a close, Ronnie had in the last few weeks not only appeared in *Seven Faces of Jim*, but made a cameo appearance in the second series of Sid James' sitcom *Citizen James*, in which the South African-born actor played a gambler. Ronnie had also utilised his funny voices for Michael Bentine's radio show *Round the Bend*. Ronnie once stated that often he played up to ten parts in one radio programme, proving why being equipped with a plethora of voices was so valuable in his trade. He explained, 'I used to keep a voice file. I'd give each one a particular designation: gruff or reedy, heavy or light. Sometimes I'd give them special words or phrases. It was a useful reference, something instant.'[1]

His career was certainly heading upwards, and as everyone toasted the new year and stumbled through the lyrics of 'Auld Lang Syne', Ronnie faced his busiest year to date, a year which would see him work across all media for the first time.

But as clocks struck midnight at 165 Lyon Park Avenue, Wembley, Middlesex, where the Barkers had been living since May 1961, Joy had entered the final weeks of pregnancy. On the last day of January the couple's second child Charlotte entered the world. But soon after the birth, Joy suffered a terrible bout of depression. Thankfully, this was short-lived and happy times were soon restored at Lyon Park Avenue. But it had been a trying period for all concerned: Joy was the light of Ronnie's life and for a time he feared their lives wouldn't be the same. He admitted in his autobiography, 'It was a traumatic period, we nearly came to blows . . . to be honest, we didn't, but I nearly struck her, out of frustration and panic that things would never be the same again.'[2] Ronnie's fears soon dissipated, though, and normality resumed with a busy schedule ahead of him.

Earlier in January he had informed the BBC of his wish to be known as Ronnie instead of Ronald Barker for all future work, and this change was in evidence as he took to the stage at the Royal Court Theatre in London's Sloane Square for the first night of *A Midsummer Night's Dream*. Tony Richardson directed The English Stage Company's production of Shakespeare's popular comedy, in association with the Arts Council of Great Britain, and audiences attending a performance during its run between 24 January and 17 March delighted at the prospect of seeing Nicol Williamson, Rita Tushingham, Corin Redgrave and his sister Lynn among the cast. Ronnie played Peter Quince, the carpenter from Athens who, along with five other craftsmen, stage a play at the wedding of Theseus and Hippolyta. The director assembled a largely youthful team, which he hoped would embody his own aspirations. One critic, however, thought the play was 'free of any elaborate tricks either of interpretation or of stage management.'[3] Unfortunately, the play wasn't well received and was universally panned by the leading dailies. A scribe in *The Times* explained that it was the first Shakespeare play presented by the English Stage Company at the Royal Court, before admitting that 'under the shock of the dire result one is almost driven to hope that it will be the last.'[4] He admonished the young cast further, because he found it difficult following the plot, believing it was hampered by an inability to hear the lines clearly, as the actors were given to 'gabbling or shouting'[5]. Robert Muller in the *Daily Mail* thought the play 'lay back groaning and gave itself up to laughter. Poetry, grace, subtlety and charm it lacked the strength to give.'[6] Other reviews were equally scathing and Ronnie found his name mentioned just once, and then he was referred to as 'Ronnie Parker'.

Ronnie was not the kind of actor who deeply desired to play Shakespearean roles, and after the Royal Court experience one could, perhaps, understand why. Of course, in reality this didn't influence his attitude – after all, every actor appears in a production, whether screen or stage, which fails in terms of its performance; it was just that Ronnie admitted later that he never felt the need to prove himself through the Bard's matchless lines. Perhaps this was a factor when, in later years, he never got around to accepting Sir Peter Hall's constant offers to bring him back to the London stage in the shape of Falstaff. Ronnie did, however, return to Shakespeare's

A Midsummer Night's Dream once more, this time on television a decade later, playing Bottom in a BBC *Play of the Month*.

The second entry on his big-screen credit list arrived with an appearance in the 1962 film *Kill or Cure*. A comedy spotlighting an incompetent policeman's attempts at investigating shenanigans at a health club, it featured a stellar cast from the British film industry, including Terry Thomas, Dennis Price, Peter Butterworth and Patricia Hayes; Ronnie played Burton, assistant to Lionel Jeffries' Detective Inspector Hook. A slow-paced comedy, it disappeared rather quickly from the cinema circuit, only to resurface in recent years for the occasional late-night screening on obscure satellite channels. Its release earnt a few brief compliments, with Nina Hibbin classing it as a 'perky little whodunnit'[7] and Margaret Hinxman an 'engaging comedy idea'[8].

A string of television appearances was scattered through the rest of the year, including a role alongside Prunella Scales in an unusual strip-cartoon segment within the *Tonight* programme, in which he played Uncle Leslie and Scales Awful Evelyn. Written by Bernard Levin, it showed the duo – while pushing their heads through a cartoon backdrop – reflecting satirically on events deemed insufficiently strong to warrant a full-blown interview on the programme. In addition to *Tonight* Ronnie was seen in, among others, *The Benny Hill Show*, *Brothers in Law*, *The Rag Trade* and an episode in the third and final series of *Citizen James*.

To top off a busy year professionally, he was heard on two radio broadcasts – *It's a Stereophonic World* and *Discord in Three Flats* – on the same day (22 September), and provided more comedy voices for another season of *Variety Playhouse*. The following year the team of Leslie Crowther, June Whitfield and Ronnie Barker would regroup for a new show: *Crowther's Crowd*.

In February 1963 Alastair Scott-Johnston was tasked with finding a show for Leslie Crowther. Realising he faced a challenge centring a programme on an actor not regarded as a leading name, he penned a memo from his office at 327 Aeolian. As the rain beat against the windows, he concentrated his thoughts, detailing his plans to J. H. Davidson, the then Assistant Head of Light Entertainment (Sound). 'Faced with the problem of projecting a character man as the lynchpin of a show, we suggest that each week, under some such title as "Crowther on . . .", we take one subject (politics, National Health Service, police, etc.). The show must be held together by Crowther, who really must have something not only funny but worth listening to to say on the subject.'[9]

Written (again) by George Evans and Derek Collyer, *Crowther's Crowd* had Mickie Most and the Minute Men providing the music, while the tight-knit trio played students – Ronnie a trainee chef – intent on reforming the world, masterminding their plans in the El Aroma coffee shop in Bloomsbury. Again produced by Alastair Scott-Johnston, recordings were held at the Paris Studio. The first of two series – in which the team utilised every conceivable character voice and accent – hit the airwaves in September 1963, running for fourteen weeks. In an interview for the *Radio Times* Scott-Johnston introduced the series, saying, 'They'll argue about anything and illustrate their points with impersonations. There'll be plenty of scope, too. After all, one can sit over a cup of mud and froth a long time. Each programme will give these artists a chance to exploit their versatility with eight or nine character sketches on a particular theme.'[10]

Leslie Crowther, meanwhile, thought the BBC were on to a winner 'letting the three of us loose for a whole half-hour'[11]. Providing an insight into the jovial and relaxed atmosphere within the team, he added, 'As for our conferences with the scriptwriters . . . they're a riot. We meet in each other's houses and then carry on in the nearest local over darts. If our arguments on the air sound true to life, that's why.'[12]

Unfortunately, BBC Radio's Light Entertainment Department's high expectations weren't realised, as *Crowther's Crowd* failed to attract the sizeable audience the Beeb's hierarchy had anticipated. In an Audience Research Report conducted after an episode transmitted on 23 November 1963 a housewife's comments typified those of virtually all respondees. She believed 'the sketches in this programme are often good, but never really come up to the standard one thinks it will . . . it lacks real sparkle'[13]. Leslie Crowther and Ronnie, however, were praised for their efforts.

The producer was adamant that much original comedic thought

had been utilised in the programme, as much as he'd heard in the last eighteen months, and hoped it would be given another chance. In a memo to the Head of Light Entertainment (Sound) he stressed, 'I think that in terms of appreciation, it did score sufficiently well, and showed sufficient promise for the future, to deserve our earnest consideration.'[14] But realising something was required to draw a bigger audience, the writers suggested bringing a 'star name' into the fold, although Scott-Johnston warned of the dangers of such action. He wrote, 'If we add a bomb of a personality like Jimmy Edwards or Frankie Howerd, then it must essentially become their show, and I think this would be a complete waste of what we have so far built up.' While accepting the need to attract a genuine anchorman, he suggested someone with a distinctive voice, such as Eamonn Andrews, while Evans and Collyer floated the idea of signing up the likes of Stanley Baker, Trevor Howard or Robert Morley.

Sadly, nothing materialised and it seemed as if *Crowther's Crowd* would fizzle out with just one series to its name. In July 1964 a letter from C. J. Mahoney dropped through the scriptwriters' letter-boxes commiserating with them over the show's apparent ending. He explained that its return had been discussed at length but, sadly, this wouldn't happen due to lack of support. Closing his brief note, he admitted, 'It was indeed a promising first series and to some extent I share your disappointment that we are not attempting a rerun with a changed format.'[15] But it was all change within a year when the team was reunited for a second – and final – season, with another fourteen shows recorded in late 1965 for broadcasting the following spring.

Before 1963 came to an end, Ronnie added two further film credits to his CV: a 'blink and you'll miss me' moment in *Doctor in Distress*, sharing a scene with the inimitable James Robertson Justice at Windsor railway station, and Yossle in the Peter Graham Scott-directed *The Cracksman*. Starring Charlie Drake, George Sanders and Dennis Price, it told the story of a guileless locksmith who's dragged into a safe-cracking scheme by gangsters before, ultimately, managing to turn the tables. The film received a lukewarm reception from the Press, most agreeing that it was an example of stretching a flimsy idea too far.

To round off his radio work for the year he was heard in further episodes of *The Navy Lark* and *Variety Playhouse*, as well as adding to his earlier appearance on *The Arthur Haynes Show*, earning him twenty guineas. His only other notable television work saw him playing Henry Wallace in the Easter Day broadcast of *The Holly Road Rig*, which screened at 9 p.m. as part of *The Sunday Play* series. Written by Martin Woodhouse and starring Avis Bunnage and Peter Butterworth alongside Ronnie, the comedy featured Henry, who resided at 38 Holly Road, and his faithful assistant, Reg, spending an inordinate amount of time in his cellar, much to his wife's despair, while promising his beloved that he's planning to make their fortune.

The Sixties was becoming an increasingly busy decade for Ronnie who, even though still not a household name or face, was turning out fine, polished performances in every medium. But his big break would happen in 1966 on joining the team of a new satirical show, *The Frost Report*, which would set him on the road to stardom and see him become recognised by a steadily increasing number of fans. Although this breakthrough was still a couple of years away, Ronnie's diaries for 1964–5 looked healthy as his growing reputation within the industry attracted new offers of employment.

Ronnie and his family had just moved to 124 Eastcote Road, Pinner, Middlesex, when he was asked, at short notice, to appear on the Light Programme's comedy series *Listen To This Space*, hosted by Nicholas Parsons. Producer John Bridges appreciated Ronnie being able to accept the job at the eleventh hour. He dropped him a line, thanking him for his efforts. 'I just want to underline my very great appreciation of what you did for us on Sunday. I am well aware that you must have been tired, having just returned from Cambridge when you got our call, and quite apart from that it was a very splendid piece of fire-brigading that you did. To pick it up like that, and to pull out such a performance at such very short notice was something I shall never forget and never cease to be grateful for.'[16]

To prove that his track record was being noticed by potential employers, we need look no further than radio producer John Fawcett Wilson, who recruited Ronnie for his 1964 summer revue and sketch show *Not to Worry*. 'I knew Ronnie was good, because I was aware of other material he'd done, but I didn't realise just how good until he worked for me,' says Fawcett Wilson, who described the nine-part series, running between July and September, as 'summer-weight, tailored to fit a light-hearted, easy-going mood'[17]. Cyril Fletcher was the anchorman, but other performers were required to make up the team. 'I wanted two good character actors and I booked Ronnie and Joan Heal, who was more or less the female equivalent. My two juveniles were David Kernan and Eira Heath.' It was Ronnie's budding reputation which led the producer to pick him. 'I talked to colleagues, saying I wanted someone who was a versatile actor. Various names were mentioned, including Eric Barker and Peter Jones, but I knew Ronnie's work from *The Navy Lark*. However, I was very much flying blind, because we didn't know each other and hadn't worked together.'

Fawcett Wilson saw the programme as 'cutting his teeth' in his new department, but enjoyed working with Ronnie so much that he devised a new idea, which, if greenlighted, would be led by Ronnie. Before long, the producer received the go-ahead for *Let's Face It*. 'Ronnie told me that this was the first series which "starred Ronnie Barker". We made an initial nine programmes, but when the head of the Light Programme came down and enjoyed watching a recording he immediately extended the series to nineteen.' The show's extension saw the programme run from 8 January 1965 until 14 May. You would have thought that the extension was music to Fawcett Wilson's ears, but he regarded it as a 'big mistake'. He explains, 'When you're doing a new show it's one thing to have a good run like that, but this was Ronnie's first starring role and sometimes you need a bit of a break to sit down, regroup and discuss what worked and what didn't, rather than plough on with more. Also, I was a relatively new light-entertainment producer.'

John Fawcett Wilson had joined the BBC as a music producer, but after a few years fell in love with the medium of radio; wanting to do more than just make music shows, he joined Light Entertainment. He enjoyed producing *Let's Face It* and recalls Ronnie frequently ad-libbing during the series. 'Once, he and Patricia Routledge, who had replaced Gwendolyn Watts, ad-libbed for about five minutes, right away from the script. I remember one of the blokes, I can't remember who, tearing away in the middle of it; one of the commissionaires told me afterwards that the man had actually wet himself laughing so much!' Unfortunately, the series, which Fawcett Wilson designed as a vehicle for Ronnie within a revue-style format, was only moderately successful and a few eyebrows were raised when it was extended so generously. The Audience Research Department compiled its usual report and it didn't make particularly enjoyable reading. As the report's author pointed out, the first episode had attracted a Reaction Index of 52, when the previous year's average was 57 for 'less sophisticated comedy team shows'[18]. While plenty of people acknowledged the wit and entertainment level in the first show, a sizeable number of respondees weren't impressed. 'Some condemned it as downright silly, but most were content to call it feeble in places.'[19] Many in the sample enjoyed what they heard, though, and made a point of praising Ronnie's versatility.

When the report landed on the desks of Roy Rich, the then Head of Light Entertainment (Sound), his assistant head Con Mahoney and script editor Ted Taylor it caused a flood of memos to flow between their respective offices. Mahoney questioned the idea of extending the series, a view backed by Taylor. In a memo to Roy Rich, Taylor agreed that it 'seems inconsistent to extend this series when the early results are poor. In particular, it seems a strange policy compared with that accorded to its predecessor *Not To Worry*, which was, to my mind, a better show.'[20] He didn't agree with Con Mahoney's suggestion to augment the cast in an attempt to try and boost its appeal. He advised Rich that he would 'sooner see those already involved left to make a success of it or else withdraw, having made a laudable effort. I should have thought the original nine was sufficient scope for them to do the one or the other, or at most, perhaps an extension of two or three.'[21]

Roy Rich, though, had decided on the extension, although he did have a suggestion for the producer: he thought it was a propitious time for Ronnie to take on the warm-up duties from Fawcett Wilson. Dropping the producer a line on 3 February 1965, he felt it would definitely help the show's fortunes. He explained, 'When the red light goes on, he virtually opens "cold" and it often takes the first five minutes for the audience to warm to him – whereas I think the rapport which he eventually establishes on air, should be achieved before the red light. This is not an isolated attack on you, but simply one memo in an overall scheme to encourage bigger audiences generally.'[22] The extended run went ahead and although audiences didn't increase substantially, it remained a show enjoyed by many, even if it was never regarded as the most original series aired.

The experience didn't stop Fawcett Wilson wanting to work with Ronnie even more; but if there were to be a next time, he was determined it would be in a show which would truly showcase his wide range of talents. 'Let's Face It had been an enjoyable series, but didn't show off Ronnie's particular skills – which were considerable – to the full; it wasn't doing him justice.' It would be another six years until Fawcett Wilson's plans materialised, but when they did it was based on an idea he'd hatched back in his music-producing days. Although lacking a title, the producer had formulated the basic premise sufficiently in his mind to present to his bosses; having liked what they heard, a series was commissioned. The programme emerged as the unusually titled *Lines From My Grandfather's Forehead*, to be discussed in a later chapter.

During 1964 Ronnie took to the stage in two plays. The first saw him playing Bob Acres in *All in Love* at the Mayfair Theatre. Based on Richard Sheridan's comedy of manners *The Rivals*, it was set in and around Bath in the late eighteenth century and featured Annie Ross, Margo Cunningham, Peter Gilmore and James Fox among the cast. Sadly, when it opened on 16 March many of the national critics didn't have a good word to say about it. Eric Shorter in the *Daily Telegraph* regarded it a 'mediocre travesty'[23] while *The Times'* drama critic wrote that 'this artless off-Broadway musical based on Sheridan's *The Rivals* glaringly illustrates the dangers of attempting to transform a classic into a piece of popular entertainment.'[24] But among the disappointing notices Ronnie's efforts were recognised, with Eric Shorter acknowledging his 'spirited little performance . . . as an amusingly terrified Acres'[25], while *The Times'* unnamed critic thought Ronnie had played his role with 'enjoyable confidence'[26].

During his Oxford Playhouse days in September 1954, Ronnie (second left) was best man at the wedding of fellow performers Derek Francis and Ann Elsdon.

Ronnie (left) and Gary Raymond admire the screen they decorated in their dressing room at the Lyric Theatre while performing in *Irma La Douce* in 1958.

Ronnie (right) and John Buckland in the Oxford Theatre Players' production of *The Shop at Sly Corner*, circa 1947.

Donald Hewlett (left) as Hastings and Ronnie as Poirot on stage at the Oxford Playhouse.

Ronnie, Ronnie Corbett, David Frost and the rest of the team celebrate *The Frost Report*'s success in winning the Golden Rose at the 1967 Montreux Festival.

Jon Pertwee and Ronnie Barker were key members of the BBC's popular radio series, *The Navy Lark*, and said their goodbyes to HMS Troutbridge when the frigate left for the breaker's yard in 1969.

Fletcher (Ronnie) and Godber (Richard Beckinsale) gave Barrowclough (Brian Wilde) a hard time in *Porridge*.

Ronnie (2nd left) joined a host of stars for a fund-raising event in 1969.

Ronnie scored another hit playing northern shopkeeper Arkwright in *Open All Hours*.

Ronnie received an award from Princess Anne for Light Entertainment Performer of 1978.

Ronnie B and Ronnie C filming the 1980 serial, *The Worm That Turned*.

Ronnie's original handwritten contribution for the *Two Ronnies'* sketch, *Jolly Rhymes Limited*.

The two Ronnies became
not only a great team
but true friends.

The two Ronnies celebrate
being named joint
Show Business Personalities
of 1980 by the Variety
Club of Great Britain.

Ronnie and his wife, Joy, smile for the camera.

Ronnie and David Jason chat to Donald Sinden during the annual get-together at Ronnie's Oxfordshire home in 2004.

The two Ronnies talk during the annual get-together at Ronnie's Oxfordshire home in 2003.

Richard Briers shares a joke with Ronnie in 2003.

Ronnie, during the 1990s, relaxing at a caravan site near Kidlington, Oxfordshire, where he was visiting his friends, Paul and Pamela Jocelyn.

Two months of the summer were taken up with his other theatre show of the year: *Mr Whatnot* at the Arts Theatre, in which he played Lord Slingsby-Craddock. The Alan Ayckbourn comedy was directed by Warren Jenkins and joining Ronnie in the cast were, among others, Judy Campbell, Judy Cornwell and Peter King. Although it only ran for around three weeks it did receive a few favourable reviews. After sitting in the audience on the opening night Eric Shorter wrote, 'The great and abiding merit of . . . *Mr Whatnot* . . . is a refreshing and unsullied theatricality. Reading it would be a waste of time. Seeing it, on the whole, isn't . . . But the manner of their presentation in a series of lightly fantastic, flicking tableaux gives the simple fable an amusing invigoration.'[27] Although some of his contemporaries submitted pleasing notices, his view wasn't indicative of what all his contemporaries felt. There were many stinging comments, especially from Bernard Levin; considering this was Ayckbourn's first experience of the London stage, the extent of the criticism dented his confidence and contributed to the 25-year-old playwright deciding to work as a radio drama producer at the BBC in Leeds for six years; although he continued to write during this period, his output wasn't as prolific.

Glancing through the reviews, one notices the *Sunday Telegraph*'s critic studying Ronnie's performance, commenting that he 'milks all he can from the role of the old-fashioned buffer'[28]. The description rings a bell in terms of recognition. One of Ronnie's most famous character creations was the aged Lord Rustless, who made his television debut in a one-off episode in ITV's *Ronnie Barker Playhouse* series before appearing in two seasons of *Hark at Barker*. He later resurfaced in the BBC's 1970s series *His Lordship Entertains*, although this character's characteristics were commonly employed by Ronnie in future sketches and productions, such as *The Picnic* and *By the Sea*. But the character originated before any of these screen appearances, in the 1950s, according to Ronnie. He once explained that while scriptwriter Alun Owen first wrote the character into a script for an episode of the aforementioned *Ronnie Barker Playhouse*, the character dates back to his time at the Oxford Playhouse. 'The part was originally written for a woman, a strange county lady. But because of the balance of the cast we changed her sex and I played him as a retired military man. Equally odd, of course.'[29]

Ronnie could turn his hand to most characterisations, but portraying old men was one of his specialities. Earlier in the year he'd joined the cast of Eric Sykes' comedy *Sykes and A . . . .* In the episode 'Sykes and A Log Cabin' Ronnie played a tramp and was so effective he fooled Sykes, who thought an elderly actor had been cast in the role, not some 34-year-old. 'That was my first meeting with Ronnie,' recalled Eric Sykes, while being interviewed in 1996. 'I really thought that he was an elderly actor, but he was younger than me; that shows the brilliance of the man – I was getting up to give him my seat!'[30]

Mr Whatnot was written partly in dialogue, partly in mime. While some props were real, others were imaginary; the same formula was applied to conversations, with some mimed while others were audible. The mime sequences were supervised by Julian Chagrin, a mime artist and leading authority in the field, who found Ronnie to be 'charming, hardworking and serious'. Ronnie, of course, could tap into the experience gained while touring with the Mime Theatre Company in 1950. Although it had been a brief excursion into the art of mime it gave him a head-start when learning the moves under Chagrin's supervision. Reflecting on one particular scene in the play, Chagrin says, 'I helped them with miming a tennis match. The rackets were real but, of course, they had to mime the ball – it was very funny. I taught them how to animate the imaginary ball just with the head. Ronnie was a natural comedian in everything he did and took to it like a duck to water; he knew everything already, it was innate – just a case of reminding him.'

Remembering the tennis scene well, Judy Cornwell recalls, 'We had sounds of tennis balls going over the net, things like that, and had to have all our movements in synch with the sound recording. In other scenes, the doors were simply the shapes of the door frame and we mimed opening and closing it, again with the sounds on tape. It was a lovely story about a piano tuner who turns up at an English stately home and has to cope with the idiosyncrasies of aristocratic life.'

It was Judy's second time working with Ronnie and she became another performer who benefited from his knowledge and willingness to help others. 'Not only was he marvellous in the play, he was a marvellous director – or could have been. I was playing a maid and wondered what to do with my part, so he gave me some wonderful tips and brilliant comedy direction, which subsequently brought the house down. It was obvious he was extremely talented and I kept telling him that he should do some directing because his notes were so good.'

Amongst his radio work in 1964 was a final series of *Variety Playhouse* and more adventures with *The Navy Lark*, while he appeared in other television series, including *Bold as Brass*. On the big screen, meanwhile, he appeared in three films: *A Home of Your Own*, *Father Came Too!* and *The Bargee*. The last was filmed in Hertfordshire, along the Grand Union Canal, and told the story of a Casanova of the canals, played by Harry H. Corbett, who finds himself trapped into getting wed. The screenplay was written by Ray Galton and Alan Simpson, experienced writers best known for penning *Hancock's Half-Hour* and *Steptoe and Son*. Their rag-and-bone-man sitcom had just started when they wrote the script for *The Bargee*. When ABPC, for whom they had already written *The Rebel* as a vehicle for Tony Hancock, requested other ideas, they suggested something for Harry H. Corbett. Simpson explains, 'They didn't want to make a film about *Steptoe*, because they thought it was too soon. The French writer/producer Marcel Pagnol wrote some lovely little comedies during the 1930s and Ray and I, who'd always been fans, tried to make a film based on his style.' Once the casting of Corbett as a real rascal with a girl at every lock was finalised, attention turned towards finding someone to play his partner – in fact, his cousin – on the barge. 'We had the idea of Ronnie Barker, who dyed his hair jet black for the film, playing the role. He was a consummate comedy actor and slotted in well.' In fact, Ronnie was an estimable supporting actor in the film, an adroit feed.

Galton and Simpson spent time at Southall Docks researching the film, which took around seven weeks to shoot. Also, they edged along the canal network from Southall to Birmingham for a week in order to experience life on the water. Filming happened in and around the Hertfordshire village of Marsworth and hamlet of Bulbourne. The lockhouse featuring heavily in the film was occupied by Evelyn Barber, then thirty, with two young sons. She recalls the day someone came calling. 'Someone knocked on the door and said they were making a film and asked if they could use the house for seven days – they ended up staying seven weeks!' smiles Evelyn, who recalls Ronnie hanging around the house. 'He'd come in while waiting to film his scenes and play Lego with my son, Stephen. He seemed very friendly.' While the lounge became a makeshift make-up studio, the house's exterior was utilised, including shots of Harry H. Corbett clambering out of the window when Hugh Griffith's character arrives home, unaware that Corbett's character, Hemel Pike, has been with his daughter in the bedroom. 'The actual window he came out of was, in fact, our bathroom,' says Evelyn.

The film didn't break any box-office records, admits Alan Simpson. 'It didn't set the world alight, but was a pleasant picture to shoot.' Unfortunately, it took a beating from some film critics, a scribe in *Monthly Film Bulletin* explaining that it proves that 'what may make a genial bit of fun on the small screen sounds – and looks – intolerably vulgar on the big one'[31]. In the entertainment magazine *Variety* the reviewer felt that the *Steptoe* influence – same actor, same writers and even same director in Duncan Wood – loomed too large over the film, preventing it from creating its own identity. But not everyone posted negative reviews. Ernest Betts in the *Sunday People* regarded it as an example of 'how much fun you can get out of a picture without spending millions'[32]. Others highlighted Ronnie's contribution as Corbett's canal-boat mate: a 'very good mate judging by the performance of Ronnie Barker, who is just behind [Hugh] Griffith in the first three home with acting awards'[33], wrote Ann Pacey in the *Daily Herald*. The *Sunday Times'* Dilys Powell viewed his contribution as 'trim comedy'[34], while Nina Hibbin in the *Daily Worker* felt the humour was sluggish despite some 'engaging support'[35] from Barker.

Rank's release of the Julian Wintle-Leslie Parkyn production *Father Came Too!* saw Ronnie playing Josh, an archetypal cowboy builder, alongside Stanley Baxter and Sally Smith as newly-weds moving into their first home; their naïvety, however, sees them end up with a duff house, full of problems; attempts to repair it with the help – or hindrance – of a bunch of idiots see the picturesque little cottage go up in flames. Ronnie was back working with Leslie Phillips again, and the role of Josh turned out to be one of his biggest jobs, in terms of screen time, in the world of cinema. Despite a rather feeble storyline and a compendium of frolics and jolly japes, it was an entertaining film in parts, although its director Peter Graham Scott believed it ended up like a 'ragbag of *Carry On* comic postcard gags'[36].

When it came to finding a cottage that would be literally razed to the ground and torched in the process, all offers from interested parties who'd replied to an advert asking for a suitable property were swiftly withdrawn. Therefore, the art director Harry Pottle had no alternative but to design and build his own country cottage. On a plot in Hedgerley, Buckinghamshire, a group of workmen constructed the property in a fortnight at the expense of £2,000. The £1,000 garden, meanwhile, was ablaze with colourful plants and trees, which were nothing more than plastic flowers and plaster trees. So impressive was the end result that passers-by even made offers to buy it once the film crew had departed, not realising there wouldn't be much left of the dream home.

Both *The Bargee* and *Father Came Too!* had been enjoyable little comedies for Ronnie, but although his roles translated into much visibility on screen, they weren't particularly groundbreaking or memorable in terms of the impact on his career. Although the same, in some ways, could be said of his involvement in his third film of 1964, *A Home of Your Own*, it did introduce him to a style of filming he'd use to great effect in later years: the almost-silent, 'grumble and grunt' approach, as Ronnie branded it; it was a style he employed later in, among others, *Futtocks End* and *The Picnic*.

In *A Home of Your Own* Ronnie played a workman in charge of mixing cement on a building site. On first viewing, his contribution didn't seem particularly significant – after all, he didn't move very far or do very much, other than become increasingly ireful as more and more people trampled over his newly laid patch of cement, which, incidentally, had corks dropped into it to prevent the cement setting, thus allowing it to be used time and time again during the filming. But on closer inspection of Ronnie's efforts you notice a finely drawn vignette oozing comedy and characterisation.

The film about a newly-married couple – with Richard Briers playing the husband – buying a house on a spanking-new housing estate was, in many respects, a satirical glance at the building industry. What a journalist in the *Monthly Film Bulletin* described as 'evocatively photographed . . . a bright, if unpretentious, piece of film-making'[37] was directed by Jay Lewis and produced by Bob Kellett, whose credits include directing the Frankie Howerd films *Up Pompeii*, *Up the Chastity Belt* and *Up the Front*. Kellett was employed by Dormar Productions, who were financed by Tersons the well-known building company, and was in charge of producing a short publicity film annually for the company, highlighting its successes during the last twelve months.

One year, though, Kellett decided to take a different approach by injecting a little comedy. 'A film was required for this gathering of four hundred people at London's Grosvenor Hotel. A colleague thought that Tersons were big enough now to make a proper comment about things, from a different point of view.' Titled *Tersons Were There*, the same style of commentary was retained. 'In the beginning, no one seemed to be listening much, but eventually one or two people started to laugh, because they realised that it was a complete spoof on the usual thing that went on.' The film was warmly received by the audience, but Kellett was worried when afterwards he was ordered upstairs to talk to the bigwigs. 'The man in charge said, "You've really put your foot in it now, because people enjoyed that new publicity film."' After further discussions an idea was hatched to make a more extensive picture about the building trade.

Needing a director for the project, Kellett's PA suggested Jay Lewis – whom she'd been working with – whose CV contained a string of titles, including the war film *Morning Departure* and military comedy *Invasion Quartet*. 'She rang him up and said I had a project he might be interested in. My assistant and I took him to the Ritz for lunch, telling him after a very nice meal that we wanted to make a comedy about a building site – and there was one just outside London we could use. He thought it sounded interesting and went off to Ibiza with a writer, John Whyte, to write the screenplay.'

The initial £5,000 budget was eventually raised to £20,000, and when Kellett received the script he knew it was going to be fun to make. 'When you read it you could tell it would be interesting. Even those with small roles were happy to join in. Nobody got paid more than £100 and sometimes not as much as that, but everyone had a percentage of the takings written into their contracts, hoping that it would make a profit.' And it did, with the actors making more money than if they had been paid their normal fee upfront. Bob Kellett has only one regret, though. 'It's a pity we couldn't have made it in colour, but that cost a lot in those days.'

Finding a distributor wasn't easy, either. Kellett hawked it around Wardour Street, the centre of the British film industry where most major distributors had offices, but to no avail. 'A lot of them, including Rank, thought it was a load of old nonsense and not their kind of thing; that was a bit off-putting.' Then he struck lucky with British Lion, who promised one thousand outlets. The film's appeal, however, extended beyond British shores and was in demand around the world. 'We even won a prize at the Berlin Film Festival,' says Bob Kellett, who was very happy with how Ronnie performed. 'He was wonderfully funny with brilliant facial expressions.' They would team up again six years later in *Futtocks End*.

Chapter 9

Since turning professional, Ronnie had experienced only two years which were void of stage engagements: 1962 and, now, 1965, a year in which he was seen in only one film, too. Clearly, his focus was veering towards the small screen, a medium in which he felt comfortable, at ease and, increasingly, at home. Barry Cryer, who wrote and worked with Ronnie on numerous occasions, says, 'People used to say he could have been another Peter Sellers in films, with his talent and skill. But he told me once, "I've had this marvellous time in television. This is what I do. I'm a television man." He was perfect for TV, he found his natural home.'

In all his years in the profession, Ronnie never hankered after the life of a big-screen luminary, jetting to Hollywood to star in another blockbuster, pocketing mega bucks in the process. As for everybody, earning a decent living was important, but Ronnie always treasured his family life and remained content achieving as much as possible on home soil. He had ambitions, of course, and was determined to produce the best-quality work, but reaching the top of his profession wasn't the be-all and end-all of everything. Although assignments occasionally took him to foreign shores, such as Down Under with *The Two Ronnies* and Spain for the film *Robin and Marian*, Ronnie was largely a homebird in terms of professional engagements.

Away from work, Ronnie's life was thrown into turmoil for a while when his son Laurence became seriously ill. Aged five he caught measles and, worryingly, his condition didn't improve; in fact, it worsened and on contracting bronchial pneumonia he was rushed to hospital, where he was placed in an oxygen tent. Ronnie – who had just recorded an episode of the children's programme *Crackerjack* for a £52 fee – was beside himself with worry and for a time thought he was going to lose his son. One night, while sitting next to his son's hospital bed, Ronnie noticed that the supply of oxygen had run out. 'At one point the nurse couldn't change the oxygen and I had to summon up the strength of ten men to open the new oxygen tent.'[1] Thankfully, Laurence was soon on the road to recovery and back running around the garden at their house in Eastcote Road, Pinner, but the traumatic period left its mark on Ronnie, who from that moment became extra-conscious of his children's health.

His solitary film role in 1965 was Mr Galore in *Runaway Railway*, made by Fanfare Films Limited for the Children's Film Foundation. The story concerns a group of children saddened to hear that their local railway line, the Barming Loop, is closing and their beloved engine Matilda being scrapped. They attempt to delay the closure by a minor act of sabotage, but in doing so almost destroy the treasured train. When the eccentric Lord Chalk promises to take over the running of the line, so long as everything remains in working order, the children have the unenviable task of trying to repair the mess, aided by Mr Jones (Sydney Tafler) and Mr Galore (Ronnie), who claim to be railway enthusiasts; it's all a ruse, of course, because they're really criminals intent on using the little locomotive in a proposed mail-train robbery.

While scenes involving special effects were filmed at Pinewood, the rest of the picture was shot in Hampshire, with Bordon Station transformed into Barming Station and the army allowing the production team to film on a stretch of military-owned railway line at Longmoor, built by the Royal Engineers in the early twentieth century to help train soldiers in railway construction.

As well as spending a few weeks in Hampshire, Ronnie was kept busy on the radio and remained in demand on television. Among his appearances he played Jerry Cruncher, a porter at Tellson's Bank of London, in BBC's Sunday afternoon production of Dickens' *A Tale of Two Cities*, which ran to ten episodes from the beginning of April.

Exterior shooting took Ronnie to various locations in and around London, including All Saints' Churchyard in Parish Road, Old Isleworth, Middlesex, and Shere Manor, Netley Heath, in East Horsley, Surrey. Unfortunately, his performance didn't attract individual praise in the Press, unlike his time as Grimwood a month earlier in *The Keys of the Café*. Reviewing the instalment of ITV's *Armchair Theatre* series Lyn Lockwood at the *Daily Telegraph* described Ronnie's performance as 'excellent'[2]. Equally complimentary was an unnamed reviewer in *The Times* who wrote, 'Mr Ronnie Barker, whom we usually see as drolly eccentric, gave Grimwood the sort of deliberate, semi-Napoleonic but innately uncertain determination which is the ineffective man's way of hiding his ineffectuality.'[3]

Four months later Ronnie appeared in a similarly titled programme, this time *Gaslight Theatre*, a season of six old-fashioned melodramas delivered in the mood of the Victorian theatre. Resembling a little repertory company, the actors, including Eira Heath and Warren Mitchell, appeared in each of the six plays, all adapted for the screen by Alec Clunes and directed by Bryan Sears. The BBC2 series began with *Maria Marten* on the evening of Saturday, 31 July. Ronnie was kept on his toes in the one-hour show, playing three separate characters: Mr Marten, father of the heroine; Ishmael Lee, a gipsy; and Pharos Lee, the juvenile lead.

As Ronnie revealed, the series necessitated his getting involved in editing when the scripts ran over time. Then, after yet another attempt to cut one of the scripts down to an hour's duration failed, Ronnie reacted. 'I stood up – I've never done this before or since – and Warren Mitchell always remembers it, I said, "OK, Alec, it's two hours. When it's an hour, give us a ring and I'll come in again." And I walked out. I was amazed at my own courage then. I remember their faces as I went out, they were frozen.'[4] Clunes later contacted Ronnie, admitting something had to be done; asking for his views on how the script could be trimmed, Ronnie was happy to help, suggesting deleting a subplot running the extent of the script, but not crucial to the main storyline. Ronnie's advice was accepted willingly and did the trick. The series, says Warren Mitchell, was 'rather disastrous'. He explains, 'There was a lot of fighting going on, and Ronnie should have had a job at the United Nations because he was such a wonderful peacemaker. He'd shuffle up to you and say, "Come on, it's not all that serious."' Reflecting further, Warren believes it was a 'daft idea the BBC had of having a theatrical director and a television director trying to work hand-in-hand, and it didn't work.' He does, though, have happy memories of working with Ronnie, particularly seeing him in drag during one of the instalments. 'He took to it like a duck to water. I think he was a frustrated pantomime dame!'

Eira Heath was aware of the impasse which led to Ronnie walking off in frustration. 'The television director and theatre director were so good in their own fields, but it didn't quite work bringing them together.' She also had her own mini-confrontations with each, recalling a moment in the strangely titled episode 'The Drunkard, or the Sins of the Parents Shall Be Visited . . .'. 'I was required to sing a song and cut out some of the verses to make it the right length. Ronnie agreed with that. But because some changes were required to the show, the television director asked if I minded singing all of the verses and they would cut afterwards. I objected, because it would give a different dynamic to the performance. But Ronnie sat down with me over a coffee and completely rewrote it, verse after verse, just like that – new words to sing to the same tune.'

Although Ronnie's involvement in reworking the scripts was born out of necessity, it would become an increasingly important element of his craft: writing sketches, programmes, one-liners, knocking scripts into shape to maximise the comedic or, at times, dramatic potential were all components he became famous for, and something at which he was particularly adroit.

Directors, script editors and producers accepting advice from Ronnie, even so early in his career, isn't something which surprises his friend Barry Cryer. 'They all listened to Ron, because he knew what he was talking about; he was an amazingly versatile man. He was an actor with solid experience behind him who had a flair for comedy and could write and virtually direct; he was singular in that way, I don't remember another performer like him.'

They first worked together on *The Frost Report*, which Ronnie identified as one of the chief milestones in his career. The satirical show would catapult him into the public psyche: yes, he had become a familiar voice and, to a lesser extent, face in the world of entertainment, but largely in minor and supporting roles – that was about to change.

During the final weeks of January 1966 Ronnie was rehearsing at the Theatre Royal in London's Stratford East. He was cast as Alf Always in the Stephen Lewis-scripted comedy *Sweet Fanny Adams*. The shortlived play ran between 7th and 19th February, with Ronnie's confidence in his own abilities having reached the point where he'd happily add the occasional amusing line to his dialogue. 'He was very assured and adept, even then, at adding the odd funny line to his part,' recalls Brian Murphy, who played a character called Liz. 'My role was supposed to have been for a woman, but then they thought it would be a marvellous part for me, played as a man, except they never bothered changing the name!'

When Joan Littlewood's Theatre Workshop wasn't actively in residence at the Theatre Royal, the venue was occasionally let; it was during one of these gap periods that Lewis's play, set in a pub, was staged. Ronnie played the landlord in the cheery, lighthearted comedy directed by Kenneth Parrott, who recalls Ronnie, again, making suggestions to help the production. 'There was a scene in which a pub party atmosphere developed. We were working on this one day and next morning Ronnie, with typical modesty, said, "I hope you don't mind, but I thought that if we were going to have a song, I've got a suggestion." It was a song he'd written.' Kenneth remembers a 'natural air of experience' about the 36-year-old actor. 'But he was by no means pushy, self-assertive or egocentric. He was a joy, wonderfully common-sensed and a "let's get on with it" type of guy.'

Unfortunately, Ronnie was unable to finish the short run because a bigger opportunity presented itself, and one he couldn't refuse, leaving his agent to negotiate his release from the stage contract. The golden opportunity was a part in *The Frost Report*, which followed on nicely from the David Frost-presented *That Was The Week That Was* and the less successful *Not So Much a Programme, More a Way of Life*; another satirical show of quality, *The Frost Report* offered an assortment of sketches, music and monologues: Ronnie experienced his first real taste of delivering the latter in the show, something which would become one of his fortes. Each week, the programme focused on a particular subject: from holidays and sin to crime and education, it seemed nothing escaped the Frost team's attention.

Producing and directing the programme was Jimmy Gilbert, already an admirer and extensive user of Ronnie's talents. Bill Cotton, the then Assistant Head of Light Entertainment, asked Jimmy what he thought of Frost and received the thumbs-up from the Scottish-born producer/director, who – a couple of years earlier – had shared the same flight back from the Montreux Festival. 'Over a glass of champagne we said we'd have to work together some time,' recalls Jimmy, who embarked on a mini-tour of Europe in the name of *The Frost Report*. 'I was given a completely open brief to do what I wanted.' All that Tom Sloan, the then Head of Light Entertainment, stipulated was that he wanted it to be variety 'with a small "v" not a capital'. It was suggested Frost and Gilbert grabbed their pass-ports and set off on a talent-spotting tour of European cities. 'Tom said we should go and see all these amazing acts and meet their agents in preparation for bringing them over to appear on the show. We went to Paris, Amsterdam, Copenhagen, Berlin, Brussels, visiting clubs and theatres, supposedly looking for new talent; I don't know what we thought we were going to end up with, but it worked well, if only because we had a great time and got to know each other extremely well.'

By the time the pair reached Amsterdam's Schiphol Airport they had agreed on the show's format, as Jimmy explains. 'We decided to concentrate on a different subject each week, with Tony Jay writing a developing monologue which would be given to the writers, a learned essay providing background to each subject.' Once the format had formulated in Frost's and Gilbert's minds attention turned, initially, to the writing. A crop of young British talent, including Michael Palin, Terry Jones, Marty Feldman, John Law, Eric Idle, David Nobbs, Graham Chapman and Barry Cryer were brought in to provide material. Casting, meanwhile, saw Frost hire John Cleese and Ronnie Corbett, while Jimmy Gilbert signed up Ronnie. 'I had a tall one in Cleese and a tiny one in Corbett, so Ronnie seemed an obvious choice. I rang him and asked if he'd be interested. He said he'd love to do it, but was at Stratford East, so we'd have to speak to his agent to see if he could get out of the show.' Fortunately, he was released from *Sweet Fanny Adams* in time to begin filming and planning for the first series, having already been released to rehearse for the pilot episode, for which he was paid £126, and its subsequent recording on the 6 February.

As the actors and writers braved the cold January air to reach the Addison Road Boys' Club for the first rehearsal at 10 a.m. (subsequent rehearsals took place at the West Kensington Church), Jimmy Gilbert had no doubts Ronnie would settle in. 'It was a tiny cast and all shone.' He acknowledges, however, that the writers struggled to find suitable material for Sheila Steafel, who was brought into the team as the female lead after impressing Jimmy with her performance in Michael Bentine's *It's A Square World*. Despite lack of air time – the writers found it difficult writing for women, according to Jimmy Gilbert – Sheila enjoyed working on the series. 'It seemed to gel from the start, one of those lucky moments. It was fun to work on, partly because we all had a similar sense of humour. Ronnie Barker was very pleasant and clever, a marvellous character actor.' Each performer had their own unique qualities, claims Sheila, who classes a 'quick eye and wit' among Ronnie's. 'He was very observant, too.'

One factor behind the show's success was the relaxed atmosphere generated among cast and crew. Everyone worked diligently and turned out high-quality work, but there was always room for fun and humour, such as the obligatory game of football before the day's proceedings began. 'All the lads, writers and actors, including David Frost, played football with a tennis ball in the hall before we did anything,' recalls Sheila, smiling. 'Then we'd go upstairs and read the sketches. We decided between us if they were funny; Jimmy Gilbert tended to rely on our reaction as to whether he'd put them in the show or not.'

Barry Cryer concurs with Sheila regarding the easy-going atmosphere. 'It was a very warm set-up.' He adds that he was one of those who enjoyed the kick-around in the downstairs hall. 'David [Frost] was usually in goal. Ronnie B. joined in, but wasn't the most agile; Ronnie C. was darting and weaving about much more nimbly.'

The pilot episode was eventually shown as the first of thirteen in Series One, running between 10 March and 9 June; the audience reaction was positive from the beginning: the opening programme, spotlighting authority, was watched by 15 per cent of the population and, via the BBC's audience survey, scored an impressive Reaction Index of 72, compared to an average of 63 for Frost's earlier show *That Was The Week That Was*. The Audience Research Report, covering the opening episode, stated that many viewers rated the programme 'much more clever and entertaining . . . than the cruel barbs and blue jokes of his [Frost's] earlier programme'[5]. The pleasing results weren't just a fluke based on a curious audience tuning in to the first programme of a new show before returning to their normal viewing pattern. By the middle of June nearly 24 per cent of the population were watching and the Reaction Index had climbed to 76.

The *Radio Times* described Ronnie as a man who had 'launched a thousand laughs in many BBC TV comedy shows'[6] when previewing the first episode. Ronnie appeared in sketches, particularly 'quickies', the term given to small pieces lasting ten to sixty seconds; arguably, the most famous is, of course, the class sketch, written by John Law. It was so successful Jimmy Gilbert requested one each week. 'Other people wrote them, including Ronnie, but they never had the same impact,' he admits. 'John Law, who'd worked on the Michael Bentine series I directed before becoming comedy advisor for Light Entertainment, wrote it specifically for John Cleese, Ronnie Barker and Ronnie Corbett. I recognised immediately that it was pure gold.'

In many ways *The Frost Report* was instrumental in shaping Ronnie's future. First, it was regularly watched by up to fifteen million people, ensuring his face and voice became well and truly recognised by the viewing public. This, of course, had its downside, particularly for an intensely private man like Ronnie. His daughter Charlotte once revealed how his increasing fame affected day-to-day events taken for granted, such as holidays. 'I suppose I was six or seven and we were going over to the beach . . . with my mother we walked across the road and walked across the green that led on to the beach and I remember turning around and my father waving to me from the window. He couldn't come on to the beach, there were too many people who'd recognise him; it wouldn't be a relaxing time for him.'[7] Nonetheless, Ronnie was receiving plenty of televisual exposure, which he welcomed.

The series, which was almost universally complimented by the Press, also afforded Ronnie the chance to indulge himself increasingly in the monologues, initially stepping in when John Cleese was unavailable, which became an integral part of the programme. They highlighted not only Ronnie's verbal dexterity but his ability for wordplay. One particular scene well received by the critics saw him present the Exchequer's post-Budget television broadcast. It was a segment of the 'Parliament' episode transmitted in the second season on 4 May 1967 and many reviewers regarded the sketch as the episode's finest. Richard Last in *The Sun* regarded Ronnie as 'one of the funniest natural comics on television, doing a politician getting hopelessly entangled with his teleprompter'[8]. The show's quick pace and originality won it many admirers in the newspaper world, with its team of balanced regulars becoming one of the cornerstones of its popularity.

The aforementioned chancellor monologue was penned by Barry Cryer, who believes it exemplified Ronnie's incredible agility with words. 'It was just a parade of clichés that contradicted each other,' he explains, 'but Ronnie was incredibly disciplined and knew every syllable.'

Most crucially for Ronnie's continuing career, *The Frost Report* introduced him to someone with whom he'd forge one of the most successful partnerships in British television – Ronnie Corbett. The conjunction of their names happened long before they were officially dubbed The Two Ronnies. Barry Cryer says the chemistry between the pair was evident from the moment they began working together. 'The first thing they ever did was set in a police station. Mike Palin and Terry Jones wrote a sketch and the opening two lines saw Ronnie Barker coming in and saying to the superintendent, who's Ronnie C., "Morning, super," with Ronnie C. replying, "Morning, wonderful." The rest of the sketch was cut and just those two lines used as a quickie on the programme.'

It may have been the first time the Ronnies had worked together, but they had met three years earlier in 1963 at the Buckstone Club, an actors' watering hole in London's Suffolk Street. Ronnie C. worked as a barman between jobs in the basement club, which became a focal point for those plying their trade in the entertainment business, including Ronnie B. who would pop in for a quick drink with his wife Joy after recording *The Navy Lark*.

As soon as the Ronnies began performing together on the show, which won the coveted Golden Rose of Montreux in 1967, Ronnie C. knew he'd get on with his namesake. 'We had kindred spirits. We'd both been in the theatre since our teenage years: Ronnie in rep and me in concert parties and pantomimes. Being experienced stage performers, we warmed to each other quite quickly. I knew I'd be able to work with Ron. We were very comfortable together.' Their comedic styles complemented each other's. 'Ronnie had more character-acting skills than me, whereas I was more vaudeville, so we were a good mix. Our tastes regarding humour were always similar, too, so there were never any clashes.' Ronnie C. believes that they gravitated towards each other because neither had been to university, unlike the majority of people working on the show, giving them something else in common.

During the two years *The Frost Report* aired on BBC, Ronnie Barker was heard on a host of radio programmes, including his final two series of *The Navy Lark* and various other television shows, such as *The Saint*. In the episode called 'The Better Mousetrap' Ronnie played the ineffective Alphonse, tasked by the French police to tail the Saint, who becomes chief suspect when a series of thefts occurs at a South of France hotel. In another series to eventually attract cult status, *The Avengers*, he popped up as cat-lover Edwin Cheshire in 'The Hidden Tiger'.

Meanwhile, in the sitcom genre, Ronnie adopted a Russian accent during September and October 1966 for his role as Grischa Petrovich in *Foreign Affairs*, a comedy focusing on the conflicts between the British Foreign Office and the Russian Embassy in London. While Leslie Phillips played Dennis Proudfoot, a lecherous personal assistant to the Administrator for Foreign Relations, Ronnie was the bumbling, pro-British personal assistant to the commissar for Foreign Relations. The six-part series began on 16 September, but wasn't recommissioned for a new season.

Writers Johnnie Mortimer and Brian Cooke were asked by Frank Muir, the then Head of Light Entertainment, to help write the series. 'We were writing a radio series called *Men From The Ministry*, which had a similar premise, so I can see why Frank approached us,' says Cooke. 'I'm not sure who thought of the sitcom idea, but I suspect it was an in-house thing, because several writers were involved. It wasn't working properly, because each writer had a different idea of what kind of humour it should be. It meant taking scripts from various people and making them into a successful series – it was our first rewriting job.

'The initial script we had to deal with was basically not funny and we rewrote practically the whole thing. When Frank Muir handed over the next script we noticed quickly that it was a badly written whimsical story involving things like fairy boots being mistaken for ferry boats and was more suitable for radio. We puzzled over it for several days before telling Frank that we couldn't adapt it for the series. He agreed with us and a very well-known writer's material was assigned to oblivion.' It became clear that reworking existing scripts that were, frankly, unsuitable for the series wasn't going to work, so Mortimer and Cooke were commissioned to write the remaining five scripts.

When it came to shooting the episodes, one in particular sticks in Brian Cooke's mind. 'It involved night filming outside the Russian embassy. Obviously we couldn't use the actual embassy, so the locations manager found a high whitewashed wall surrounding a big house in Hampstead to suit our purpose. Johnnie and I went along in my car to find out what filming actually involved. It turned out that the house was owned by Bob Monkhouse, who invited Leslie, Ronnie and the director in for a glass or two of Glenfiddich. It was a bitterly cold night and Johnnie and I, huddled in my car, watched our colleagues cheerfully swigging whisky in the warmth of an upstairs room while we went thirsty; it was a reminder that the writers aren't actually considered to be as important as they think they are. I told this tale to Bob Monkhouse decades later and he was horrified. He said, "You should have knocked on the door, I would have given you a glass of water."' Regarding working with Ronnie on the series, Brian recalls a 'charming man, very friendly and open'.

The first episode received a warm welcome from those quizzed for the BBC's audience survey, with one woman declaring it bode well for the future because it was, in her opinion, the best comedy programme for some time. But the decision-makers at the BBC obviously didn't agree and the series never returned after its initial outing, despite its moderate success. Reaction from critics was mixed: many, though, felt Ronnie and Leslie worked well together. Although he thought the show over-strained credulity, an unnamed critic in *The Times* commented that it offered the pair 'another occasion to show how amusing, in a light, sophisticated way, they can be'[9]. But Philip Pursar in the *Sunday Telegraph* wasn't enamoured of Ronnie's performance, writing, 'The Russian who apparently is to be a regular foil and opposite number is played by Ronnie Barker, a performer I would have thought it impossible to make unfunny. It just goes to show how wrong you can be.'[10]

When the closing episode of the second season of *The Frost Report* was screened by the BBC on 29 June 1967 it was never to return, except for a one-off festive special, *Frost Over Christmas*, transmitted just three days before Ronnie and Joy were celebrating the birth of their third child Adam on 29 December 1967.

Despite the series having been a tremendous success, there were changes afoot. In 1967 the Independent Television Authority reviewed its network of franchises and many changes to the televisual map took place, including London Television Consortium (later to become known as LWT) winning their region's weekend viewing from 7 p.m. on Fridays, with programmes networked to other areas of the UK. David Frost, still not yet thirty, had formed a consortium of high-powered individuals whose bid was accepted. After winning the franchise, Frost launched a three-part package of programmes: *Frost on Friday*, looking at current affairs, *Frost on Saturday*, concentrating on celebrity gossip and *Frost on Sunday*, focusing on entertainment. Switching stations from BBC to ITV didn't just apply to Frost; the majority of performers and writers associated with *The Frost Report* decamped, too, with Ronnie being signed up by Frost's own production company David Paradine Productions, which would guide his television career for a period of time.

The main players in the Sunday show were none other than the two Ronnies. While John Cleese had decided not to make the switch in order to concentrate on other projects, particularly writing, Sheila Steafel didn't transfer, either. The main female roles in *Frost on Sunday* were picked up by Josephine Tewson, with whom Ronnie B. would share a long professional relationship. Meanwhile, some of the writers, such as Michael Palin, would crop up in cameo roles, too.

But before he debuted on the new ITV programme Ronnie appeared in his solitary theatre role for 1968, playing Birdboot, a theatre critic, in Tom Stoppard's short one-act play *The Real Inspector Hound* at London's Criterion Theatre. The rather surreal plot centres around two theatre critics – Moon and Birdboot, originally played by Richard Briers and Ronnie respectively – who are sitting in a theatre watching a ludicrous murder mystery before becoming involved in the plot and sparking off a series of unfortunate events.

When theatre producer Michael Codron acquired the rights to Stoppard's play and suggested Ronnie Barker for the role of Birdfoot, the lubricious tabloid-style critic, the play's director Robert Chetwyn had only seen Ronnie on television. 'When I met Ronnie in Michael's office he seemed a very nice, intelligent man and I had no worries at all. Sure enough, he was an extremely professional guy with an excellent acting technique. Tom's play is a bit intellectual and you had to be subtle. For comedy, some performers would have played it over-the-top, but Ronnie didn't, he always kept his performance on an incredibly tight rein; his comedy technique was wonderful.'

Robert was pleased with how the play panned out, although he has one regret. 'It was a one-act play and Michael Codron had seen a very funny production called *The Audition*, so he began the evening with that. But it was a comedy at a different level and the wrong kind of humour, in my view, to go before *The Real Inspector Hound*. People laughed outrageously at the first piece, so trying to get them to think rather more deeply for *The Real Inspector Hound* was difficult.' Robert wasn't alone in this way of thinking, with the *Guardian*'s critic Philip Hope-Wallace remarking that the play suffered by following a curtain-raiser. As usual, reviews were mixed. W. A. Darlington in the *Daily Telegraph* thought it was acted with 'great gusto'[11] by Richard Briers and Ronnie Barker. At the *Sunday Times* Harold Hobson described their performance as one of 'gaiety, petulance and wit'[12].

The cast were contracted for six months, long enough for Ronnie, who trod carefully after the bad experience of *Irma La Douce*; now he avoided long runs in the theatre like the plague, something acknowledged by Richard Briers, who played the intellectual critic, a pretentious man who found meaning in everything, even fourth-rate thrillers. The repetition of saying the same lines night after night, as well as the discipline of leaving home every evening at the same time takes its toll. 'There's only so much of that you can stand,' he says. 'I think Ronnie wanted to write and become famous rather than just being a stage actor.'

Of course, Ronnie eventually concentrated his energies on the small screen, a medium which suited him down to the ground, says Richard Briers. 'He did early radio work, but in a way you need him to be there, to see him, otherwise you just hear a voice, which although very clever and comedic in its tone, you forget five minutes later. Once you've seen him, with his rather large presence, you don't forget him.'

Richard enjoyed working alongside Ronnie, who became a great friend, and remembers the times he made him laugh 'Being critics in the play, we both had programmes. When the focus was on the actors performing in this appalling play, which Stoppard wrote so beautifully, Ronnie would draw rather naughty pictures of women and show them to me to try and make me laugh. He was a talented artist and enjoyed showing off his drawings; but he was clever at so many things.'

Richard experienced Ronnie's wit away from work, too. Once, while arriving for lunch at the Barkers' Oxfordshire home, Richard and his wife, Ann, were shown through to the garden. Ronnie was nowhere to be seen. Suddenly, a voice boomed: 'Get off my land!' Richard recalls: 'It was Ronnie, in his best squire's voice, shouting from behind a hedge. He then emerged with a big smile on his face.'

Playing Mrs Drudge, an elderly housekeeper in *The Real Inspector Hound*, was Josephine Tewson, who would go on to appear with Ronnie in various television shows, including his final sitcom *Clarence*. Although she had seen Ronnie and admired his work, this was the first time they had appeared together. 'I was playing a sixty-year-old, even though I must have been in my twenties,' says Josephine, who was acutely aware that Ronnie was intent on avoiding the agony of another long run. 'Ronnie had experienced staying in a play that went on and on. It was in the days when sometimes you couldn't get out of it. You had to stay until the play closed. There were people who had nervous breakdowns because they found themselves stuck in plays. You can go potty performing the same scenes night after night after night, doing eight shows a week.'

The Real Inspector Hound ran until the beginning of December 1968, by which time cinemagoers had seen Ronnie in two earlier produced films, playing George Venaxas in the American-distributed *The Man Outside* and Mr Prendergast in the Children's Film Foundation's *Ghost of a Chance*. Television viewers, meanwhile, were also watching Ronnie and Josephine on the box, because for the last four months of the play's run they were appearing in *Frost on Sunday* and *The Real Inspector Hound* simultaneously. As Josephine points out, it's down to Ronnie that she got the chance to work on Frost's programme. 'They needed a girl in the series, someone who could do sketches and play different parts. Ronnie mentioned me to the director and I did several things, eventually being offered a contract.'

For the launch of London Weekend Television's coverage, the newly printed schedules revealed that Frank Muir would start the ball rolling at 7 p.m. on Friday, 2 August 1968 with a programme titled *We Have Ways of Making You Laugh*, with the first piece of action from the *Frost on Sunday* team planned for Sunday at 9.10 p.m. Unfortunately, chaos ensued when industrial action among the technicians' union led to viewers being greeted by nothing more than black screens, delayed programmes and management swapping hats and becoming temporary crew members in a desperate attempt to salvage what they could of the disastrous first few nights.

Chapter 10

When you're launching something new you can usually expect a few teething problems, but sheer bad luck and wretched timing were behind the fiasco which greeted the first few days of London Weekend Television's spanking new schedule. An industrial dispute between technicians and management over extra pay for working weekends led to walkouts and strikes, ensuring the early days of *The Frost Report* were uneasy.

Philip Casson, the programme's producer, recalls the chaos in the studio on that balmy August evening, when members of management stepped in to operate the technical equipment themselves. 'Being a union member, I wasn't allowed to direct or produce the show. Many of the executives who didn't belong to the union took over. They were people who had been cameramen, floor assistants or sound engineers. I was expecting something to go wrong every moment, which, of course, it did.'

The chaos didn't help the first-night nerves for the *Frost* team, as Michael Palin explains. 'It was nerve-racking. We were asked to move to a smaller studio, so all the sketches were done live in a different place from where we expected to do them. I realised then that somebody like Ronnie's great skill is his absolute dependability. Even in the midst of all this we managed to get a show together.'[1]

When the dispute was settled and Casson returned to his director's chair, Philip adored working with Ronnie B. 'He was an extremely funny man – very mild and professional. Being that the show was live, which could be terrifying, especially during commercial breaks when we were all chasing around and the sets had to be changed, you always knew you were in safe hands with him.'

Ronnie, like any true professional, gave his utmost in whatever he did. As Barry Cryer explains, the comedy actor's life was a combination of compartments. 'He loved his home life and his family, that was kept very separate. He wasn't a man obsessed with work when he wasn't working; he was very disciplined as far as that was concerned.' Ronnie wasn't a party animal, desperate to prop up the bar for a few hours after the final scene had been filmed. He was more interested in getting home. Josephine Tewson recalls a conversation she had with him while waiting for a train on the London Underground. 'What I loved about him was that he was so good and marvellous to work with and had his priorities absolutely right: top of the list were Joy and his family.

'One day, we were travelling to Wembley to rehearse *Frost on Sunday* when he told me he'd been offered a prestigious part on television. I can't remember what, but he couldn't do it. I asked why and he replied, "It's during the school holidays." I said, "What do you mean it's during the school holidays? It's television, you'll be rehearsing during the week, so you can see Joy and the children at weekends – and it's only for three weeks." He was adamant, though, explaining, "No, no, it's the holidays and they'll be at Littlehampton." OK, he didn't play this wonderful part, but it wasn't a sacrifice for him. It was just the natural order of things. The family came first,' says Josephine, who remembers a time she dined out with Ronnie and Joy at Beotys, a restaurant in London's Covent Garden. 'We were going to watch a film, but had a meal first. Ronnie asked what I was going to have and when I said the veal sounded nice, he gave me a long lecture on why one must never eat veal because of the terrible way they treated the calves. I ended up choosing something else. I remember Joy saying from time to time, "Oh, let her have veal if she wants it." I replied, "No, no, I'll never eat it again, it's all right." He was very serious about it.'

When in work mode, he was equally serious, giving his best and expecting everyone to follow suit. 'He was a perfectionist,' says Richard Briers. He knew what he wanted and became a real expert in comedy business, comedy timing and, of course, comedy writing; he understood what worked and what didn't. Ronnie extracted the best from fellow performers not by demanding and stamping his foot in rage, but by presenting a pleasant demeanour and encouraging. Richard adds, 'He was very kind and amusing. And when he became a big name and began to really direct his own sketches, I think he was then very strong, meticulous and disciplined. He believed in the old-fashioned values of standing still and being clear in diction.'

Ronnie was also becoming increasingly interested in the mechanics of programme-making: it seemed there wasn't an aspect of creating a show which he didn't want to become involved in, and this came to the fore when starring in his own shows and working alongside Ronnie C. in *The Two Ronnies*. 'He was a worrier,' says Barry Cryer, affectionately. 'He'd turn up at the editing of the shows with his sandwiches and bottle of milk, and he virtually directed some of the filming when they went on location.'

From his early days in repertory theatre Ronnie had revealed an ability to understand the technical side of acting and how a production should be constructed. As he gained more and more experience in his trade, this interest and knowledge became increasingly evident – something film editor Ray Millichope can vouch for. He first met Ronnie on *The Frost Report* and will never forget his visits to the editing suite with Jimmy Gilbert and David Frost. 'In the cutting room there used to be trim bins, each containing several strips of film, and he'd rummage through them looking at all the out-takes. I found it incredible that this man could look at these tiny frames and try to figure out what they showed. I found it irritating at first, because I wondered what he was looking for.'

Some of the writers from the Frost stable who continued penning sketches and 'quickies' for *Frost on Sunday* found themselves becoming more involved with Ronnie and the rest of the team. David Nobbs, who was later to write, among others, *The Fall and Rise of Reginald Perrin*, says, 'I'd go into the studio and meet people, one of them being Ronnie, who was a mainstay of the sketches. My first impression was what a brilliant actor he was, although a very shy man.'

Ex-Python Michael Palin often wrote with Terry Jones, criss-crossing London to work at Jones' house in Camberwell, South London or Palin's in Gospel Oak. Their association with the Frost team began as 'junior writers' on *The Frost Report*. 'The three of them together (Ronnie B., Ronnie C. and John Cleese) were a writer's dream, because they played material so well,' explains Michael. 'It was a wonderful feeling knowing you were in good hands. Ronnie B. was very amiable. He didn't seem particularly complicated, just a nice guy.'

Frost on Sunday ran to two series, the initial season finishing during the first week of January 1969, the second beginning a year later and ending in spring 1970. By the time the second series was screened, some critics felt that the formula was beginning to tire. The *Daily Express'* James Thomas wrote, 'How can you cross David Frost, two top comedians, three singers and eighteen script writers, and turn up with a show as obvious as this one? I don't really feel very funny about it.'[2] He felt it was a 'rehash of an ageing formula and it looks like it.'[3] However, he did, like many of his contemporaries during the two series, praise the Ronnies, stating, 'Here in support are two of the funniest men on TV . . . the bulky Barker and the tiny Corbett, both of whom can play a good piece of nonsense for all they are worth.'[4]

Being live television, there were some fraught moments, as Josephine Tewson recalls. 'Every Sunday frightened you to death, because if anything went wrong it was there to be seen.' She will never forget the moment disaster nearly struck during a monologue Ronnie was reading. 'Admittedly, he read it from the autocue, but he needed his glasses. He had a hell of a quick change from the previous sketch before and no sooner had he ran on than "action" was called. Ronnie said, "Good evening," looked up and realised he didn't have his glasses. He patted his jacket pockets in a kind of "Oh my god!" way and, fortunately, noticed they were in there. He covered it up beautifully. Little Ronnie and I had fits and had begun to run around the dressing room looking for them. In fact, both Ronnies had tried using contact lenses instead of glasses, but were so grumpy because neither could wear them that we told them to go back to glasses!'

Watching a dress recording at LWT's Wembley Studios one day was a teenager who would become one of the most prominent writers for *The Two Ronnies* and pen a string of hit programmes, including the classic sitcom *One Foot in the Grave*. David Renwick had first become aware of Ronnie while watching him on *The Frost Report*. 'It was pretty much cult viewing at Luton Grammar School when I was in my mid-teens. In fact, I eventually managed to organise an outing to see one of the shows, in 1967, when they were going out live from the Television Theatre in Shepherd's Bush. And a couple of years after that I got tickets to *Frost on Sunday*. At the dress recording they would test out their material on an invited audience to get a measure of what was working and what wasn't.'

One particular segment sticks in David's mind. 'It was called "Sayings of the Week and the People Who Said Them", where they would cut away to one of the two Ronnies for some bit of dialogue or little vignette, then back to Frost for the tag. At the end of the spot I remember Ronnie B. came on in a vicar's dog collar, calling out, "Right, all you Charlies. This way Charlies. Welcome Charlies, one and all . . ." And Frost had the pay-off: "Charlie Chaplain." There was silence as it died on its feet, then Frost ad-libbed, "Probably *not* the joke to finish with." And I can still see Ronnie leaving the floor in his cassock muttering, "Not the bloody joke to *start* with . . ."

'It was the first time that – even as a schoolboy – I had a glimpse of the underlying steeliness with which Ronnie always approached his comedy. In that tiny unguarded aside you could read the frustration of a supporting player being assigned material he was clearly unhappy with, and it made sense of the very strict and proprietorial way he would approach the selection of his scripts once he had acquired complete control. At that point in my life, of course, I was simply a young, star-struck observer, and had no idea how gracious he would be about my own writing many years later.'

In addition to the regular pool of writers contributing sketches and 'quickies', envelopes from an unknown writer began arriving at the television studios, attributed to a certain Gerald Wiley. The name was unknown to everyone reading the scripts, which came via his supposed agent, who just happened to be Ronnie Barker's, too. But all took notice, because they were of a high standard and certainly useable. The story has been told many times in print and on television, so most readers will know that the man behind the pen name was, in fact, Ronnie Barker. After becoming frustrated at some of the sketches being used on *Frost on Sunday*, he decided to write a few himself. Adopting a fictitious name avoided the embarrassing situation of his work being accepted simply because no one wanted to hurt his feelings. Anonymity meant his contributions could be judged purely on merit without extraneous influences coming into play. Not wanting to reveal his own name as the author of the sketches, Ronnie and his agent went to great lengths, almost setting up contingency plans, to cover every eventuality. If Frank Muir wanted to meet Wylie, he would be informed that the writer was a recluse; later, when Muir kept pressing to meet the mysterious man, Ronnie told his agent to convene a meeting, but to later phone and cancel it. The next challenge to retaining Gerald Wiley's anonymity came when Ronnie Corbett, wanting to buy the rights to a sketch Wiley had written, titled 'Doctor's Waiting Room', for his next summer show, asked Ronnie Barker whether he thought Wiley would sell? There was only one way to find out, write to his agent, said Ronnie B.

Ronnie Corbett put pen to paper and his request winged its way to Wiley's agent; it wasn't long before a reply arrived. 'The request from the writer came back saying he wanted £3,000. I told Ronnie and he said, "Oh, my god, £3,000!" Then Gerald Wiley gave me the rights in perpetuity for the lovely way I performed the sketch. I thought that was very nice of him, so bought some cut glasses with "GW" engraved on them; I left them for him at the reception in London Weekend Television, only to find that Ronnie B. was to end up with glasses in his cabinet marked "GW"!'

Ronnie C. explains that the writer's true identity was revealed to him before the rest of the *Frost* team. 'It was in the afternoon, in the dressing room, but only about eight hours before anyone else.' Ronnie admits he had no inkling it had been his namesake all along, although once informed, it didn't surprise him. 'I knew he had always been very clever with words, but it was a fascinating moment.'

The *Frost* team had begun questioning the validity of Mr Wylie, thinking he must be a well-known writer using a pseudonym. Tom Stoppard and Nöel Coward were just some of the names being bandied about. It was clear that Gerald Wiley's time was up, the secrecy couldn't last any longer, so Ronnie B., using his self-made Gerald Wiley headed notepaper, dropped a line to everyone, inviting them to a Chinese restaurant, opposite the studio, to meet Mr Wiley in person. There was a big turnout, everyone keen to meet the man who had supplied so many high-quality sketches. One writer eagerly awaiting his arrival was Barry Cryer. 'We all assembled. It was like an Agatha Christie: *Who's Gerald Wiley?*. Frank Muir, our boss at the time, stuck his head in and we all shouted, "It's you!" Then there was the theory that it was Tom Stoppard enjoying himself, because he was with the same agent. But then Ronnie Barker stood up and said, "All right, it was me." And we all shouted, "Shut up and sit down!" So he sat down. A bit later, he stood up again and said, "No, it was me." We all booed and laughed, and then I stood up and said, "The toast is, 'Nobody loves a smart ass.'"' Barry respects why Ronnie created the entire Wiley saga. 'He had blown his cover, so started writing under other names, too. But he wanted his material to be accepted on its own merits rather than to be used purely because Ronnie wrote them. I don't think that would have happened, though.'

Ronnie continued with the Wiley pen name, particularly during the days of *The Two Ronnies*, which is covered in due course. Before then, he enjoyed a run of shows on ITV in which he was the sole star. Contracted to David Frost's production company led to both Ronnies being given solo series, in addition to the *Frost on Sunday* programmes. For Ronnie B. it was *The Ronnie Barker Playhouse*, which afforded him the much-enjoyed opportunity to create a host of different characters for six playlets, a style of programming he would repeat in the future with *Six Dates With Barker* and *Seven of One*. The *Playhouse* was a programme Ronnie enjoyed recording. Made for Rediffusion and networked across the ITV regions, it was screened between 3 April and 8 May, with the individual instalments ranging from *Tennyson*, about a failed Welsh poet, to *The Incredible Mister Tanner*, concerning an escapologist who deludes himself about what he can realistically achieve. The *Tanner* instalment was written by Brian Cooke and Johnnie Mortimer, who also penned *The Fastest Gun in Finchley*, transmitted third in the series. Regarding *Tanner*, Brian Cooke says, 'The episode was inspired by what I'd seen at The Pier Head in Liverpool years before. It was brilliantly exploited by Ronnie, his overweight, physically and mentally square Mr Tanner hailed in the Press as something to be put in the same class as Steptoe and Alf Garnett.'

Ronnie followed up the *Playhouse* with projects for London Weekend Television: two series of *Hark at Barker* and one of *Six Dates With Barker*. Both titles were produced by Humphrey Barclay and directed by Australian Maurice Murphy, who first teamed up on Michael Palin and Terry Jones' *The Complete and Utter History of Britain* and hospital sitcom *Doctor in the House*. Humphrey joined the LWT payroll when the channel started in 1968 and recalls the day he was called to the office of Frank Muir, head of comedy. 'I was a baby producer back then, reporting to Frank, and to my great pleasure he said he was giving me Ronnie Barker, which was good, but had no idea what show to make for him. Although vastly inexperienced, I was in charge of trying to create the programme – that turned out to be *Hark at Barker*.'

The first series ran during April and May 1969, with Ronnie officially giving his blimpish, bumbling Lord Rustless character his own series. He had first introduced Lord Rustless in *Ah, There You Are*, an Alun Owen script televised as part of *The Ronnie Barker Playhouse*. Two series of *Hark at Barker* spotlighted the aged peer in a pleasant formula. After welcoming viewers into his home to hear him expound on various issues, his ramblings were constantly interrupted by domestic problems and his faithful staff, resulting in Rustless spinning off into ideas, comments or triggers for sketches. Considering it's over forty years since the series was made, many sketches were technically inventive, as Humphrey explains. 'One had a set built on its side, so the characters appeared to be walking on the ceiling. Another was an old silent film called *Abdul the Filthy* in which a character escaped in a chase from one frame of the film to another. In the gallery, everybody was keeping very quiet, praying that Maurice knew what he was doing, and it turned out that he always did.'

When it came to explaining to Ronnie what was required for the *Abdul* sequence, with the character trapped inside the film, Maurice Murphy didn't have to say too much. 'It was very complex and with most actors you'd have to explain everything in words of one syllable, but not Ronnie. He knew all about the technicalities and was always able to make such things better.' Maurice admits he learned much from him. 'It was joyous, because I knew virtually nothing because

I hadn't done much television. He taught me a lot about comedy.' One thing he quickly learnt about Barker was that he didn't hang around when shooting a scene. 'When I was suggested as director, I had to go out and meet him at his house. We had a nibble of something and talked about the programme. What I remember most clearly was him saying, "I'm happy for you to do the show, but there's one condition." I asked him what it was and he replied, "I only do it twice." I didn't know what he meant, so he explained, "I'm happy to rehearse as long as you like, but in takes I can only make it work twice – and even better if we can get it on the first one." That was fine with me and I don't think it ever took more than two takes, he was so professional.'

Being that this was Ronnie's show, he was understandably involved in virtually every component, including costumes and sound effects. 'It fascinated me how meticulous he was with things. He was concerned from an early stage who the characters were going to be, what shoes they could wear, those kind of things. On days off I found it fun scouring second-hand shops to find items which I could bring back for him. Once we started doing the post-production on the shows, he became very inventive, turning up with old discs he'd found in a shop somewhere, saying, "This is a good backing track for it."'

Film editor Ray Millichope, who worked on several of Ronnie's BBC shows, also experienced the actor's interest in sound effects. 'He liked visiting my editing suite, which he called the Fun Factory, and would always arrive carrying a brown cardboard suitcase. Inside he'd have, among other things, a football rattle, triangle, swanee whistle, pots and pans, hooters – this was the Barker effects library. Everywhere he went, he'd carry this suitcase into the dub. On one occasion, he opened it and there was a cabbage inside. I asked what it was for, and he replied, "If you whack it, it sounds like a thump on the head."'

Ray admits that working with Ronnie could be hard work. 'He was very demanding, but at that level you're entitled to be. There were never any bad words between us. When he was demanding, normally it was in the dubbing theatre, not so much the editing process, because I could put right things he wanted to change. But in the dubbing, time would run out. I was freelance, but in the dubbing theatre they were BBC employees who worked until 9.30 p.m. We'd get very close to 9.30 and he'd become a bit short, because it was out of his control. He expected everybody to be able to work endless hours, but, of course, they didn't work that way at the BBC. We weren't the most popular people to walk into a dubbing theatre: they always knew it was going to be hassle and late nights; people were apprehensive, because Ronnie wasn't easy.'

The two series of *Hark at Barker* gathered a small cast, which became a close-knit team. Josephine Tewson played Rustless's secretary, Mildred Bates; Frank Gatliff the butler; Mary Baxter the cook; and David Jason the aged gardener. 'Ronnie wanted Jo Tewson and Frank Gatliff and we found this funny little actress Mary Baxter, who wasn't very experienced but just the right caricature figure for the cook,' recalls Humphrey Barclay, who also cast David Jason. 'Then we hatched the idea of this 100-year-old gardener called Dithers, who couldn't hear or speak coherently. Very early on, I pushed for David Jason, who I'd discovered for *Do Not Adjust Your Set*, and that's how David and Ronnie were introduced to each other. They were more or less strangers, but got on so well from the word go.'

Ronnie enjoyed teaming up with fellow actors or crew members he'd worked with before, as he once explained to me. 'You've often got such a short rehearsal period that you've got to know from day one that the person is OK; you needed to feel safe and know that no one was going to let you down.'

The second series of *Hark at Barker* introduced Ronnie to Moira Foot, with whom he'd work on the later series of *Six Dates With Barker* and *His Lordship Entertains*. Moira's father Alistair Foot was a well-known writer and lived in Pinner, Middlesex, five minutes' walk from Ronnie's home. One day Ronnie mentioned the series to Moira's father and said there might be a part in it for his daughter – that materialised as Effie, the maid. Apart from a handful of adverts, the role marked her television debut. When it came to preparing for the second series, she didn't have to walk far for the initial meeting. 'We all went to Ronnie's house. He invited the whole cast for coffee and we read all the scripts in one go. It took about three hours and my abiding memory is of continuous laughter until tears were rolling down our cheeks. It was the funniest three hours I've ever spent, a wonderful introduction to my television career.'

It was Moira's first taste of television, having just left Aida Foster's drama school, and she found Ronnie a pleasure to work with. 'It's well documented that he was very generous and if he thought that somebody else would be better saying a particular line, he didn't mind giving it up – I think his ability as a writer made him like that.' She'll never forget the encouragement and advice he freely passed on, recalling an occasion when the subject of teeth came up. 'Once, I went to see a casting director for a film and was told that I should get my teeth fixed. I happened to mention this in rehearsals and he said, "Don't do it. You'll end up with a mouthful of china and lose all your character." So I never did get my teeth fixed. Mind you, I never worked much in films, either!' says Moira, who classes the worst part about playing Effie as having to squeeze into high heels. 'They were four-inch heels, too, which made me about six-foot four. The shoes crippled me, because I wasn't used to wearing them. Apart from that, the show was pure joy.'

Reflecting on how the two series were received – the first attracted viewing figures of 1.3 million, rising to 5 million in the second season – Humphrey Barclay admits it was never going to be 'break-through material, but kept everybody happy and was very jolly entertainment'.

The series certainly kept the critics happy, many lauding Ronnie's performances. The *Daily Telegraph*'s Sylvia Clayton pinpointed Ronnie's skill in character acting. 'Ronnie Barker has the sort of versatile talent that is an asset to any revue, for he can assume contrasting characters at a moment's notice.'[5] Mike Kerrington in the *Daily Mirror*, meanwhile, felt it was time Ronnie's contribution to the world of comedy was recognised officially. He wrote, 'It is about time Ronnie Barker got among the TV awards. This could be the series that puts him there.'[6]

During 1969–70, the years he was starring in *Hark at Barker*, Ronnie was seen in a handful of other television productions. Among these was the role of Stephen Spettigue, alongside Danny La Rue in the title role in *Charley's Aunt*, shown as a BBC *Play of the Month*, with one reviewer regarding Ronnie's performance as an elderly suitor as 'more credible than usual'[7]. He made a guest appearance in the third season of Dudley Moore and Peter Cook's *Not Only . . . But Also*, too, and was seen as a music-hall performer in the Michael Mills produced *Wiltons – The Handsomest Hall in Town*, in which Victorian music hall was brought to life in an original setting, for which Ronnie donated his fee to help the refurbishment of the music hall situated in the London borough of Tower Hamlets.

There were no stage or radio appearances during this period, but Ronnie did venture on to the big screen, transferring his Rustless-style character to the film world in the shape of General Futtock in *Futtocks End*. It was a return to the grunts-and-groans-style favoured by Ronnie, with Futtock inviting an assortment of oddball guests to stay at his country mansion for the weekend, where, as expected, chaos ensues. The film was directed by Bob Kellett, who'd worked with Ronnie on *A Home Of Your Own*. One of his first tasks was sourcing a suitable mansion for the filming, which he found, thanks to the Harrow District Council, at Harrow Weald, Middlesex. The script was written by Ronnie. 'We stuck to it very closely, apart from getting rid of a big sequence at the end where the village fête, which is held at the mansion annually, was struck by a thunderstorm, flooding the entire location. It would have been a very funny sequence, but far too expensive.'

The film, which saw Michael Hordern playing the lecherous butler, was distributed by British Lion and, as Bob Kellett explains, was a successful second feature. Once again, he enjoyed the experience of working with Ronnie. 'He and I worked as a team. Ronnie was always by my side. If I had an idea I'd discuss it with him; it was easy and great fun.' While some critics agreed with the director's assessment of the film, others were less enthusiastic about the picture, which was released as an 'A' certificate. A reviewer in the *Monthly Film Bulletin* felt that although some jokes worked well, 'they are far too thinly spread, and the whole venture reeks of ancient music-hall jokes . . . the cast seem to be enjoying themselves, but their over-emphatic performances and bits of speeded-up action hardly communicate the fun to the audience'[8].

After two series of *Hark at Barker*, Ronnie desired to make more half-hour, stand-alone shows, similar to those recorded for *The Ronnie Barker Playhouse*. Humphrey Barclay dreamt up the title *Six Dates With Barker*, and between January and February 1971 the six shows were screened, each embracing a different era and premise. One of the scripts came from Spike Milligan and was titled *The Phantom Raspberry Blower of Old London Town*. 'It was a wonderfully rude, nonsensical Victorian romp and we had great fun with that,' recalls Humphrey. 'There was also a funny piece with David Jason called *The Odd Job* from Bernard McKenna, and a wonderful piece from John Cleese, titled *Come In And Lie Down*.'

Although none of the single-episode comedies triggered a full-blown series instantly, five years later *The Phantom Raspberry Blower of Old London Town* resurfaced as a serial within the fifth series of *The Two Ronnies*; while the opening episode, *The Removals Person*, written by Hugh Leonard, was turned into a series titled *Clarence*, with which Ronnie bowed out from the world of sitcom in 1988. Moira Foot was back for the *Raspberry Blower*, playing six characters. One was particularly memorable: Maureen Body, the prime minister's secretary. 'I had to play that with two balloons pushed up my front, which had to explode on cue, which was rather alarming,' she explains, grinning. 'I had an elasticated blouse on at the time and there was a little man with a plunger and long cable, thirty feet away. On countdown he pressed the plunger and the balloons exploded. Thank goodness, it worked first time.'

One episode of *Six Dates With Barker* that was well received by the public was Bernard McKenna's *The Odd Job*, a delicious black comedy in which Arthur Harriman (Barker), distraught after his wife leaves him, hires an odd-job man (David Jason) to bump him off; trouble is, Harriman changes his mind, but is unable to stop Clive, the hit man. Bernard had started writing for Ronnie on *Hark At Barker*, as he explains. 'Around 1968 I got a job at London Weekend Television as a script associate. I had a little office and was tasked with collecting sketches for people like Leslie Crowther and Ronnie Barker, who was going to do the *Hark at Barker* series. I was also asked to contribute and immediately started getting material accepted. He liked the stuff I did and I liked the way he performed it; he always brought a little extra to it and was always very good at letting you know nicely if he didn't think something would work. I started with thirty-second sketches before moving on to longer sketches requiring filming. My first experience of being on location with him was great, because he always came up and asked how you thought the sketch had gone; I felt very embraced by him.'

Bernard feels Ronnie had the ability to spot material that would work straight away and to discard anything that wouldn't. 'Ronnie always liked a bit of naughtiness in the work he did,' admits Bernard, smiling. 'He had a touch of the Benny Hill about him. I tried not to encourage him, but in *Hark at Barker* you'd always have the maid bending over and there would be a remark of "cheeky" or something – that wasn't my kind of humour. But Ronnie collected all the Victorian postcards and liked the naughty McGill stuff.'

The half-hour episode earned much praise. 'Ronnie loved it,' enthuses Bernard, who was disappointed with just one aspect of the final cut. 'Ronnie made a few tweaks, but the only time his Benny Hill side came into play was at the beginning.' The opening scene was meant to show a boring man heading home on yet another tedious bus journey, but the scene ended up involving a short-skirted young lady who alights from the bus at the same stop, only for Ronnie's character, realising he's forgotten the bunch of flowers he's bought his wife, to bump into the busty brunette, his head sinking into her cleavage. 'Ronnie put that in and whenever I watch it, it always annoys me, because I didn't write it; there were bits of that going on,' admits Bernard.

The series showcased Ronnie's versatility and endless supply of characters, even if some were first and second cousins of each other. 'He was terribly rewarding to work with and always very funny; he always lifted your spirits when you went into a rehearsal room. You never had to lift his,' says Humphrey Barclay. 'He knew exactly how he wanted a sketch shot, particularly if it was on film. I remember a "quickie" about a woodman chopping down one of two trees we could see. He chopped, stood back and the other tree fell down. He was very particular and dictatorial with Maurice [Murphy] about how it must be shot. He had a clear idea as to how the joke would work best, a very clear visual image.' But

Humphrey points out that even Ronnie could be wrong occasionally, recalling a scene involving him and David Jason. 'In rehearsals, we couldn't get beyond one joke; every time we tried, Ronnie and David couldn't look at each other without collapsing in fits of giggles. On the show, the line was delivered and the audience didn't murmur; there was such a silence that you could hear a high-pitched noise from Ronnie as he struggled to keep the laugh in. In those days, we didn't use dubbing machines as much as they do now to sweeten the show afterwards, so you can still hear that noise.'

Six Dates With Barker became Ronnie's ITV swansong and the majority of critics writing in the national press were upbeat in their reviews. In essence, most applauded the depth of his talents, with Brian Boss in the *Daily Sketch* regarding it amongst the best work Ronnie had ever done, writing, 'The six-part series offers his wide acting talents much scope.'[9]

Nothing remains static in the world of television and Ronnie was soon on the move; all his future work on television would be with the BBC, a move forced upon him by Paradine Productions and London Weekend Television's parting of the ways; although Stella Richman wanted to retain the services of the two Ronnies, they were contracted to Frost's production company and so were under his direction in terms of future employers. But Ronnie didn't have to wait long before the dawning of a new era, a period which for the extent of their remaining television career would be spent at the BBC, a career which would be full of rich pickings.

Chapter 11

It takes skill, confidence and courage to step into the breach and laugh in the face of adversity, but that is what Ronnie Barker and Ronnie Corbett had to do one cold March evening in 1970. They were attending the annual BAFTA awards ceremony – compèred by David Frost – in a heaving London Palladium when a technical hitch brought proceedings to a grinding halt. Unaware how long it would be before normal service resumed, the two Ronnies stepped up to the mikes and gave an impromptu performance that had the audience in stitches; little did the Ronnies know that their off-the-cuff performance would play a major part in shaping their small-screen careers. In the audience that night were Bill Cotton, who became Head of Light Entertainment in May 1970, and Sir Paul Fox, Controller of BBC1.

Although stories differ regarding how long the Ronnies were asked to hold the fort, there is no doubting the impact their performance had on those listening, as Sir Paul Fox explains. 'They did an improvisation and during the performance, Bill Cotton turned to me and said, "How would you like those two on your channel?" I told him I'd be delighted, but thought they were contracted to LWT. Bill replied, "Leave the contract negotiations to me. Do you want them?" I said, "Yes, please!" They were exceptionally funny and very different, and anyone who can improvise for that long and keep a professional audience entertained and roaring with laughter will do for me.'

When Bill Cotton subsequently held discussions with David Frost and the two Ronnies, who were still contracted to Paradine Productions, he had no idea that they had just parted company with London Weekend Television and were, in fact, open to offers. 'I turned up at David's office and made an offer for a three-year contract,'[1] recalled Bill Cotton. The two Ronnies, trying to show restraint, informed Cotton that they would consider his proposal, although privately were over the moon with the offer on the table; it would be some years before they informed him that their ties with LWT had been severed before that fortuitous meeting.

With Barker and Corbett in the bag, Bill Cotton called Jimmy Gilbert, executive producer in Light Entertainment at the time. Jimmy will never forget that morning phone call. 'Bill said, "Hi, Jim. Have you got a minute? Come round and have a glass of Frascati, I've got some exciting news." And he certainly had: the Ronnies were coming back to the BBC. He had agreed a contract spread over three years, which, apart from the sketch show they would do together, would provide each with a comedy series and a special. This would give them a separate existence and not lock them exclusively into a double-act like Morecambe and Wise. Bill then said, "And by the way, they want you as producer. Do you want to do it?" "Yes, please," I replied. We had several glasses of Frascati after that!' Jimmy was taken off all other projects for a year, his sole priority being to devise a big comedy series and special for each of them, plus a variety series in which they would both appear. Reviewing their individual talents, Jimmy Gilbert says they couldn't have been more different. 'Ronnie B. was a brilliant comedy actor who could play dozens of different characters with total reality yet still make them funny. Ronnie C. is a personality performer, who really enjoys being on stage doing his act in front of a live audience, something Ronnie B. could never do. They were a perfect complement to each other and good friends.'

Although it was spring 1970 when the BBC secured the services of the two Ronnies, just under a year would pass before either appeared in their specially devised solo specials and joint show which, of course, was christened *The Two Ronnies*. Before then, the second season of Ronnie Barker's *Hark at Barker* and *Six Dates With Barker* for LWT were screened, having been recorded before he switched channels. Ronnie would also be heard on the radio in what would become his final show for the medium.

The first series of episodes of the strangely titled *Lines From My Grandfather's Forehead* was broadcast between Monday, 15 February and Monday, 5 April 1971. The Radio 4 programme saw Ronnie reunited with producer John Fawcett Wilson, who had been at the helm for *Not To Worry*, *Let's Face It* and *Young Pioneers*, a series set in nineteenth-century Australia spotlighting a young English couple who had inherited a property in New South Wales. Ronnie played an Australian sheep shearer and, says Fawcett Wilson, was 'absolutely wonderful'. A particular moment typifies the seriousness and dedication Ronnie invested in his portrayals. A scene saw Ronnie's character embroiled in an altercation with a professional man, played by Kenneth J. Warren. Fawcett Wilson recalls, 'Afterwards, Kenneth said to me, "You know the scene where if it had been visual Ronnie would have grabbed his sheep-shearing shears and pointed them at me, well, he might have just as well had those shears with the point at my stomach. We were standing there, in front of the radio mike with scripts in our hands, but he turned to me and, literally, I was frightened for a moment."'

For *Lines* . . . the producer assembled not only Ronnie but Terence Brady, Pauline Yates and, on piano, Gordon Langford for this zany, off-the-wall series offering a sequence of comedy sketches, monologues and comical songs. John recalls receiving a favourable response when discussing the original idea with Ronnie. 'He was still working with London Weekend and didn't want to do an audience show, because he was busy doing those for LWT. I told him that what I had in mind wasn't in front of an audience and would, hopefully, explore different ways of presenting humour and comedy; Ronnie thought the idea sounded terrific.'

John will never forget the day he visited London Weekend's studio to catch up with Ronnie. 'Humphrey Barclay said Ronnie was editing. I asked him what he meant – editing? He replied, "He's downstairs, he likes to edit the programme himself."'

Humphrey explains, 'When you're working happily together as a team it's not out of resignation that you let the star of a show go and be the editor as well – not in the mechanical sense of pushing the buttons, of course, but in saying, "It will be funnier if this shot comes before that one." You're completely happy to use all the talents you can and nobody needs to get jealous about their own territory – that comes out of insecurity. Ronnie was a talented all-rounder and a good decision-maker in terms of what was and wasn't funny.'

The subject of editing caused the only argument Fawcett Wilson and Ronnie had in all the time they worked together. When the pilot episode of *Lines From My Grandfather's Forehead* had been recorded, Ronnie said he'd like to undertake the editing. John, however, didn't agree. 'I said, "No, I'm afraid you won't." This little disagreement went on for a time, before I finally said, "I've been sitting, thinking about the shape of this programme for years before joining Light Entertainment – it's my baby."' John, though, appeased Ronnie somewhat. 'I said, "I'll tell you what, I'll strike a deal: I'll edit the programme and if you have any strong objections and don't like the finished product, you are then at liberty to edit the series in consultation with me." He bought that and when he heard the pilot he liked it and from thereon I edited them all.'

Each episode was recorded in isolation, affording Fawcett Wilson the chance to construct the programme afterwards, providing maximum flexibility. The half-hour shows were packed with sketches from a host of writers, including Gerald Wiley, with the selection process frequently taking place at Ronnie's house in Pinner, as John recalls. 'I used to separate the scripts into about five categories, put them into folders and go over to Ronnie's place. We'd work through them, only going with those we both liked. Ronnie would sit at his end of the table with about three boxes of cigarettes piled up and I'd be sitting with one box next to me. We'd start at about ten in the morning and work through until around six, by which time the air was rather fuggy!'

Cigarettes helped Ronnie concentrate on the job at hand, so when he finally ditched the habit on health grounds he struggled to cope through the transitional period, as witnessed by Barry Cryer. 'He had a bit of a health scare and was told to stop smoking. His concentration went and he started fluffing lines, which had never been known. He was my neighbour: I was in Hatch End, he was in Pinner, just down the road, so I'd go over and sit with him. We'd drink endless cups of tea and write something together; it was only a brief period, but he got very worried. I remember him saying, "I can't concentrate on anything, including the writing." He had been a happy smoker. But it was only a matter of weeks before he was back on form.'

Ronnie's decision to quit cigarettes happened around the time a second series of the radio programme was being planned, and in between the first two series of *The Two Ronnies*. The original and longest-serving producer/director on the show, Terry Hughes, recognised how tough it was for Ronnie. 'He found it very difficult to write for that second season. He told me that the loneliness of sitting in his room, trying to come up with ideas without being able to turn to a cigarette, was hard. Although Ronnie's work in that series was really good, I don't think it was as wonderful as he had been or would go back to being; of course, we're talking a matter of degrees; no one else would have noticed.'

With Ronnie quitting cigarettes, John Fawcett Wilson knew his visit to discuss scripts for the second series could become rather awkward. 'My wife said, "What's going to happen? If he can't smoke, what are you going to do?" I said I wouldn't smoke, either, but she didn't think I'd cope – it was a necessary fuel for me.' Arriving at Ronnie's home in Pinner, John was ushered up to the study. 'There wasn't the usual pile of cigarettes on the desk, and I wasn't going to smoke, either. As we discussed the scripts he got a cigarette holder out and began chewing and sucking it; it was a way of filling the gap in his mouth. On several occasions, he said, "John, are you not smoking?" I told him I'd decided to give it a break. I was making all sorts of excuses and he knew that. I'm sure he was dying for me to light up, so he could sniff the tobacco!'

The programme title for *Lines . . .* was Ronnie's idea. One afternoon, sitting in Fawcett Wilson's office, the producer suggested *Listen To This Space*, but the idea wasn't picked up; then Ronnie came up with *Lines From My Grandfather's Forehead* and the matter was resolved. John says, 'It was an odd title but, then again, it was an odd programme, not like any other sketch show.'

The small team creating this unpredictable and inventive sketch comedy, which won a Writers' Guild award for Best Light Entertainment Show (Radio), had a ball each week while preparing and recording the show. Gordon Langford says he'd return home in Finchley with his sides aching, realising just how lucky he was to be paid for working on one of his easiest engagements.

Robin Spicer, a studio technician when *Lines . . .* was recorded in Studio 8 at London's Broadcasting House, revelled in the inventiveness of the performers and writers, particularly Ronnie. 'Apart from Ronnie B., the cast was never more than two actors (one of each sex), Gordon Langford, another one or two musicians and me on coconut shells, swanee whistle, etc.' One particular scene sticks in Robin's mind. 'It concerned the retirement of an attendant of the directors' retiring room, and the handover to his young successor. Ronnie B. played the outgoing attendant. As there was a gents' adjacent to the studio, I suggested playing the sketch in there to get the proper acoustics and correct background sounds: flushing WCs, taps on and off, roller towels and such like. So in we went. Halfway through the sketch, the house foreman arrived in great dudgeon and demanded to know what was going on. Ronnie, hardly deviating from the script, which he'd written himself, immediately included the house foreman, accusing him of being unaware of his own bailiwick, and carried on to the end, with the man leaving, and apologising for God knows what was going on in his small empire. That for me was the genius of Ronnie B.'

Someone else who witnessed the brilliance of Barker was fellow actor Terence Brady, who first met him on the day they arrived for the opening rehearsal. 'We did the programme on Sundays, which infuriated Ronnie because he was such a family man he wanted to be home doing the roast – so did I, for that matter.' Terence concurs with Gordon Langford regarding the fun-filled recordings. 'The trouble was, Ronnie discovered very quickly that I'm easily corpsed, so there was lots of bad behaviour from Ronnie, because he wanted to see how far he could push me,' says Terence, laughing. 'We ended up at one point with John Fawcett Wilson so infuriated with us that he built two special cells inside the studio, out of huge screens, so we couldn't see each other. They were soundproofed and had cue lights but, to be honest, only made matters worse. It was childish, though, so I had to get a grip and try to be grown-up!' Terence, like many of his peers, acknowledges that Ronnie was a generous performer, giving up lines if he felt they would be better delivered by another performer. 'He was not only generous but kind and unpatronising.'

During the programme's run, Audience Research Reports were

conducted, with the response favourable. Many people found the programme clever and humorous, the general consensus being that 'with the variety and pace of the items, there was no time for boredom'[2]. And the majority of respondees classed Ronnie as a 'clever and versatile comedian'.[3]

The programme closed at the end of Series Two, in 1972, by which time Ronnie was focusing almost exclusively on television. John Fawcett Wilson enjoyed the time they had spent together. 'He was a fine actor with an absolute talent for comedy; I'm sure there's nothing he worked on where his input wasn't immense.'

During this period, Ronnie didn't just wave goodbye to the medium of radio: he made his last appearance in a stage play, too. Although he donned the greasepaint for *The Two Ronnies'* theatre shows in 1978 and 1983, his last play was *Good Time Johnny* at the Birmingham Repertory Theatre in December 1971. This musical version of *The Merry Wives of Windsor* was written by Jimmy Gilbert and Julian More, with Canadian Alan Lund, fresh from the West End success of *Anne of Green Gables*, hired as director and chore-ographer. The cast, meanwhile, saw Ronnie playing Falstaff and Joan Sims as Mistress Quickly. 'The story was brought up to 1900, post-Boer War, and Falstaff, instead of coming back from the European wars, as he does in Shakespeare's version, was returning from the Boer War,' explains Jimmy. 'Rather than touring the show, which would have been expensive considering the sets and size of cast, we struck a deal with the Birmingham Rep who'd just opened their brand new theatre – I think we were the second show staged.'

Performing in the afternoons at the theatre was a stage version of the classic children's show *Noggin the Nog*. Most of the repertory company members working on *Good Time Johnny* also donned beards and wigs to become members of the Nog army. Of course, neither Joan Sims nor Ronnie Barker was expected to join the army's ranks, yet they surprised everyone by making a one-off appearance, as actor Adrian Lawson remembers. 'One afternoon, as the Nog army assembled, I noticed there were two strange faces: they belonged to Ronnie and Joan. They were hilarious and, needless to say, had come in to send the rest of us up.'

Back on *Good Time Johnny*, a junior cast member was Malcolm

Rennie who appreciated Ronnie's approachability. 'All my experience had been in straight theatre, where your leading man can be distant and rather snooty. It was such a relief to find Ronnie nothing like that: he was totally approachable, even to us juniors. He enjoyed having a natter and cup of tea with us; there were no airs and graces with him.' Malcolm saw Ronnie's writing abilities coming to the fore, too. 'During rehearsals there were many times when he'd make suggestions about changing little bits of script or something, and all were spot-on. I thought, "Gosh, that's very clever." It was great being with somebody who was working on those two levels: as a creative writer and a performer, coupled with the fact he was an extraordinarily nice chap – we all warmed to him.'

As Malcolm states, no one was offended when Ronnie suggested tweaking scenes. 'He did it with such diplomacy, tact and goodwill that it was impossible to take offence.' It wasn't as if his suggestions were fatuous, so for the production team not to have accepted his advice would have been churlish.

From the outset, Ronnie's other commitments meant John Baddeley, who played Forbes, would replace Ronnie as Sir John Falstaff for the last two weeks of the eight-week production. Unfortunately, worrying events unfolded and Ronnie was forced to pull out of the show just days after its opening, much to the dismay of everyone involved in the production and the public who had expected to see the main man. 'Ronnie was to play Falstaff, the biggest larger-than-life character in the Shakespeare canon. He had about eight or nine songs to sing or be involved in, plus dancing,' says Jimmy Gilbert. 'It was a huge part. Unfortunately, Ronnie had been working in television for a few years and I think he found projecting to a large theatre a strain; soon, it started affecting his voice in rehearsals. By the time it came to opening night, he'd lost his voice completely and had to be given a personal mike, whereas everyone else just used stage mikes.'

For John Baddeley it was clear after a couple of days that Ronnie was having problems with his voice. 'We became friends, thanks – basically – to an insult I threw at him; on his first day, I saw him sitting alone in the café drinking coffee. I introduced myself, and then he asked how the bookings were going. I said the last two weeks – when I was playing the part – were sold out, but the others weren't doing *too* badly. He enjoyed my joke and we became friends.'

When, later, Ronnie admitted to John that there must be something wrong with his voice and perhaps he should see someone, John suggested his cousin, Michael, who worked as a consultant in Birmingham. An appointment was convened at Baddeley's cousin's home. On recognising a problem with Ronnie's vocal chords, the consultant referred him to a colleague, a specialist in the field, who recommended an operation immediately. 'No one, at this stage, knew he was ill. Ronnie carried on for a couple of days, but I didn't think he'd make it.' Realising he might have to take over earlier than expected, John began rehearsing the role of Falstaff. 'Ronnie had been told not to speak, so for nine tenths of the rehearsals sat watching me play his part.

'The first night was a full house, so Ronnie came on. He was miked, but even then I could tell his voice was duff. We opened on the Thursday night with Ronnie playing the character. He did Friday evening and then asked me to do the matinee on Saturday, with Ronnie taking over again for the evening. That was his last show – he was forced to leave after just three performances.' John recalls an emotional Ronnie singing his final number in the production, 'The Laugh's On Me'. He says, 'It was a sad number about regrets and I saw tears in Ronnie's eyes as he sang; it was as if he was thinking about whether he'd ever be performing again – his throat problem could have been very serious.'

The specialist confirmed Ronnie was suffering from nodules on the vocal chords. 'Everyone was frightened he had throat cancer,' admits Jimmy Gilbert, who remembers a downbeat conversation he had with Ronnie. 'He said, "The specialist is 75 per cent sure that it's not malignant, and of the 25 per cent he's 23 per cent sure he'd be able to treat it. But when you wake up at two in the morning, it's the 2 per cent you think about."'

An operation was carried out at Birmingham's Queen Elizabeth Hospital and, thankfully, was a complete success with no cancer present. Feelings of shock and worry were replaced by relief and happiness. He had been working his voice too hard and was ordered to rest. Sadly, he never returned to *Good Time Johnny*, marking the end for the musical. 'It was two years' work down the swanee, because the show never recovered. I never wrote another theatre musical after that experience. It put me off,' admits Jimmy Gilbert.

Actor Malcolm Rennie agrees that the play's future was bleak once Ronnie left the fold. 'Although it did well in Birmingham and could have gone into the West End, we lost a huge commercial draw when he had to pull out. John Baddeley was a senior member of the rep company and took over the part at short notice. He made a very good attempt at it, but the whole thing had been tailored for Ronnie. Most tickets were sold on the back of him being in it, so there were many disgruntled patrons once they found out Ronnie wasn't performing.'

It wasn't only the public who were disappointed; the local rag wasn't enamoured of the show. The critic accepted it might provide cheery entertainment over the Christmas period, but it wasn't the kind of success story he was hoping for, explaining, '*Good Time Johnny* is not the smash hit, the exportable product, that the Rep badly needs to match the new theatre and spread its reputation abroad. The basic trouble is that updating *The Merry Wives of Windsor* never looks all that strong an idea. This ragtime Falstaff is a bit of a ragbag of a story.'[4]

By the time the review hit the newsstands, Ronnie had already left the production and was recovering from his throat operation, while beginning to prepare for the second series of *The Two Ronnies*. The eight-part opening season had transmitted between 10 April and 29 May 1971, watched by, on average, 25 per cent of the population, equating to 12.6 million viewers. The series had kicked off just three weeks after Ronnie had appeared in the one-off special that was part of the contract which brought the Ronnies back to the BBC. Partly written by Ronnie B., adopting his famous Wiley pen name, *The Ronnie Barker Yearbook* was screened on BBC1 at 8.20 p.m. on Saturday, 20 March 1971. Structured as an almanac, the programme focused on the months of the year, with Ronnie C. making a guest appearance; Ronnie B. reciprocated the following Saturday when Corbett's special went out.

The author of the BBC's internal Audience Research Report – reflecting the views of the sample audience providing feedback on the *Yearbook* – commented that most respondees found the show amusing, one person stating that Ronnie was 'one of the few really funny men on TV'[5]. While the lion's share of the people were pleased, there were a few less enthusiastic people, some claiming that they 'could take Ronnie Barker only in small doses'[6]. Fortunately, they were in the minority.

Four weeks later *The Two Ronnies* came into being. Although people had already started referring to Corbett and Barker – who during the year was also seen on the big screen in *Sloth*, a segment of the Graham Stark-directed film *The Magnificent Seven Deadly Sins* – as the Two Ronnies, it seemed the obvious choice when selecting a programme title. Their first official engagement in this capacity, however, took place on Saturday evening, 10 April 1971, when the opening credits on their new comedy show began to roll and we were introduced to Messrs Barker and Corbett sitting behind desks, welcoming viewers to their new venture; little did they know that the format would become such a monumental success story that twelve series and a host of specials spanning sixteen years would follow.

For the story of how *The Two Ronnies* came into being, we need to return to 1970. Bill Cotton had struck the deal with Paradine Productions to reclaim the services of Barker and Corbett, and Jimmy Gilbert, then executive producer, had been pulled off other projects to focus entirely on devising programmes for the pair. While the specials came about relatively easily, the joint variety show would need much more thought and planning – or so you would have imagined. But as Jimmy Gilbert relates, the structure was resolved relatively quickly. For two mornings, Barker and Gilbert were holed up in Gilbert's office on the fourth floor of Television Centre, during which period the format was virtually drafted. 'Ronnie Corbett was, as ever, happy for Ronnie B. to represent his interests, because he trusted him totally,' says Jimmy. 'So I dealt with just one person: Ronnie B., who I'd know for years and whose career I'd been involved in since he came into television.'

Jimmy acknowledged the success David Frost had enjoyed on his shows using a news desk for comedy items and wanted to utilise something similar in *The Two Ronnies*. 'I thought we could use the double newsreader format of the old *News at Ten* to open and close each show; it was a great way of delivering jokes disguised as news items – and worked well.'

As it transpired, the programme's format wasn't particularly original and, as Jimmy Gilbert admits, 'Another pinch from *The Frost Report* was the party sketch, written by Michael Palin and Terry Jones. They became another constant and we did them, on and off, through the entire series. Also, we had a centrepiece. Ronnie B. had written a send-up of a classic serial, which we would film, giving us eight ten-minute segments in the middle of each show. It would be useful on the night of recording when you could show the film to the audience, while everyone was involved in scene changes and other such things. I liked musical sequences and Ronnie B., again, had an idea for writing a pastiche using existing music but fresh lyrics; he had it firmly in his mind what he wanted to do. We thought a big musical ending would work well. I remember enjoying the finales that *Round the Horne* did regularly on radio, taking a subject like folk music, brass bands or morris dancing and then doing musical parodies around it, which is what Ronnie was thinking, too.'

Then, it was agreed that each Ronnie would do something on their own: Ronnie B. to write and perform elaborate bits of tongue-twisting wordplay and Ronnie C. to sit in a chair spouting humorous, rambling monologues, written initially by Spike Mullins and later David Renwick, that would stray all over the place but eventually get back on course at the end. 'Finally, we would leave a space for any sketches or "quickies" submitted by other writers,' says Jimmy Gilbert. 'And that was it, basically.' Each of the individual components had been explored and used, in one form or another, elsewhere; but the show didn't set out to be groundbreaking or at the cutting edge of entertainment. That wasn't what *The Two Ronnies* was all about.

The next task for Gilbert was to pick someone who would produce and direct the series on-going: that man was Terry Hughes, who, when asked to take on *The Two Ronnies*, had been mulling over an offer to join ATV. Hughes had been producing and directing *The Val Doonican Show* on BBC and when the Irish singer moved channels, Hughes was invited along. 'At the time it was the biggest show on television. When Val left to go to ATV to do the show, which was going to be shown in America, he wanted me to go with him.' Terry was leery of moving, because he didn't think it would work, plus the BBC didn't want him to leave. 'Part of the way the BBC tempted me to stay was to offer me the chance to produce and direct *The Two Ronnies*. Jimmy Gilbert would be there at the beginning as executive producer. His help was invaluable, but after we got going he wasn't that involved because he was producing his own shows. Ironically, Val's show was also on Saturday and *The Two Ronnies* premiered within weeks of it, and we absolutely blitzed Val's programme from the word go,' says California-based Hughes, who was acutely aware of the Ronnies' desire to maintain their individuality. 'Ronnie Corbett, in particular, was very anxious, understandably. At that point, I think it was more important to him than for Ronnie B. He did a lot of work outside *The Two Ronnies*, such as summer shows and pantomimes, and wanted to maintain that individuality.' The Ronnies, however, would never become a double-act in the same way as Morecambe and Wise, Mike and Bernie Winters or Little and Large where, traditionally, they performed as a unit, interlinked inasmuch as one played the funny guy, the other the straight guy; with the Ronnies, each was funny in his own right and had established a successful solo career, which would continue, despite working closely together for over a decade; theirs was a fluid partnership: together they were a brilliant duo, their individual styles complementary, while out on their own they could perform equally well.

Retaining their independence happened regardless, because they continued to work separately, but it was a desire which was even reflected in the new-style graphics accompanying Series Three of *The Two Ronnies*. Rowland Morgan was the graphic designer responsible for updating the titles in 1973. Morgan was an assistant designer at the time, a holiday relief artist seconded from the Open University. When Terry Hughes asked him to design the new titles, he came up with the glasses idea. 'My brief was to come up with something showing their individual personalities, even though they were together on the show. I came up with the glasses idea and they went for it immediately. I remember thinking how different the Ronnies' spectacles were and how they suited their personalities. I thought that was a good way of showing segregation and togetherness all at once: the glasses travelling left and right and through the screen to symbolise their individual personalities, but then coming together, with the two photos appearing.'

The agreed format for the show, for which Ronnie was paid just over £5,000 per episode in the beginning, would prove popular and remain virtually constant throughout the show's history. 'The only thing that changed was that in the early days we had more variety acts, including jugglers and conjurors,' says Terry Hughes. 'That didn't last for two reasons: we found we didn't need them and, also, we wanted to squeeze more material into the show.'

And what a packed show it became, with a wealth of opportunities for Ronnie Barker to exploit his verbal dexterity, his staggering talent for characterisation and abilities as a comedy writer.

Chapter 12

Just before 8 p.m. on Sunday, April 4 1971 an anticipative audience filed in to Studio 8 at Television Centre, excited about watching the first recording of *The Two Ronnies*, ready for screening the following Saturday. During the day the final camera rehearsals had proceeded without a hitch before everyone stopped for dinner at 6.30 p.m. The two Ronnies and director Terry Hughes headed for the BBC canteen, where Ronnie B. ordered what would become his regular pre-show meal: sausage, egg and chips. As Terry confirms, it became a ritual. 'There were a lot of rituals and this was one. Every week, without fail, he would have this meal; it was like a superstition: I'm sure he thought that if he didn't have it, it wasn't going to be a good programme. He'd make a joke of it, but it was ritualistic, nonetheless, a kind of comfort food before doing the show.'

Standing alongside him in the queue occasionally was David Renwick, who would become a regular writer on the series. 'In those days, I was a junior member of the writing team, content to remain a hanger-on when the Ronnies and some of the others would adjourn to the canteen during the break. There was something unreal about standing next to this towering celebrity as we slid our trays along the rail, while in accordance with his weekly routine, he ordered a plate of egg, sausages and chips. "I never have it any other time," he told me. "Only before a recording."'

Editor Chris Wadsworth, who worked on many of the *Ronnies* shows, witnessed Ronnie's need for sausages, too, and remembers the time it looked like the canteen had run out. 'I was behind him in the queue that evening and they didn't have any left. There were lots of, "Oh, I must have my sausages!" from him so the canteen staff fried some specially.'

David Renwick says his other big culinary preference was a decent curry. 'In later years, when I was privileged to join the two of them and their wives for a meal after the show, I remember him settling down in a restaurant in Westbourne Grove and declaring that Indian food was far and away his favourite. "Chinese comes a very poor second."'

Terry Hughes enjoyed the moments he shared with the Ronnies, away from the immediate pressures of recording and filming. 'Ronnie C. was the performer, the song-and-dance man. Having said that, he was very much a thinking-man's song-and-dance man. He was very smart, which has, at times, been underestimated over the years. He's got great instincts, good taste and would see a lot of theatre.' Terry always thought that he was very cognisant of what was going on around him in the industry. 'He just enjoyed the business.' As for Ronnie B., Terry knew he was very aware, too, but 'led a much less showbizzy life', adding, 'Ronnie would be home with his collections of postcards and books, doing a lot of the lonely work of writing. He wrote because, firstly, he wanted to, and, secondly, it gave him confidence that the right material would be there for the programme.'

Terry thinks it may have been superstition which saw Ronnie continue to contribute sketches under the Gerald Wiley pseudonym, even though the fictitious writer's identity had already been revealed. His sketches were an integral part of the series from the beginning, with other sketches and news items contributed by experienced, reliable writers, many of whom had written for *The Frost Report*. 'For the first year, we went to the established people like Dick Vosburgh, Palin and Jones, Barry Cryer, David Nobbs, Ian Davidson and Peter Vincent,' explains Terry. 'But once the show was up and running we'd receive submissions. It was a show that everybody wanted to write for, especially the news items. They came from far and wide. We'd go through a big editing process each week to get down to the ones we wanted to use.'

The selection process was an exhaustive task, coordinated by a script editor. 'The news items would be submitted by current writers and others; sometimes, we'd receive sixty or seventy a week and cull them down to the eighteen or so needed,' recalls Terry. 'Sat around a table, sometimes at the rehearsal room in Acton, the two Ronnies and I would read them; all three of us had to agree, though, before any were accepted. Something else which became a rule was that whoever read the item at the meeting, read it on the show.'

The script editors during the comedy series' sixteen-year history included David Nobbs, Peter Vincent and Ian Davidson, all of whom supplied sketches, too. Although, as Terry Hughes explained, a culling process usually took place to select suitable news items, there were odd weeks when the script editor struggled to garner sufficient quantities to show Hughes and the Ronnies. 'It could be a terrible job,' admits Peter Vincent. 'Lots of writers sent material but getting them just right was very difficult. I used to call David Renwick and would put in just about everything he sent, because they were so good. David Nobbs was very good, too. On the whole, the news items were of a high standard and became the stamp for what *The Two Ronnies* was like.'

Peter worked at the BBC's script offices, where he was paid to find and edit scripts for not only *The Two Ronnies* but also *The Dave Allen Show*. Each morning, a pile of envelopes would arrive on his desk, many bringing more additions to the 'news items' pile. 'I'd sift through them, knowing quickly if they would work or not. Usually, I'd end up with about twenty possibles. Those were taken along to a midweek meeting with the Ronnies and Terry Hughes, who'd read them without smiling. Then they would say "yes" or "no". Most were rejected and sometimes I'd leave with just half a dozen acceptances, when about eighteen were needed. The Ronnies were difficult to please, in terms of the news items, and quite rightly.'

Many writers' career began in earnest on *The Two Ronnies*, such as David Renwick, who would later gain success writing, among others, *One Foot in the Grave* and *Jonathan Creek*. In 1974, while earning a living as a reporter on *The Luton News*, he had started selling sketches on radio. On hearing that Peter Vincent was looking for jokes and 'quickies' for the show, David submitted a sample. He was invited along to Vincent's office at Television Centre, where he met the show's producer, 'the improbably handsome and statuesque Terry Hughes', recalls David. 'It was the first time I had any kind of dialogue with people who worked in television, and they couldn't have made me feel more at home. To my delight, Terry said Ronnie Barker had really liked a sketch I'd written called, "The Yes Man", and that he'd taken it away to "tickle" it. By this time it was well known that Ronnie was a writer of considerable talent and just to know he felt the idea had potential was a thrill in itself. In fact, the sketch didn't turn up on the air for another three seasons, but that marked the beginning of my long association with the show, where I began with a trickle of jokes for the newsdesk before graduating to sketches, monologues and film items.'

Another top-class writer given his big break on the show was John Sullivan, who subsequently wrote the likes of *Citizen Smith*, *Only Fools and Horses*, *Just Good Friends*, *Dear John* and *Green, Green Grass*. He has Ronnie to thank for helping to launch his writing career. John, then twenty-nine, was working as a scene-shifter on *Porridge* – which was made during the run of *The Two Ronnies* – when he sought Ronnie's advice on how to get started in the profession. 'I was building and dressing the set and Ronnie was lying on the bottom bunk in the Slade Prison cell, reading his script. You're warned not to annoy the stars, and not knowing what Ronnie was like, if I interrupted him and he told the director to get me out of the studio, I would have been in trouble. But I took a chance and approached him, asking, "Do you read sketches from *anyone*?"' Fortunately, Ronnie didn't mind the interruption and asked John what he'd written. He hurried to his locker, grabbed the sketches and gave them to him. The following week, John was again assigned to *Porridge* and Ronnie called him over. 'He asked if I could do any more and, bravely, I said "yes", even though I wasn't sure.' When it was proven that he was able to deliver more material, Sullivan was placed on a contract and worked for the Ronnies for several years. 'The same year, I sold the *Citizen Smith* pilot, so suddenly had two major contracts within three weeks of each other – after ten years of trying.'

The sketch John showed Ronnie involved Sid and George, two would-be philosophers who sat in the bar talking 'cobblers', says John; he based the first piece on his father. 'He was a member of the local servicemen's club and would often drink there and play dominoes with friends. As the drink went down, the talk became hilarious, even though they were trying to be deadly serious. That first sketch was based on the things my dad said to me after he'd had a few.' Sullivan couldn't believe his luck when the Sid and George sequence was turned into a serial, with the characters' wives, Lily and Edie, brought in – played, of course, by the Ronnies in drag. 'Ronnie B. was tremendous and always had time for you.'

Realising in hindsight the power Ronnie B. held within the Corporation, John wishes he had shown him a pilot he'd written in which he suggested casting Ronnie alongside David Jason. 'After the first season of *Citizen Smith* I wrote this script called *Dear Old Pals*, based on two eighty-year-old men who'd been friends since infancy; now they were in their eighties and facing the end.' The men were rapscallions and spent much of their life in the pub, reminiscing. Unfortunately, the BBC didn't like the idea. 'I made a big mistake, because I should have taken it to Ronnie. It might have got off the ground that way. When I told him about it, years later, he said he liked the sound of it and wished he'd read it,' says John, who also wrote news items for *The Two Ronnies*. 'There wasn't much money in them, but you had the wonderful kudos of being with the Rons.'

Longer sketches used within the main body of the programme were submitted by a string of writers, including most of the regulars, such as Peter Vincent, Ian Davidson, Barry Cryer, David Nobbs and, later, David Renwick. Normally, these scripts were directed to Terry Hughes' desk, who would weed out any that failed to hit the spot before passing them on for the Ronnies to read. But even a commission didn't guarantee they would be used, such was the high standard insisted upon. 'There was a high rejection rate and I think this upset some of the writers, because they started thinking Ronnie B.'s material was favoured over other people's,' says Terry. 'I don't think that was true. We chose the best available. We'd have been crazy to have turned down something wonderful just to do a Ronnie Barker sketch. He wouldn't have wanted that, either.'

Ronnie Corbett says that Ronnie B. rather regretted admitting to being the man behind the Gerald Wiley sketches, before adding, 'Anything Ronnie wrote was always a treat to do.'

Terry Hughes was right. Some of the regular scribes did, at times, become frustrated writing for the show, and, in particular, with

Ronnie B. 'Ronnie Barker, the actor, was great and we thought how wonderful he was, but Ronnie Barker, the writer, did slightly step on our toes,' admits David Nobbs. 'He wrote some brilliant sketches, including "Four Candles", probably the most famous sketch they ever did. I admired his writing and none of us resented any of the really good sketches he wrote that were used in the show. But as time went on, he wrote more and more and we felt it wasn't a level playing field any more, because he would take an idea – and both Dick Vosburgh and I suffered this – and write more sketches, using the same premise.

'I wrote a sketch called "Pispronunciation", a monologue about a bloke who couldn't pronounce his "worms" correctly. But Ronnie wrote at least two sequels to it, and he did this to Dick Vosburgh's "Dr Spooner" sketch, but we felt we owned the copyright. Therefore, the very good intention he had at the beginning, as expressed by him, that he didn't want to take advantage of being Ronnie Barker, the star of the show, changed. In the end, I felt he did take advantage of this fact, which we slightly resented.' One of the consequences of this, says Nobbs, is that 'it meant others didn't have so much of a chance getting material accepted as we once had. It wasn't anything to fall out over, and I don't know that he was aware that we felt he was doing anything wrong, but it was a slight irritation to us.'

While discussing his life and career with Bob McCabe, Ronnie said he only wrote the additional 'Pispronunciation' sketches after consulting with David Nobbs. It's suggested that Nobbs said that not only was he unsure about whether he could supply any more sketches using the same theme, but that he didn't mind Barker writing further pieces. The same kind of discussion was, apparently, held with Vosburgh. David Nobbs, however, doesn't recall such a conversation. 'I have no recollection of Ronnie ever asking me that question, and it's pretty inconceivable that I would have given that reply. I would have had no problem writing sequels. I know that Dick was upset at Ronnie writing Spoonerism sequels, so I can't believe that Ronnie's version of that is correct, either.'

Sadly, Dick Vosburgh died in 2007, but his widow Beryl remembers how angry her husband was when he saw Ronnie had written new Spoonerism-based sketches. 'Dick was absolutely furious. He phoned up about it and was told that an idea is transferable. Dick protested, saying that if they had wanted another sketch like that, they could have asked him.' When Dick was told Ronnie Barker had written the sketch, he asked for half the money. 'And, what's more, he got it,' confirms Beryl. Dick Vosburgh was an incredibly witty man and wouldn't let the matter pass without a final chance of a joke, utiliting spoonerisms, as Beryl confirms. 'He sent either a postcard or a telegram which said, "Ronnie Parker, you're a brick". It was certainly very funny in the circumstances.'

Peter Vincent and Ian Davidson were two other writers vexed by the situation. 'It annoyed us that he tended to see a good idea and then do a version himself, which was probably very good, but we felt he should have left it alone,' says Peter.

'There were no confrontations, but he was gathering more and more influence for himself,' adds Ian Davidson. 'At a certain level, he was a bloody clever man and a wonderful performer. But it was very unfortunate that he brought about this unfair situation. We were all chewed off, especially Dick, who wrote this wonderfully ingenious sketch based on Spoonerisms – reversing the sentence – which became a real winner. The next year there was this sketch, written by Barker; no one had ever asked Dick for another one. It was a great sketch, but was the same damned idea, and it was Dick's idea, although there is no copyright on ideas, so you can't really argue on that basis. But the decent thing didn't come into it, that was our gripe. Amongst writers, taking an idea and doing it yourself is unforgivable.'

Another writer who experienced the surprise of seeing a sketch idea he'd created subsequently resurrected was Bernard McKenna, who had written for Ronnie on *Hark at Barker* and *Six Dates With Barker*. Ronnie's film *The Picnic* had just been screened when Bernard met Graham Chapman, whom he was working with at the time. 'I hadn't seen it and the following day Graham, who could be pretty scathing about other people's comedy, said, "Oh, it was pretty dreadful, but there was one bit that made me laugh – it was when Ronnie walked into the middle of a field and saw a sign saying DANGER. He looked around, couldn't see any danger, but then the sign fell on him."'

Recognising the sketch instantly, Bernard bellowed, 'I wrote that!' He explains, 'I'd written that for *Hark at Barker*, so I got straight on to my agent and after several weeks I was paid. Ronnie said he thought he'd written it. We all knew what we've written and for Ronnie to say that, you feel like saying, "Come on." But there was no protest and I was paid. But what I had done was go to London Weekend's script archive to find my original script, which had my name alongside it, and kept a copy, just in case we needed it – but we didn't. I think Ronnie just thought that as he'd performed it, it was his almost.' Peter Vincent acknowledges that, as Gerald Wiley, Ronnie wrote 'some of the best things in the show', before adding, 'and some of the things which weren't the best in the show. The things that we wrote which weren't the best didn't get in. You can't really complain, because his standard was pretty high, but there were one or two dreadful things – and some of the films weren't great.' But there is one 'superb' Wiley joke, in particular, which he remembers clearly – partly for its simplicity. 'Some people were digging a hole, but dug it in the wrong place. When told that they would have to move it, they just dragged the actual hole along to the right place – it was a terrific joke.' But Peter wasn't enamoured of *The Phantom Raspberry Blower* and *The Worm That Turned* (starring Diana Dors, in a world where women rule and men are relegated to subservient roles) serials. 'At his best, Ronnie's writing was terrific, but I think these serials dragged, and he had a tendency to write long scenes which didn't help.'

Ian Davidson wasn't a fan of *The Worm That Turned* serial, either. 'I thought it was horrid and shouldn't have got on television; there was a slight concentration on women's bottoms, I noticed. I'm all for them, but I didn't think it was necessary,' admits Ian, grinning. At times, Ronnie's liking for the McGill-style postcard humour, including bum-and-tit jokes, surfaced in many of the sketches, and, at times, according to Ian Davidson, the guidelines issued to writers contributing scripts to the show didn't seem to apply to Mr Wiley. 'We were given harsh limits and told that sketches had to have a good punchline; if it didn't, the sketch wouldn't even be looked at. So we spent ages beating our brains about punchlines, but I always remember a famous Gerald Wiley sketch which didn't have a punchline. It was a lesson, because it showed you could have very good sketches without punch-lines; but Ronnie's got through and ours didn't. The famous "Four Candles" sketch had no punchline, either. I'm not saying that's a reason it shouldn't be done, I'm saying why couldn't some of ours be done?'

When asked about the use of ideas dreamt up by other writers, Terry Hughes says, 'I don't think Ronnie even stopped to think about it. He thought, "We need some material. Here's an idea. I could take this and run it." Not for a moment would it have been for financial gain – that was never part of his thinking. He needed good material for the show and in doing so probably deprived, say, Dick Vosburgh of a cheque or chance to write something else. But my guess is that he probably just sat down with that idea one day and said, "Let's see if I can go somewhere with this." He then came up with something he liked and submitted it. At the time, I didn't even think, "Oh, this is originally Dick's idea." In retrospect, maybe it wasn't the right thing to do, but it was about getting material for the show, not stealing credit or making money, just about filling up the programme with the best stuff possible.' Terry says that the whole reason some writers were 'bitter' is the reason why Ronnie adopted the Gerald Wiley pseudonym when he began working for David Frost. 'He didn't want people to think he was getting favouritism. I'd say categorically that we never passed over another writer's better piece of material for something less good of Ronnie's. It was all about what's the best material, regardless of the source. Writers may not agree, but we didn't think any other way.'

Something else writers had to get used to was Ronnie polishing sketches, making them – in his view – as effective as possible for the show. Michael Palin recalls this happening to him even before *The Two Ronnies* – on work submitted for *The Frost Report*. 'You'd send something in and on the actual night realise that it had been quite subtly changed: Ronnie was not above tinkering with other writers' work. Sometimes, I felt he'd gone a bit far, perhaps because one feels that sense of ownership, but generally he did it because he knew he could make it funnier – and he did. He never changed anything which didn't get laughs. But we had no great battle. We licked our wounds every now and then, but were just glad the material was used.' Michael admits that a little of Ronnie's style of working rubbed off on him and Terry Jones. 'We were journeymen writers at the time, writers for hire. Once we started on *Python* we were amongst a group who wanted to do it their way, so maybe the spirit of Ronnie B. went on into *Python*, because that gave us our chance to do our stuff, and we were very particular with material, working on it like Ronnie did.'

Another writer who saw his work amended was John Sullivan; not that it worried him, because he felt it put him in good stead for the future. 'Through Ronnie I discovered that the only way of working is to show by example. I'd write a sketch and be paid, then I'd go along to see it being made and notice he'd added or adjusted it. But you would look and say, "I see. I know why he's done that now." He taught me through example, so much so that when I write now or get other people writing for me, instead of sitting down and saying, "You need more emphasis here" or "this character isn't doing enough" the only way I can show the technique is by just rewriting what they've written and hope they'll learn from that. I learnt a tremendous amount from Ronnie.'

Reflecting on the relationship between Ronnie B. and the band of writers, David Renwick says it would be 'disingenuous' to pretend that resentment didn't exist occasionally amongst members of the writing team regarding Gerald Wiley taking the lion's share of script credits. 'Ronnie would regularly write all of the long-running serials, many of the musical items and songs, and a fair share of sketches and monologues. Writers can be a fairly embittered breed and there would be occasional rumblings in the BBC bar about Ronnie B.'s strike rate on the show compared with their own. There were a few of my own sketches I thought were "certs" which never made it to the screen. But that's how it always is on a sketch show, you can never totally predict the taste of the performers, and at the end of the day they have to feel comfortable with the material if they're to do it justice. I'm sure Ronnie was astute enough to be aware of that discontent behind his back, and Terry Hughes certainly was. I remember him declaring once, "If it wasn't for all the stuff Ronnie produces, we'd be in one hell of a mess."'

Ronnie's contribution in terms of material increased as the series moved along, bringing with it additional pressures. This was, in part, due to worries about the standard of some of the material being received; as the years passed, many of the established and long-serving writers became busy on other shows and, therefore, the quantity of sketches they were able to supply reduced. David Renwick was aware of this fact. 'On a couple of occasions Ronnie B. sketched out an idea for an end item he'd come up with, and asked if I'd like to write it up for him. One was called *Caribbean Nights*, set on board a cruise ship, and the other was the demonic Christmas finale *Pinocchio II, Killer Doll*. That was the extent to which we ever collaborated on any material, and I wouldn't say either of those pieces was the strongest thing I wrote for them. But I think by that time Ronnie was growing a little tired from the sheer volume of stuff he was having to produce to fill up the programmes. Over the years they had had many top-name writers working for them – the *Pythons*, David Nobbs, John Sullivan and many others – but most had moved on to other things and the burden inevitably fell back on Ronnie's shoulders.'

Although it could be argued that Ronnie's increasing power and influence saw him claiming more and more control of the show in terms of direction and content, it must be remembered that the two Ronnies were the stars, and it was their reputations on the line when they performed the show each week. Any sub-standard work, in the eyes of Ronnie B., would reflect on him and his partner: ultimately, the majority of viewers disappointed with a particular week's output wouldn't cogitate and come to the conclusion that it was, in fact, the writers behind the sketches who had delivered a disappointing script, they would blame the artists, perhaps showing their dissatisfaction by reaching for the OFF button on their remote.

Many of those who wrote for the series – and worked on it – freely admit that Ronnie B., in particular, was demanding; however, they're also keen to acknowledge his brilliance as a performer and the qualities he brought to his work. 'During the recording of the show, you'd become aware that he was very much in control. If a sketch wasn't going well, he'd make a deliberate mistake, which the audience thought was terrific. Then they would start again and get a much better response – he was very clever,' says Peter Vincent. This was a tool he used to great effect in other shows, too.

Ian Davidson concurs with Peter. 'Yes, he was a very clever performer, and also an extremely quick learn in terms of lines. Like Ronnie Corbett, he was a writer's dream, because he was so good and accurate with the material you gave him.' Ian recalls a party sketch he wrote with Paul MacDowell in which the Ronnies' characters spoke in unison. 'It was about two men being introduced to each other at a party; they couldn't stop speaking in unison, and at the end, as they turned and walked away in opposite directions, they said, again in unison, "boring bugger". They did it beautifully and got it to work by Ronnie B. having his foot on Ronnie C.'s and pressing when he was just about to talk, allowing them to synchronise their speech. It was an absolute joy and people were talking about it the following day.'

David Nobbs has no hesitation in classing Ronnie B. as 'not only one of the best actors of his generation, but of any generation'. He says, 'Ronnie was a rare comedy actor in his facility of words and ability to create characters of depth.' Such was David's respect and admiration for the man, he wanted to cast him as Reggie Perrin in his hit sitcom *The Fall and Rise of Reginald Perrin*. And, if circumstances had been different, we might have seen him cast as accident-prone Frank Spencer in the sitcom *Some Mothers Do 'Ave 'Em*. Regarding Perrin, Nobbs says: 'I would loved to have worked with him more. He shared with Leonard that enormous affinity with words. Long speeches and tongue-twisters, both did these brilliantly.' In hingsight, David realises his comedy about a stressed executive, bored with life's mundanities, who fakes his own suicide – twice – and returns with a new identity, couldn't have been any more successful than with Rossiter heading the cast, but believes Ronnie B. might have been just as good.

As co-writer – along with Terry Jones – of many of the party sketches in *The Two Ronnies*, Michael Palin was impressed with Ronnie B.'s sharpness, something he witnessed first-hand. 'He was very good at absorbing what was funny about a situation and how it could be made funnier. When he wrote some of the party sketches himself, it was difficult to know which were his and which were ours.' Being a founding member of the *Python* team, many of Palin and Jones' sketches had a surreal quality. 'You wrote knowing Ronnie

B. would perform the lines perfectly – and Ronnie C. was marvellous, too. But Ronnie B. liked the form of a traditional sketch. I think he was conventional, and if one tried doing something a bit different, he'd bring it back to how he could deal with it best, that being in a slightly more conventional way.'

The teaming of Barker and Corbett, which started in earnest when the pair moved to the BBC, worked beautifully in *The Two Ronnies* and a high standard of programming was achieved, even when the show began to run out of steam towards the end of its life; by then, time was, sadly, catching up with its style of comedy. 'The Ronnies were very different in the way they performed and the characters they could play,' remarks Palin, 'but they complemented each other well – and both were supreme deliverers of a funny line. While Ronnie C. had this engaging Scottishness about him, Ronnie B. was always slightly cooler; he might be doing a character brilliantly, but it was almost like a piece of science he'd developed in the lab, whereas Ronnie C. was much more instinctive when delivering material.'

Ronnie B. was one of the best comedy actors Ian Davidson had seen, his deftness at delivering complicated sentences – exemplified by many of the popular monologues which became one of his trademarks – being one of his finest assets. 'Take the Spoonerism sketches. It's the devil's own job saying those lines quickly, because if you utter them too rapidly you're likely to Spoonerise them back the other way, meaning they'll make sense again. But there was never any question of him becoming unstuck on things like that; he was marvellous on the most complicated sketches.'

The famous monologues – influenced by a trend in the 1970s for government officials to appear regularly on the box, talking about a host of topics – became a popular part of the programme. They came in all shapes and sizes, but usually saw Ronnie playing a po-faced official, such as a stern-looking spokesman appealing on behalf of the Society for the Very Clumsy, the moustached and bespectacled official from the Ministry of Pollution and the popular spokesperson appealing on behalf of those who can't pronounce their words properly. Many were complicated to deliver but, being a skilled technician, Ronnie carried them off with aplomb. 'Ronnie was amazingly quick-witted,' says Ian Davidson. 'There was an occasion when he was in the BBC bar with Eric Morecambe, and Eric said, "He's quicker than me." Barker was able to fire stuff back at Morecambe.'

John Sullivan can testify to the speed at which Ronnie's brain worked when it came to comedy. 'I remember a scene where Ronnie Corbett was a patient and Ronnie Barker a psychiatrist with a nameplate on his desk. As they were recording it, it went wrong, because Corbett knocked the plate off. Ronnie B. said, "You little name-dropper, you." He was that fast. It was so good it was left in.'

Another impressive monologue was 'Nows at Ton', written by Barry Cryer and Peter Vincent, in which a typewriter typed the letter 'O' instead of 'E'. Barry and Peter thought Ronnie B. was 'brilliant' doing this sketch, which required very precise timing. Peter says, 'It was quite short and only took about ten minutes to write. It's a corny idea, but I'm sure it came from personal experience, because typewriters often play up like that.'

Another popular segment of the series was the extravagant musical strand, usually written by Ronnie. The standard was high, although time constraints prevented the Ronnies learning the lyrics, so autocue was employed and the song recorded the day before. Terry Hughes never saw anyone use autocue as well as Ronnie B. 'He used it a lot. You had to, because there was so much material to learn. But where some people would be like robots using it, he would only use it as an aide-memoire.'

The weekly schedule for recording episodes of *The Two Ronnies* remained largely unchanged throughout its sixteen-year history. The working week began on Monday morning, when many of the sketches selected for that week's instalment would be read. Any additional actors needed would be present, plus members of the production team – such as Mary Husband, the long-serving costume designer, and representatives from the Make-up Department – would pop across to the rehearsals, which normally took place at the BBC's Acton site.

Rehearsals began in earnest on Tuesdays, with everyone working in marked-up sets using dummy props, such as old beds and chairs hauled up from the mini-prop house in the basement. 'We'd rehearse the sketches up to four times and invariably alterations were made, perhaps cuts made or jokes added,' says Terry Hughes. During Tuesday afternoons the musical numbers were rehearsed with Ronnie Hazlehurst, the musical director, making notes for the orchestration.

Wednesday was another solid rehearsal day with time allocated for reading the proposed news items, which would be delivered to Hughes and the two Ronnies by the script editor, followed by further rehearsing, allowing Hughes the chance to make notes on his camera script. Thursday saw more polishing of the sketches before a technical run in the afternoon, when all the technical departments involved in the recording would be represented. Hughes explains, 'Everyone would be there, including the lighting director, who would be busy making notes on his floor plan to show where lights were required.'

Friday morning meant more rehearsing before everyone trotted over to the Lime Grove studios where much of the music for the big musical numbers was pre-recorded. The following day, Saturday, the performers would rehearse in front of the cameras within the sets for the first time, fine-tuning before the day of recording. Sunday began at noon and involved rehearsing in full costume until around 5.30 p.m., followed by a dinner break. Soon the studio audience began to arrive and proceedings would get underway with a warm-up artist – or even Ronnie C. – introducing the show.

For Ronnie B., walking out in front of the audience and entertaining as himself was something he couldn't cope with. If he grabbed a pair of glasses, slapped on a moustache or beard and called himself John Smith, he'd be fine; once in disguise and adopting the persona of a fictitious character, Ronnie B. was in his element, able to entertain for hours. But even for each episode's closing scene where, sitting behind a desk alongside Ronnie Corbett, he said goodbye, Ronnie still couldn't be himself, as David Nobbs explains. 'I was script editor for the first series and we had this decision to make about how to end the show. I suggested the two Ronnies simply said, "Goodnight," nicely and sincerely. But Ronnie B. said he couldn't do that as himself. He wouldn't appear as himself in the show. So the joke of using the "Goodnight from him" comment was devised – that was his way of getting around the embarrassment of addressing the audience as himself.'

Nobbs cites the monologues as a perfect way of illustrating the fundamental differences between the two artists: Barker, an actor seeking refuge in character, hiding behind accents and make-up, while Corbett was delighted just to be himself. It was an aspect of Ronnie B.'s character which had affected his career from the early days. Actress Eira Heath remembers his reluctance to face the audience before a recording of the radio show *Not To Worry.* 'Because Ronnie was making a name for himself as a funny guy, John Fawcett Wilson, the producer, asked him to do the warm-up, but he hated the idea. He kept saying, "I'm not a comedian. I can't do this." Everyone kept telling him he was so funny, but he insisted he couldn't do it. The producer wanted him to do it so much it was eventually agreed that Ronnie would go on with a book of Victorian jokes and read from the book. Being an actor, he could do it as a character, but not just go on and present a comedy act.' Ronnie collected joke books and admitted dipping into them from time to time for use in his sketches. 'Someone wrote a sketch about two yokels and I thought they would be marvellous to do these old jokes. So I literally cut up the book, laid them all out on paper and stuck them down with Sellotape. In between, I wrote linking lines and it worked a treat – it got a lot of laughs.'[1]

The inability to reveal anything of his own persona when faced with an audience is something which remained with him. He explained once, 'I'm very shy, I have to hide behind a character. I can't be myself. I feel I have no personality so I pull on a character.'[2]

Good friend Richard Briers acknowledges that the clamouring for a disguise was borne out of shyness. 'It was real chronic shyness and, of course, being creative as well, unlike actors such as me who are just interpretive, he was creative and wrote; so he had a sensitive side to him, which was more artistic than just being a performer. That's why some of the funniest things he did in *The Two Ronnies* were the drag acts, because he could put the lot on. He always wore a disguise, so he could walk on with some confidence. He was a retiring man and no one knew him that well, other than Ronnie Corbett and Joy. He was a great collector, which is a form of protection in itself – he'd collect everything from bus tickets and stamps to paintings and postcards.'

This shyness, coupled with the fact that he was an intensely private man meant that you rarely found Ronnie accepting invitations to open fêtes, cutting the ribbon when a new supermarket was opening its doors or attending festivals as guest of honour. But Barry Cryer, who lived nearby, recalls his surprise at stumbling across him in Harrow. 'Locally, Ronnie was always being asked to do all these kind of things. Invariably, he'd decline, but would send a cheque, so he was in very good standing. Then, one day I noticed he was going to open a local fête and thought, this is a first. It was a rainy day, but I went along and Ronnie was signing autographs. I got a bit of paper and for a laugh tried to make it look disgusting by rubbing it on the floor with my foot. I turned my coat collar up and shuffled along in this queue. Ronnie was signing at great speed, hardly looking up, and I shuffled up and said, in a strange voice, "Would you put, 'To Marjorie', please?" He scribbled on the bit of paper and gave it back to me. I walked away and thought the joke was over, but then I looked at what he'd written and it said, "Piss off, Cryer, I'm busy." It was typical of him. I'd never noticed that he'd seen me. That was how clever he was.'

Cleverness was just one of the man's many qualities which endeared him to millions – in fact, above twenty million as *The Two Ronnies* gained momentum, establishing itself as a national institution within the world of entertainment – who tuned in to watch Ronnie deliver endless performances of real class.

Chapter 13

Nearly a quarter of the United Kingdom's population switched on to watch the first episode of *The Two Ronnies*, transmitted at 8.15 p.m. on Saturday, 10 April 1971. Opinions of the viewing public after the episode's screening revealed most regarded it as an entertaining show, with the two performers forming a welcome combination; one person commenting that 'either Ronnie is good, but together they're absolutely marvellous'.[1] But it wasn't just the public who enjoyed *The Two Ronnies*. It was respected by the industry as a whole and, in 1975, the show won a BAFTA for 'Best Light Entertainment Programme'. Accolades came Ronnie B.'s way, too, when he won the 'Best Light Entertainment Performance' category in 1977 and 1978.

The opening series, like the other eleven to come, followed a similar path, including a filmed serial; the first, *Hampton Wick*, was a pastiche of the classic serials in vogue during the 1970s. Appearing with the Ronnies was twenty-year-old Madeline Smith, a model-turned-actress whose far from bulging CV contained just the occasional play and appearances in the Hammer horror films *Taste the Blood of Dracula* and *The Vampire Lovers*. Madeline was delighted to be offered the Henrietta Beckett role. 'I was still an inexperienced sketch lady, really. I'd just worked as Arthur Lowe's daughter in five episodes of *Doctor at Large* for London Weekend when the call came, informing me I'd got the part.' As well as excitement, a sense of relief must have coursed through her veins, considering the audition. 'When I reached the BBC at White City I bounded up the stairs to meet Ronnie Barker and Terry Hughes. I sat down and Ronnie angled me so I faced this lurid sun. He put me through my paces while staring at me intently – I was surprised to find him such a serious man.' Madeline didn't realise that Ronnie had written the serial, explaining why he directed her throughout the eight instalments. 'Every time I opened my mouth Ronnie had told me what to do.

Terry Hughes was instrumental in making the programme fizz along, but the serial and, in particular, my performance was directed by Ronnie. He was very serious and highly intelligent.'

Ronnie's increasing involvement with directing didn't worry producer-director Terry Hughes. 'Material that he wrote, like the film serials, he'd visualise in a certain way. I might see it another way, but it was difficult manoeuvring him.' But Ronnie wasn't obdurate and on other items was happy to take advice. As further series were clocked up, and Terry Hughes eventually left for America, Ronnie's grip on the series' shape and direction tightened. Terry says, 'I don't think he gained it. I think he took it. I was in from the beginning and, therefore, part of the team which created the programme; I was like a third Ronnie in a way.' It has already been mentioned that Ronnie could be demanding, and Terry agrees, before quickly qualifying his views. 'He gave everything of himself. He did all his homework and was always prepared; he wanted everybody else to be prepared, too. I never found him moody, difficult or obstructive, just a perfectionist in the best sense of the word. For example, if a script wasn't working, whether it was one of his or not, he'd take it home and polish it – and it would always be better for it. While everybody else went home for the evening, he'd return to his house and worry it through to make it as good as possible.' Ronnie took his responsibilities extremely seriously: during the summer hiatus, he would be sitting at his desk writing material for the next season. 'I learnt so much from him, from filming and positioning of cameras to timing and editing.'

For most people, time spent in the company of Ronnie, however brief, resulted in an improvement of their own abilities and knowledge. Madeline Smith was one who benefited. 'While filming *Hampton Wick* Ronnie and I would disappear every week to a voice studio in London's West End to put down my wretched little high voice for the narration. Ronnie took me through every word and every nuance, and then we'd jump in a cab and head back. He was a tremendously deep-thinking man, but he didn't talk very much; it was all going on inside his head.'

Madeline will never forget filming the serial, and when I mention that Ronnie, in his autobiography, described the moment she inadvertently 'popped out' while making an instalment, she laughs before recalling the incident. 'The bosom business, of course. I hadn't long had those attributes. They were like strangers tacked on to me and I hadn't got used to them. I never mind camera crews seeing anything. They're long used to seeing all sorts of horrors. But in the studio, while recording the show for the first time, knitting it together with the filming – whoops, one did pop out and is there for all to see to this day! It's in an episode when I'm sitting between two Dickensian characters, and out it came. I was so squeezed and nipped in, and while I was sat there, looking from one character to the other, I felt it come out. But there was nothing I could do, as there would be nothing more ghastly than me stuffing it back in again.'

Madeline always felt she was treated with the greatest respect, especially as she filmed what, she believes, was her only ever totally nude scene. 'We were filming a Lady Godiva scene at the Bath Theatre Royal and I was supposed to be naked and wearing a long wig. Ronnie B. came up to me and said, "Maddie, that body stocking shows on camera. Listen, would you mind very much if you were genuinely nude? We're only going to film you from the back as you run offstage." I didn't mind, and I ran straight into the arms of the wardrobe mistress, who was holding a towel. Body stockings don't always work. So if you're doing it, go for it and don't be coy.' Madeline remembers how 'nice' Ronnie B. was. 'Obviously he loved the female form, but I never thought either man was looking at me lustily, plus there were never any revolting overtures from anybody.'

The only regret Madeline has is that the first series, unlike others, was rarely repeated while Ronnie B. was alive; she says this is because he wasn't enamoured of that first season, something Ronnie admits in his autobiography. 'I saw him at a do and said it was a shame the first series was never shown. He replied, "No, I didn't feel I was any good in it. It hadn't really come together for me." It was almost as if he wanted to disown the first season. I disagreed, but he was a complete perfectionist and I think he was still honing it and felt he was better in the other series. That saddened me. But that was what he felt in his heart and he was a completely honest guy: what you saw was what you got with Barker, so he told me straight that he didn't think it was any good.'

The Press didn't agree with him. The *Guardian*'s Peter Fiddick, for example, thought the programme had talent in abundance, using the Brooklea Hearing Aid Centre sketch as an example. He wrote, 'It's one thing to create a sketch like that between the hard-of-hearing, hearing-aid consultant and his hard-of-hearing client, quite another to perform it with the miraculous timing of Corbett and Barker.'[2]

Sketch ideas came from everywhere, including day-to-day situations, and the hearing-aid sketch is a fine example, being inspired by Ronnie's wife Joy. He explained once, 'One morning, I was sitting reading a local paper and I said to my wife, "I see that new building down the road is going to be a hearing-aid centre." And she said, "Pardon?" Well, of course, I immediately started writing the hearing-aid sketch.'[3]

It wasn't only the *Guardian* applauding the Ronnies' first show. Stewart Lane in the *Morning Star* thought they made a brilliant team, stating, 'Much funnier than when appearing separately, the two Ronnies made a triumphant opening to their new series.'[4] Without exception, the critics thought that one of the most rewarding aspects of the series was that Barker and Corbett cohered so smoothly and effortlessly. Virginia Ironside in the *Daily Mail* thought they were just as good as Morecambe and Wise, before grading the Big Jim Jehosophat and Fat-Belly Jones musical item as 'one of the most affectionate, understanding and funny little items I've ever seen'[5].

The musical numbers were one of Ronnie's favourite elements, but writing the lyrics was a complex business. Occasionally, he'd compose the tune as well, although normally he picked standard tunes out of copyright. Regarding the lyrics, he once said, 'You not only have got to rhyme it, and the metre has got to be exactly right, but also you've got to get the jokes in, and the jokes have to be at the end of the line, and have to be the right number of syllables.'[6]

Memorable musical numbers – other writers contributed, including Dick Vosburgh – over the years included the Ronnies singing their version of Chas & Dave's 'Rabbit' in one of their *Top of the Pops* spoofs. Ronnie B. was a big fan of the musical duo and asked them to write parodic lyrics for their Top Ten hit. Chas

Hodges says they were honoured to have been part of 'Ronnie Barker's creative achievements'. Concerning revising the lyrics to their song, Chas says, 'We changed the lines to "Why don't you tune up your bass? Why don't you shut your face?", etc. We were invited in to view it before it went out. I know Ronnie just wanted to clock our faces as we watched it. We fell about and Ronnie was pleased. On the day of transmission I rang my Aunt Alice in Hackney. I said, "Watch *The Two Ronnies* tonight, Alice." She replied, "Why, are you on it?" "I'm not saying, just watch it." She did, then rang back. "Chassie! You two boys were great. I knew you were going to be on it." She thought the two Ronnies were us.'

Audiences looked forward to the Ronnies' monologues each week as well. While wordsmith Ronnie B. could display his incredible appetite for the English language and its peculiarities, Ronnie C. wallowed in his chair slot, regaling the audience with stories and quips penned by Spike Mullins and, latterly, David Renwick. Producer-director Terry Hughes says, 'Apart from shortening the contributions from Spike, we hardly ever had to touch them.' Ronnie C. and Hughes looked forward to the script's arrival each week at the BBC studios. 'It was a particularly joyous moment, because they'd come in a brown envelope by motorcycle messenger. Ronnie C. would go off into a corner and read his copy, giggling, and I'd go off into another corner and read my copy, laughing, too. Then we'd get together and say, "He's done it again!" He was unfailingly reliable.'

What was pleasing, considering critics can often be ruthless and scathing, is that as the series progressed, many acknowledged that the team wasn't content to rest on its laurels, wanting, instead, to continually improve. As a correspondent in the *Daily Mail* wrote at the end of Series Two in November 1972, 'from the first to the last in Terry Hughes' production there was an exhilarating sense of a team at work trying to force the level up, rather than coast along down with what the majority will accept.'[7] And even in 1985, fourteen years after the first outing, the show was still receiving favourable press reviews and adored by millions; in fact, the final series – number twelve – was watched by, on average, fourteen million viewers each week.

There was a mix of personnel within the production team over the years, experienced individuals who were called back repeatedly and younger crew members who lapped up the chance to learn from two of the nation's top comedy performers. All had to be prepared, however, to accommodate Ronnie B.'s need for involvement and, to a degree, control. For example, he was a regular visitor to the editing suite. 'It was very much a team effort, though. I'd offer suggestions about how to make things better, then Ronnie would offer his. It was a pretty affable arrangement and not the slightest aspect of jobsworth about it,' says Geoff Hicks, a videotape editor, who will never forget Ronnie inviting him to lunch. 'Ronnie came down to the suite and we spent all morning together. Then Terry Hughes said, "OK, let's break for lunch. We'll see you back at two." But Ronnie said, "No, you won't, you're coming with us – and he'll buy you lunch." He was pointing at Terry. So we ate together at the second-floor restaurant, which, in those days, was waitress service.'

Sometimes, though, Ronnie's desire to be involved in every moment of constructing the series and subsequent programmes got him into trouble, like the time he helped out in a car park at Ealing. Leighton Turnham, who worked as a prop man, recalls the time the *Porridge* cast filmed the episode 'The Harder They Fall' at a school in Fulham. 'The school was surrounded by high fences to stop balls going out of the playground. This forty-foot lorry, full of props and scenery, was backing in off the road. Ronnie happened to be there, so tried to help. He kept indicating to the driver, saying things like, "Keep coming, you're fine." The driver kept sticking his head out of the window, asking, "Are you sure?" Ronnie would reply, "Yeah, yeah, you've got plenty of room." When it was apparent the driver was oversteering, Ronnie screamed, "Too much, too much!" Unfortunately, the driver ended up backing into some fencing, nearly ripping it out of the ground. You can imagine what the driver said!'

Back on *The Two Ronnies* one of the constants was the costume designer Mary Husband, who worked on all but the first series. She formed such a trusting and productive relationship with Ronnie B. that he requested her services for all future productions. Mary, who almost had a second sight when it came to Ronnie B., explains that their working relationship clicked from day one. Every time a new script arrived a set procedure was followed. 'I'd take it home and read it carefully. Then I'd phone Ronnie at a given time and go through it, from a costume point of view. I'd say what I felt and he'd straighten me out, if necessary; he was the driving force, but we got on extremely well.' Mary admits that it was unusual to go into such depth with an actor. 'I regarded him as co-producer/director in a way, partly because he'd written so much. I always used to say to him, "As long as I keep one page ahead, we'd be OK."'

Original costume designer, Hazel Pethig, set the tone for the series in terms of costume style; Mary developed it from there. 'Little Ronnie loved clothes and would say what he liked to wear, such as, "I thought something in lime green would be fun." So I'd do a simple jacket with the right colour shirt and tie – he'd have them made at his tailor's. Ronnie B. wasn't really interested in clothes, so the outfits he wore while reading the news headlines were left to me. We ended up with strong stripes and colours, and he loved them.'

Although working on the show was a challenge, it was great fun as well, says Mary, who treasures a poem Ronnie wrote for her when he retired from the business in the late 1980s. It read:

> By hook or by crook, I'll write in your book,
> By silver and gold, should your talents be told,
> By longjohns and vest, you provided the best,
> By needle and thread, you kept one page ahead.
> My love to you,
> Ronnie Barker

Ronnie's attention to detail was widely known by now and although Mary struck up a friendship with him, she's aware his relationship with the Make-up Department wasn't always as smooth. 'Make-up weren't too keen working with him, because he was *such* a stickler. There was an occasion when a designer was making him up to be an Irishman. She thought for a change they would give him a blond wig, but he stressed, "Irishmen aren't blond. You've got to do the right thing. It's got to be dark hair."'

Jill Shardlow, who worked on two series, agrees that Ronnie never struck up such a close relationship with the Make-up Department. 'He felt *The Two Ronnies* was very much his baby and was personally responsible for making it work, especially as he wrote so much material. For that reason, he had a finger in about four million pies and was very quick to be exacting about what he wanted. I worked on *The Phantom Raspberry Blower of Old London Town* in which, amongst many other characters, he played Disraeli. He wouldn't let me make him up to look like him, because he thought people would think it was anti-Semitic. I had to make him a papier mâché joke nose on elastic, so that it was clear that he was just joking – he was quite funny about things like that.

'The key was to try and think ahead of him. Trouble was, because he was such a bright man with an off-the-wall sense of humour, that was tricky and I didn't always make it.' Jill recalls a particular moment when he was rather curt. 'I'd really struggled and needed to talk to him about whether what I was doing was what he wanted, but he was a bit dismissive. He said, sharply, "You must remember, Jill, make-up is at least fifth in my list of priorities!" I was completely crestfallen. It was like being hit between the eyes with a wet kipper. I thought afterwards that it wasn't terribly good psychology if you want us to give of our best. That incident made me think twice about doing the next series I was asked to do. However, I did, but, to be honest, I'd had enough at the end and knew I couldn't have coped with another season.

'I don't think Ronnie B. meant that remark unkindly, because he was a very nice man. He was just very single-minded when it came to the programme and would say what he wanted without really thinking about how it might affect the other person.' His drive for perfection, according to Jill, was a double-edged sword sometimes. 'Some people, being professionals, reckoned that they should be trusted to do the best for him, which he wasn't always able to do through his own desire to have everything absolutely perfect. That was the problem, really. There's a point where you've got to let people take on the responsibility and I think they work better if you do – sometimes he couldn't see that.

'But overall, although there were times when I could cheerfully have throttled him, there were many more occasions when I enjoyed being in his company and working with him. We had some great laughs, too. Like all make-up designers I had a box of assorted moustaches that I took everywhere. He used to have one in the collection we called the "nasty moustache". He'd use it for a lot of sketches and would say, "Ah, for this sketch I want the Nasty Moustache." Looking back over the experience as a whole, despite the stress involved, I probably produced some of my best work for *The Two Ronnies* and felt real affection for Ronnie B. and Ronnie C.'

Ronnie B. made no excuses for being fastidious, realising that he was often regarded as being fussy by some people working on his productions. He inherited such character traits from an early mentor, Glenn Melvyn. He explained once, 'His first thoughts were always for the audience. Efficiency was his watchword in every facet of the rehearsals and performances . . . and to this day this has always been my goal. I know that in later years, when more in control of what I did and performed, I was regarded by many as pernickety, fussing about detail, but to me it was just getting it right, as right as it was possible to get it. Glenn taught me that and I'm grateful that he did.'

Looking back over nearly one hundred hours of *The Two Ronnies* it's near impossible to select a favourite sketch, most of which brought ineffable joy. The monologues were terrific, the party sketches hilarious – in fact, it's difficult to choose just one. But if pushed, one that would be vying for top spot is the *Mastermind* sketch, penned by David Renwick. We should think ourselves lucky, however, that we saw it at all. 'Having sat down and written this sketch, I tore it up,' admits Renwick. 'The following day, because I had no better ideas and had to deliver whatever it was I'd agreed to deliver that year, I literally fished the pieces out of the waste bin and sellotaped it together.'[8]

Let's not forget Renwick's delicious little sketch 'Crossed Lines', which saw the Ronnies making phone calls from adjacent phone booths and, seemingly, answering each other's questions. But the most famous – and voted the most popular in *The Two Ronnies Night*, screened on BBC in 1999 – is the 'Four Candles' or 'Fork Handles' sketch in which a shop assistant (Corbett) in a hardware shop is driven mad by a customer (Barker) when he continually misunderstands what he's asking for. Voted among the Top Ten comedy sketches of all time by various polls, the sketch was written by Barker, based on a real incident in a hardware shop in Hayes, Middlesex, details of which were submitted by the shopkeeper. The sketch makes full use of Ronnie B.'s love of wordplay, and a hand-written copy of it, fully verified by Corbett, turned up on an edition of *Antiques Roadshow*; it was later sold for nearly £50,000. 'In rehearsal, Ronnie C. never got through it without breaking up,' recalls Terry Hughes. 'If you look at it now, there's a moment where he's going to get something; as he turns away, you can see this half-smile form and he's fighting to control the laughter. He never thought he'd get through it.'

'If you notice, Ronnie C. tops the laugh about three or four times,' adds Paul Jackson, who went from runner to producer on the show. 'He milks the laugh and gets another laugh out of it, just with his timing and look. He walks away to get an item and glances back; that kind of thing doesn't happen until the night and you had to be very alert when you were directing them not to miss those moments.'

A major change happened at the end of Series Five when Terry Hughes, who eventually established a successful televisual career in America, was promoted, resulting in a string of director-producers taking over *The Two Ronnies*. 'I wasn't looking to get out of it, but Thames Television offered me a really good deal, with one of the things they wanted me to do being Benny Hill,' recalls Hughes. 'I was considering it when Bill Cotton, one Friday evening, said, "Don't do anything, meet me over the weekend at the golf club at Richmond." So I met him and Alisdair Milne, then Director-General, and they offered me the Head of Variety position. I was very flattered, so took the job. In truth, it was the worst mistake I ever made, because I wasn't good at it and hated it. I truly missed making shows. The Ronnies were happy for me when I told them, they understood, but they were saddened because everything was comfortable, so why rock the boat?'

By this point, though, the programme was such an established hit – you only have to consider the generous filming schedules and budgets to realise how much it was treasured by the BBC hierarchy – that the producer-director's main job from that point was to keep the ball rolling and ensure the programme remained on track. Several people were at the helm over the remaining seven series. By this time, though, the show was a running entity, so no one taking over would want to alter a winning formula. However, if there is one criticism which could be aimed at the final seasons, it's that some sketches were rather long and would have benefited from tighter editing.

One person who stepped into the producer-director's shoes after Hughes' departure was Paul Jackson, heading up Series Eight and Nine. He found Ronnie a 'joy' to work with. He says, 'He was demanding and knew what he wanted – and normally knew how to get it. He taught me how to direct and edit comedy. When I moved up to directing the shows, I used to go to his house in Pinner before a series and go through my camera scripts. He taught me how to do it. In the early days, he'd pop down to the edit and make sure everything was OK. In the end, he trusted me and didn't do it. In eight to ten years of working with him, we never had a cross word. Ronnie was very respectful of the level of professionalism around him. But he had a very clear author's view – particularly on material he'd written – on what was required.'

In the hot seat for Series Ten and Eleven was Marcus Plantin, who says, 'Both Ronnies were demanding in different ways, but why wouldn't they be, because they were consummate professionals. I enjoyed the demands. If you're in your twenties and being brushed by Barker and Corbett in their late forties, it was the best thing you could ever have.'

As it transpired, Ronnie found much of his small screen career entailed working with people less experienced than himself, a situation which almost invited him to adopt a more commanding, controlling manner.

After sixteen years of entertaining millions, the curtain came down on *The Two Ronnies* with a Christmas Special in 1987. It remained a significantly popular programme with its loyal followers and had earnt its place in the annals of British Television as one of the best comedy series of all time. Although it was never cutting edge in terms of its comedic style – in fact, it was fairly mainstream

– it was perfectly executed and subtly produced, containing some wonderful material from a host of top-drawer writers. But compared to its very high standards, the latter years weren't as bold, imaginative or innovative. A degree of repetition was creeping in and as nothing lasts forever in the world of entertainment, it was time to call it a day.

Reflecting on the ending of an era, writer David Renwick says, 'Towards the end, the comedy climate was slowly changing. Anything that smacked of Benny Hill – and there were resonances of Benny's stuff throughout the Ronnies' run – was starting to become unfashionable within the television industry and the new generation of performers. *Not the Nine O'Clock News* had savaged them with their "Two Ninnies" parody, which I know had deeply offended Ronnie B., and I'm not surprised. Personally, I found bits of it quite funny – the silly Beefeater song – but thought the smug jibes at the newsdesk, where they couldn't even get their positions the right way round, were fairly hypocritical considering their own track record of smutty innuendo. The trouble was, *Not the Nine O'Clock News* was "hip" and on the ascendant, and just as people like Mike Yarwood were now suffering next to *Spitting Image*, the Ronnies began to look dangerously old-fashioned. I remember it became slightly uncomfortable when Paul Jackson was producing the later series, while at the same time working on more contemporary comedies like *Three of a Kind* and *The Young Ones*.'

Ronnie Corbett admits they were both upset by the *Not the Nine O'Clock News* sketch. 'Ron was very upset. It seemed foolhardy of the BBC to let bright young things, as they were then, take the mickey out of the big Saturday night show. It seemed impertinent at the time and a bit daft to be hurt within your own territory.'

During the sixteen-year run of *The Two Ronnies* not much had happened in Ronnie's solo career; his radio work came to a self-inflicted halt when he decided to focus his energies on television. His film and stage work was largely non-existent, too; simply, he had long-since found his true home: the medium of the small screen and that's where he decided to spend the rest of his career.

Chapter 14

During the sixteen-year run of *The Two Ronnies* Ronnie immersed himself in a host of varied characterisations for other shows, too. The *Ronnies* occupied around half the year, from writing the sketches to recording a series, allowing time to conduct a solo career. A convict, shopkeeper and short-sighted removal man were just some of the characters that Ronnie would create from his extensive library of voices and disguises in the coming years. By now, it was well-known that he was more at ease playing someone other than himself, which he acknowledged, recalling an occasion at the Palladium, during one of the *Two Ronnies* stage shows. 'We had to come on as ourselves and I said to Ronnie [Corbett], "I'm very nervous about this." He replied, "Be someone else. Be this character called Ronnie Barker." So I came on as a version of myself, a sort of showbiz version.'[1]

The nearest his adoring public came to seeing Barker, the man, on their screens was while reading news headlines in *The Two Ronnies*. In the early days of the series each item was read without facial expression, acting as newsreaders, but as the years passed, both performers allowed themselves to laugh at the jokes, endearing themselves even more to their millions of admirers.

In 1971, four months after the first series of *The Two Ronnies*, Ronnie B. played his last Shakespearean role, this time playing Bottom in *A Midsummer Night's Dream*, transmitted at the end of September, it formed a BBC *Play of the Month*. Nick Bottom supplies comic relief throughout the play, ultimately seeing his head transformed into that of an ass by Puck. This necessitated much ingenuity from the make-up designer, as well as plenty of patience from Ronnie. It was the most intricate make-up he'd ever experienced, spending around five hours in the chair as a false snout, hair, teeth and enormous brow were applied. Then, he'd endure up to seven hours made-up, restricting him to sipping soup through a straw, while fellow cast members tucked in to their scrumptious meals.

The play, shot entirely on location at the fourteenth-century moated Scotney Castle in Kent, saw Ronnie reunited with friend Eileen Atkins, who was cast as Titania; Eileen was happy to be back in the company of her mate from the Oxford Playhouse. She recalls a day when they finished early and Ronnie, relieved of his extensive make-up, made a suggestion. 'He asked if I was going back to the hotel, which was in Tunbridge Wells,' she recalls. 'I said, "Yes", so he replied, "Fancy sausage, egg and chips? I'm sick of all this posh food."' Eileen couldn't think of anything nicer, so they snuck off and enjoyed a greasy meal at a little caff. 'He wasn't particularly voluble and it was a nice, easy and relaxed meal. I liked him a lot and I think he knew that.'

The director was James Cellan Jones, who classes the production as 'very frantic'. He says, 'It was a couple of hours long and shot much too quickly; we had four days, which was lunacy. I never thought we'd finish, but managed it, although it would have been better given more time.'

When casting Bottom, Cellan Jones considered opting for a conventional classical actor. 'But as the character is a comedian, I wondered if Ronnie would do it.' He's glad Ronnie accepted, remembering a scene which highlighted the actor's immense talent. 'There is a famous soliloquy and he approached it so seriously and executed it beautifully. Years later, I met him at a function and he said he'd like to see it again, so I sent him a copy. He rang me up, saying, "It was all right, wasn't it?" I replied, "Yes, *you* certainly were all right."

'Bottom is difficult to cast, because it's so easy to become crude and stupid. The person playing it has to believe in the fact that he's a very serious actor – then you laugh at it. If you push the jokes too hard, it's unfunny. I've seen the part played many times but never better than by Ronnie,' says Cellan Jones, who witnessed another fine display of Ronnie's, this time delivering a long solo speech, with everyone watching in admiration. 'He was always word-perfect, very intelligent and had great humility.'

In an interview at the time, Ronnie reflected on being cast in a serious role, not common during his career. 'Because you do light-entertainment series people don't think of you as an actor. But I did six years in repertory when I first came into the business and followed that with six years in the West End before I ever did any television. So I always thought of myself, really, as a "legit" actor.'[2]

His performance in Shakespeare's fantasy about love was noted by many critics. The *Daily Mail*'s Peter Black thought his was a very capable performance, while Sylvia Clayton in the *Daily Telegraph* felt that although it failed to offer any fresh insights into the text, 'within its lush, pastoral atmosphere some performances blossomed. Ronnie Barker made Bottom not just an uncouth clown but an eager amateur actor tripping over his own aspirations.'[3] Henry Raynor in *The Times*, meanwhile, commented that Ronnie 'admirably refused to make the role a vehicle for his familiar enjoyable comic tricks'[4].

After rounding off 1971 with an appearance on *Christmas Night With the Stars*, the first half of the new year was spent working on *The Two Ronnies* and more episodes of the radio show *Lines From My Grandfather's Forehead*, in addition to a comedy pilot and brushing off his whiskers to reprise his Lord Rustless character.

Transmitted under the *Comedy Playhouse* umbrella (a vehicle for testing pilot programmes before committing to a full series), *Idle at Work* was written by Graham Chapman and Bernard McKenna. Ronnie played George Idle, who pledges to deflate those who pontificate on their chosen subjects. Soon after Ronnie had joined the BBC, he asked McKenna and Chapman to dream up an idea for a show. 'We came up with *Idle at Work*, which was very colourful,' says Bernard. 'We wanted to write an anarchic piece and Graham had been working on *The Magic Christian*, about a man with lots of money who could buy anything. Influenced by that, we thought we'd write something about a bloke who goes around puncturing people's balloons – their beliefs, ideas and such like. So we made a pilot, which worked quite well, and were commissioned to write a series. But Graham was difficult to write with, plus he was involved with *Python* and I was writing for the *Doctor* series, so the scripts for *Idle at Work* weren't very good. We delivered some, but Ronnie regarded them as *too* anarchic, which was right: they didn't get in to the cosy comfort zone of half-hour situation comedy, plus were rather political.' Ronnie requested changes, by which time Chapman was holidaying in Majorca and McKenna enjoying sunny Malta. McKenna recalls, 'We were asked to come back and rewrite the scripts or Ronnie would do something of his own, so Graham sent a telegram to Jimmy Gilbert, who'd contacted us, saying, "Let Ronnie do it on his own, and good luck with the bum-and-tit jokes."' Bernard admits, however, that he can understand why Ronnie wasn't happy with their offerings. 'It needed very tight writing and was far too loose. But there's nothing you can do if your co-writer isn't prepared to knuckle down.'

The BBC compiled an Audience Research Report and noted a mixed reception to the screening on 14 January, some finding the script well-written and its humour original, while a significant number of people thought it inane and a waste of the artists' talent. Many of the critics weren't convinced, either, one so disappointed that she remarked that the show had struggled even to last the half-hour, so there was no chance the idea could be sustained throughout an entire series.

An idea which did carry an entire series was *His Lordship Entertains*, which aired during the early summer. Returning to his trusty old Rustless character, Ronnie wrote the seven-part series, his first sitcom, under a pseudonym – this time Jonathan Cobbald rather than Gerald Wiley – and spotlighted Lord Rustless turning his country mansion Chrome Hall into a hotel. Ronnie explained at the time, 'Lord Rustless is a character I first played under various names in rep years ago. He is the sort of man who watches the world go by, unaffected and uninvolved. His age and position allow him to be outrageous and he is.'[5]

Assigned to the series as producer-director was Harold Snoad, who found working with Ronnie 'a wonderful experience and one I'll never forget'. Certainly, he won't forget their first meeting to discuss the series. Ronnie was recovering from the throat operation which had forced him to leave the theatre show *Good Time Johnny*. 'I went to see him at his house in Pinner for a general discussion about the scripts, but he was unable to speak. I remember sitting at his dining-room table together with him writing answers down and passing them to me. In spite of this, he was in a great mood and we had lots of laughs. Making the series went very smoothly and Ronnie and I got on well. A couple of years passed – because he was busy on other things – before it was decided that we should make a second series. Unfortunately, this never came about because we discovered that John Cleese had written a script with Connie Booth, about a hotel called *Fawlty Towers*. Ronnie decided it wasn't a good idea to have two series about running a hotel.'

It wasn't the last time Harold worked with Ronnie. As well as being at the helm for the one-off *Idle at Work* episode, he directed three instalments in the *Seven of One* series, a comedy vehicle for Ronnie transmitted in 1973. Among the pilots, *Another Fine Mess* saw Ronnie's character (Harry) and his friend (Sydney), played by Roy Castle, entering a talent contest at their local pub as Laurel and Hardy. Although the premise didn't lend itself to more than one script, director Harold Snoad had fun making it. Location shooting took place near Snoad's home, so his house was used as unit base. 'I can still see Ronnie and Roy going up and down our lawn practising their walk, both enjoying being in character. Ronnie suggested they walked down the road to see what the reaction would be from the neighbours. They did so, laughing away, and caused quite a stir.'

Another moment Harold will never forget involved a night shoot in Kilburn. 'A lady came up and complained that our lighting was keeping her young son awake. She wasn't very pleased because he was ill with a nasty cold. She returned to her house in a bit of a huff.' After establishing it would be fifteen minutes before the next scene was shot, Ronnie slipped away into the night. 'Later, when we'd finished filming, the mother came back and told me that Ronnie had called at their house, gone up to her son's bedroom and read a story to him. She said – quite rightly – what a lovely person he was and how thrilled her son had been.'

But *His Lordship Entertains*, in which Ronnie's friendship with David Jason blossomed, remains the happiest experience for Harold Snoad. The series, shown on BBC2, peaked – in terms of viewing figures – at 3.6 million, with Ronnie paid £2,300 per episode. Audience Research Reports completed during the run identified that many viewers thought there had been some weaker scripts, with the overall response to the first episode only lukewarm. But by the time the seventh episode was screened on 17 July, most were thoroughly enjoying the series.

Critics weren't quite so kind, sadly. Halfway through the run, the *Daily Mail's* Peter Black echoed the tongue-in-cheek comments in Graham Chapman's telegram from Majorca, regarding Ronnie's liking for the bum-and-tit jokes. He wrote, 'This week's script had Lord Rustless captivated by the admittedly large and handsome breasts of the supposed French film star, Fifi. There is no time in the past 2,000 years when jokes about an old man chasing a young girl would not have found a large and braying audience, but this script showed how the inspiration has reached the bottom. There wasn't a joke that couldn't have come from the crudest provincial pantomime.'[6] The *Sunday Telegraph's* Philip Purser, meanwhile, regarded it as 'desperately silly'[7].

In the meantime, preparations were under way to find a long-lasting comedy vehicle for Ronnie. Part of the BBC contract which secured the services of the Ronnies stated that a solo comedy series would be devised, and Jimmy Gilbert was tasked with creating them – not an easy task, as he explains. 'Comedy is the most difficult thing to write, and to be successful must have the same qualities as decent drama: tight structure, real characters and good dialogue – with the additional problem: it has to be funny. Viewers will be uncritical of a play on television if it has got a good story and the acting is OK, but everyone is a critic of comedy. If it doesn't make you laugh, it's rotten. That is why the casualty rate amongst new comedies is so high.

'Ronnie C. was happy to develop a series he'd already done at LWT, until we found something completely new, so I concentrated on finding a new comedy for Barker. Usually, under these circumstances, I'd commission a script from a writer that we both liked, and if the writer got it right, commission another, to make sure the idea had "legs". But Ronnie had such a talent for playing different characters we decided to go for broke and make seven pilots from the best writers I could find, and put them all out under the title *Seven of One.*'

The series of stand-alone programmes gave Ronnie the perfect platform to indulge in his fascination with characterisation. He told me, 'I designed the characters to be as different as possible, so I drew these blank heads and then wrote the names of the characters. Next, I thought things like, "Well, he can't have a moustache, because he's got one," etc. I've done this since rep, trying not to produce the same look twice. But, of course, you can't do it after 200 plays!'

Jimmy Gilbert hoped that one episode would spin off into a series, but three emerged, as he explains. '*My Old Man* by Gerald Frow wasn't chosen by us, but went to Yorkshire Television where Clive Dunn played Ronnie's part. But *Open All Hours* by Roy Clarke and *Prisoner and Escort* by Dick Clement and Ian La Frenais, which later became *Porridge* and won two BAFTAs, were made by the BBC.'

The last programme shown in the *Seven of One* series – *I'll Fly You For A Quid*, also written by Clement and La Frenais – was the episode Ronnie liked most and wanted to turn into a series, but Jimmy Gilbert wasn't convinced. 'I felt it was like a perfect short story: brilliant, but had nowhere to go and would have to be artificially reopened.'

The then head of comedy Duncan Wood invited Barker and Gilbert to lunch at the Gun Room in Shepherd's Bush to finalise which episode would be picked up for a series. They chewed over the merits of each, until two were left in the frame: *Prisoner and Escort* – in which Ronnie played Fletcher – and *I'll Fly You For A Quid*, about a Welsh gambling family who'll gamble on anything, including how long the church sermon would be. 'By coffee time, we'd agreed to go with *Prisoner and Escort*, if the writers were keen to give it a go,' says Jimmy. Although they harboured concerns, once these were resolved, Clement and La Frenais were willing to proceed.

A positive atmosphere emanated from the *Seven of One* series and, although Ronnie wasn't any less exacting, the production was free of any ripples of unease or annoyance among members of the crew. Make-up designer Penny Delamer found Ronnie 'totally professional' and 'loved' working with him. 'He was an artist as well,' she says, referring to his seven character sketches detailing how he saw each of the central characters. 'He was very specific. It was unusual for an artist to have such views; he was always very collaborative, never dictatorial,' says Penny, who remembers Ronnie as liking a good chat. 'I found I couldn't run around to check everything was going smoothly, so eventually told Jean Steward, who was assisting me, to look after him. It was a big mistake, because then she sat in the car chatting and I was running around doing everything.'

Jean recalls Ronnie's little drawings. 'They were so detailed. For Fletcher, he wanted his hair slicked back and sprayed red. We couldn't use dye, because when we went filming, we intended filming for each episode. So we had to use spray, which never works particularly well, because you worry about it raining; fortunately, it didn't for those scenes.' Jean also remembers having to pencil in eyebrows so they met in the middle. 'Ronnie had a theory that all criminals' eyebrows met in the middle!'

Ronnie was also particular when it came to moustaches: take the brand-new one he wore for Arkwright. Jean was shocked when Ronnie asked her to give the £45 artificial moustache some rough treatment. 'They're very delicate and should be treated with respect. When I opened my box and got it out, Ronnie said, "Now, put it on the floor and tread on it lightly, like you're stubbing out a cigarette." He hated moustaches that were too well-dressed, because he thought they looked artificial. His theory was that real moustaches looked lived in. Thereafter, if ever he had sideboards or anything, you had to tussle them around a bit.'

Jean was aware she was working with an actor who knew the business inside-out. 'You couldn't pull the wool over his eyes, he was very clever.' Despite his temperate demeanour, Jean says she could tell if he was angry, because 'his mouth would set, but he was always controlled. I never heard him shout or disrespect anyone; the worse he would do is look grumpy and walk away.'

Transmitted second in the *Seven of One* series was *Prisoner and Escort*. Life in prison was a theme largely untested in the genre of situation comedy, and some people doubted it had the staying power required for a long-running show. These thoughts weren't shared by Ronnie, who had always wanted to develop a prison-based show. 'While preparing *Six Dates With Barker* I wrote down various ideas. One of these jottings simply said, "prison". I always wanted to make a prison series and couldn't believe it when Dick and Ian came up with a similar idea. They were thinking, initially, about an open prison, but I didn't think that had enough threat to it, whereas my idea was much more frivolous than *Porridge*, like *Bilko* in prison, smuggling women in – that sort of thing.'

After deliberating, a closed prison was agreed upon, with the writers exploiting the daily dilemmas facing inmates. Ronnie was happy with Clement and La Frenais' desire to write with a degree of reality. 'It was definitely the best way to go, because my idea would have been geared much more towards laughs, whereas theirs possessed more bite.' It was a judicious move, affording the writers the freedom to probe not only moments of grim reality at Slade Prison, but compensatory elements, too, such as the emergence of Fletcher as a father figure for young Godber.

As soon as Sydney Lotterby, who directed *Prisoner and Escort*, saw the pilot script, he knew they were on to a winner. 'It was wonderful and just pleading to be done – it was so clever.' Everyone hoped it was an augery.

Casting for each pilot was Jimmy Gilbert's responsibility. In addition to Fletcher, the two main characters in the script were Mr Mackay and Mr Barrowclough. 'It was Ronnie's idea to recruit Brian Wilde as Barrowclough,' explains Jimmy. 'He'd worked with him before, I believe, but I'd also known Brian from my RADA days. Ronnie thought he'd be marvellous in it, and, of course, was absolutely right.' Fulton Mackay was known to Jimmy Gilbert and became his first choice. Richard Beckinsale, meanwhile, was chosen by Syd Lotterby when a series had been commissioned, although Ronnie had suggested Paul Henry, who made his name playing Benny in *Crossroads*. The casting for *Prisoner and Escort* was spot-on. 'The three of them [Ronnie Barker, Fulton Mackay and Brian Wilde] worked well together, and they had great respect for each other,' says Jimmy.

As the pilot script centred on the transfer of the recalcitrant prisoner to the remote Cumberland prison, location shooting had to be organised. Gilbert had already travelled to Wales to record *I'll Fly You For A Quid* and knew immediately the location was ideal for *Prisoner and Escort*, despite the script being set in Cumberland.

Ronnie remembers the inclement weather endured whilst filming. 'It was terribly cold, which wasn't ideal, because I did lots of running across the moors.' Overall, though, he was pleased with how the pilot panned out. 'The filming was successful. It was well shot and the reaction from the audience when we recorded the studio scenes was excellent.'

The first of three series of *Porridge* began on Thursday, 5 September 1974, and it was soon apparent that this was more than a sitcom. It was comedy drama of the highest order, played out in a claustrophobic environment exuding a degree of tension the sitcom's writers Dick Clement and Ian La Frenais could exploit. Inmates, locked away with their freedom held in the hands of others and forced to bide their time with all sorts of unsavoury individuals, were rich veins of conflict just waiting to be tapped, as Messrs Clement and La Frenais discovered. Underpinned by many facets – including subtlety, delicacy and truth – the series was the perfect package and boasted consistently high performances from Ronnie throughout. Appearing in the prison-based programme saw him, arguably, reach the zenith of his career – this was Ronnie at his finest and this is why *Porridge* is regarded by many as Britain's best sitcom.

Even by his own high standards, Barker excelled playing Fletcher, partly because he based some of the character's traits on himself. 'There was a lot of me in there, not that I broke into post offices,' Ronnie told me. 'There was plenty of my father in Fletch, too. Although the character was a cockney and I was born in Oxford, he was working class and I could relate to him. He was easy to play and I didn't have to think much about it, unlike Arkwright in *Open All Hours*, where I had to consider a different background entirely.' Despite being a recidivist, Fletcher was a likeable chap. Ronnie agreed. 'You must always have charm in a character. Even if you're playing an old tramp you need a bit of charm.'

Everyone involved in *Porridge* worked well together, breezing through rehearsals. 'We'd often start at ten and finish by one, because we all knew what we were doing,' says Ronnie, who knew he carried a lot of responsibility on his shoulders, but also received total support from those around him. 'You knew no one was going to let you down, ruin a gag or bit of timing.'

The actors who played other inmates speak highly of Ronnie, pinpointing his generosity as a key attribute. Christopher Biggins, alias Lukewarm, remembers, 'Ronnie was enchanting and incredibly generous. If during rehearsals he felt one of his lines was better off said by another actor, he'd give it over with no complaints. It was so good to work with a star who considered the whole product.'

Echoing Biggins, Patricia Brake, who played Fletcher's tart-with-a-heart daughter Ingrid, says, 'Ronnie was a delight to work with and I learnt a great deal from him. Often, he made sure that the camera was on me for a particular moment during a scene together, very unusual in this business, and the way he could develop and add to an already funny script was pure genius.' Patricia teamed up with Ronnie in the sequel, *Going Straight*, and several episodes of *The Two Ronnies*, and he always made her feel welcome, before ribbing her about why she was given the job. 'Ronnie said it was simply because my surname began with a B, and when he'd been through *Spotlight*, the actors' directory, several times and got fed up, he returned to the front and said, "She'll do."'

Ronnie was brilliant at gauging the atmosphere on set at any given time, dreaming up ideas to relieve tension and aid fellow performers, says Philip Jackson, who played Dylan, a hippie prisoner, in the episode 'A Day Out'. 'If an actor had a good line that didn't get a laugh, he was always able to do something funny and make it look as if it wasn't you who'd messed up. This was a total comedic instinct on display and I learned a great deal from watching him.'

Ronnie has been the recipient of many awards in recognition of his services to the industry, but none is more memorable than that collected at a Water Rats' Annual Dinner. 'It was an award for *Porridge*, so I thought it would be fun if I went in my uniform handcuffed to Fulton. A limo was sent for us and just as we got to the venue we decided to put the handcuffs on, but locked ourselves around a strap inside the car and couldn't get out. Eventually the chauffeur sorted it. So in we went and as we marched into the room there were great cheers and rounds of applause. Then we faced our second problem: although Fulton had the key, he couldn't open the cuffs. One of the people attending the dinner said, "Don't worry,

I'm a member of the Magic Circle, I can get you out." He spent twenty minutes trying, but couldn't. We started to panic a bit, but thankfully someone eventually prised us out of them.'

Dick Clement enjoyed working with Ronnie, and if events had panned out differently, their relationship would have started earlier. 'When I directed my first movie, *Otley*, I tried to cast Ronnie as a professional assassin – the part eventually played by Leonard Rossiter. I was looking for a superb comic actor, my theory being that if you can play comedy you can play anything. I still believe that. I wish we'd seen Ronnie extend himself more as an actor, because I never saw limits to his talent. He brought with him a rare intelligence: first, the script, where his quick mind offered up new or improved jokes, always with great respect. "Is that all right?" he'd ask and as a rule, once we'd stopped laughing, we'd nod OK. When blocking a scene he was ahead of me as a director, usually sensing where the camera had to be for the master shot.'

His precision extended to the props he would be expected to use. Susan Belbin, who went on to produce and direct, among others, *One Foot in the Grave*, worked as an assistant floor manager on *Porridge* and remembers passing Ronnie a letter. In the episode, Fletcher reads a letter received by the illiterate Bunny Warren, and Belbin prepared the missive. 'It was on two sheets of paper and I ended up writing it up nine times! I didn't mind, but eventually I asked him if it was my handwriting. He said it wasn't, it's what the last line on the page says before he turned it over. I said, "OK," thinking, "Well, why the hell can't you turn it over and carry on?"' It then dawned on Susan that it was to do with timing and comedy effect. 'He wanted to reach the bottom of the page on a certain line, when there would be laughter and a pause as he turned it over. He decided what the line had to be and apologised when he asked me to write it out again. I said, "Please don't apologise. I'll write this out a hundred times for you. You're the one up there reading it out."'

Although at times it seemed as if Ronnie Barker was a self-assured, highly confident individual, Dick Clement was aware that on the day of recording, he wasn't dissimilar to any other actor – he, too, was nervous. 'Many actors are thrown off-balance by the audience.

They rehearse all week without them and then their response on the day of the taping throws their timing completely. It's a strange, hybrid medium – an awkward cross between theatre and film. But I can think of nobody who worked a studio audience better than Ronnie.' He refers to a scene within the pilot to illustrate. 'Fletcher, having been on the moors all night, discovers at dawn he's back in the same place he started. We artfully concealed this fact from the studio audience and it got a huge laugh. But watch the tape and see what wonders Ronnie did with the moment. Other actors would have got two laughs out of it – he got three. And without mugging or going out of character.'

Porridge, as Dick explains, was the perfect marriage of an actor to a part, even though he realises it wasn't the series Ronnie had envisaged. 'Once we'd gone round Wandsworth, Brixton and the Scrubs we knew we couldn't write the kind of *Bilko* scenario; in fact, for a while we didn't know how to write anything. Perhaps what kept us going was the thought that at a certain point Ronnie Barker was going to appear and the audience – at home as well as in the studio – would relax, knowing they were in safe hands – the hands of a comic genius.' Ronnie was aware of his talents but, according to Clement, he didn't have a 'monster ego'. He says, 'He knew he was good and what his strengths were. He didn't impose himself: he had strong views, but didn't ram them down anyone's throat.'

Ronnie became a 'warm and generous friend' of Clement and La Frenais. 'In those days, Ronnie usually had at least three years work planned in advance. He'd struggled in the early years and seemed to fear unemployment.' He feared typecasting, too. But unlike some actors who become typecast after appearing in a successful sitcom, Ronnie moved between roles with ease; yet he was always worried about outstaying his welcome, hence his decision to give up prison life. 'I think Dick and Ian would have happily continued with *Porridge*, but I didn't want to. I worried constantly about getting stuck with a character. I didn't want that. Although I went on to film the sequel – *Going Straight* – I told Bill Cotton, then Head of Comedy, that I wanted to move on and do *Open All Hours*. He tried persuading me to stick with *Porridge*, but it was no use.'

Ronnie feels he owes much to *Porridge*. 'It was probably the best and most important show I did, but *Open All Hours* topped it as far as fun was concerned. I loved doing both, but because of David Jason in *Open All Hours* it was slightly better, because of the laughs we had.'

The series about Arkwright, the miserly northern shopkeeper, was written by Roy Clarke, whose wife used to run a little shop in the South Yorkshire market town of Thorne. 'I knew the corner-shop set-up and when I met Ronnie for lunch to discuss ideas for the *Seven of One* series, he told me he'd always wanted to play a grocer. From that meeting, the idea emerged.'

When developing the main characters, Roy liked the idea of a dreamy adolescent chained to 'this monster'. But he was aware the lead character had to be likeable. 'In cold print, Arkwright probably was a monster, but when you get someone who's good, like Ronnie, the character can be as rough and as tough as you like, but you get away with it, because the quality of humour comes through. You put the wrong actor in saying those same lines and they'd be insulting and awful, but when you've got someone like Ronnie you're given plenty of freedom.' Looking back on the show's success, Roy feels the sitcom worked because it resembled 'a little theatre'. He explains, 'You had the two regulars – Ronnie and David – and all these others coming in to the shop for a short time; it was almost like variety.' The first series was transmitted in 1976 on BBC2, but it was five years before another season appeared. In an interview, Ronnie told me, 'The first series only attracted about two and a half million viewers, which it would on BBC2. I complained it was on the wrong channel and when we finally made the second series it was put on BBC1. It went on to become a massive hit.'

As well as the parsimonious Arkwright and the put-upon Granville, the other main character in *Open All Hours* was Nurse Gladys Emmanuel, the buxom nurse over whom the cantankerous shopkeeper drooled. In the pilot episode it was actress Sheila Brennan who donned the cap and apron. When it came to making the first series, three years later, the role of Nurse Gladys was recast, with actor Dennis Ramsden recommending someone with whom he'd toured – Lynda Baron. 'I was playing a rather pompous hotel manager in a sketch about inventors in *The Two Ronnies*. During a tea break, Ronnie said, "I'm doing a series and need a girl who's got to be good at comedy and have big tits." I replied, "Lynda Baron!" I'd just toured with her in *A Bed Full of Foreigners*. She was wonderful in comedy and had the required-sized boobs for Ronnie to do his double takes.'

The trouble was, Lynda was slim, while the character was described as having a bottom like the 'fenders of a Morris Minor'. That matter was resolved with plenty of padding. 'I had a whole body down to my knees made: it was like a big swimsuit with lots of Velcro,' chuckles Lynda. 'But I had this skinny neck and skinny legs coming out the top and bottom and it made me laugh. I used to wonder how she walked around. It was also alarming when I needed to go to the ladies, because I had to ask for assistance!'

While the *Open All Hours* pilot was shot in Ealing, the team headed north to Doncaster for the series, with a hairdresser's being turned into Arkwright's corner shop. At the time, Lynda was still appearing in *A Bed Full of Foreigners* at the Duke of York's Theatre in St Martin's Lane, which meant a busy schedule. After catching the late train from London on Saturday evening, she'd film on Sunday and Monday, before catching the train back in time for the evening performance. Ronnie always made Lynda feel welcome. 'Clever people are usually easy to get on with. He had no worries about his own ego or his position in the world – well, certainly no discernible worries. I don't mean he was entirely confident because nobody is, but he was confident enough in his abilities and choices to allow other people to breathe, be happy and as funny as they could be.'

Again, Ronnie found himself surrounded by a cast and crew in whom he had total confidence, allowing him to relax somewhat, as noted by Lynda. 'He expected 100 per cent from everyone, but didn't tell you every Monday morning. He wasn't a hard taskmaster, in my view, because he had a way of making everyone work that much harder without ever asking you to do so. He helped by letting you think that he thought you were marvellous.'

Lynda remembers occasions when laughter filled the air at

rehearsals and, also, during breakfast. 'We used to exasperate poor Sydney Lotterby, because we'd all talk at once at breakfast. In the end, he decided to eat at the other side of the room. Ronnie would say, "We won't talk at once, we'll press an imaginary buzzer when it's our turn." What happened was that we still all talked at once, but were also pressing imaginary buzzers simultaneously. Then there was the time that Ronnie and I couldn't stop laughing, so had to pack up early for the day. It was a wonderful series to work on.'

Producer-director Sydney Lotterby enjoyed it immensely, too, recalling times when Ronnie and David Jason would arrive on set. 'When they came to rehearsal, the set was nearly always finished. Being a cornershop there was always ham or bacon on the set. Ronnie wasn't really allowed bacon, because he put fat on very quickly, but both he and David would slice some off and get the prop boys to cook it for them. They'd be standing there stuffing themselves before we rehearsed.'

Lynda Baron has nothing but respect for Ronnie and remembers an occasion when she began probing him about his many attri-butes. 'I once said, "You can't be good at everything, there must be something wrong with you. You love your family, have a very happy family life, you've got enough money to live on and you're talented – there must be something wrong with you?" And he replied, "I'm overweight and these are not my own teeth." And that was it.'

The character of Arkwright possessed a sporadic stutter and was adored by the huge audiences for whom it became essential viewing; fortunately, only a couple of letters of complaint trickled in complaining about Barker adopting a speech impediment. Another was complimentary. 'It came from a family of five stutterers who'd watched *Open All Hours* and fallen off the sofa watching it; they spent the next two days sending each other up,'[8] recalled Ronnie.

Porridge and *Open All Hours* occupied much of Ronnie's diary over the coming years, the former running between 1974 and 1977, the latter between 1976 and 1985. On *Porridge* a party was normally organised to celebrate the end of a season. On one such occasion, Susan Belbin remembers the time the crew presented him with a table, which had been gathering dust in the BBC prop room. 'In the rehearsal room you have all this tatty furniture to represent what will be used in the recording. We had this small pub-style table covered in Formica. While waiting for the next scene, Ronnie began picking at a corner and noticed that underneath was copper – he was impressed with it. We forgot all about it and finished the series. Then, he invited us to his home at Pinner for a do. Everyone agreed we should get him something, but didn't know what, so I said, "It's a wacky idea, but he loved that table." Everyone thought it was horrible, but I told them it was copper underneath. With the BBC's blessing, we took it to a chum for restoration. It turned out to be a magnificent beaten copper-topped table.' Ronnie was so touched when it was presented to him; the fact people had taken the trouble to think of him – and it was a much better present than the ubiquitous bunch of flowers or bottle. 'If tears weren't actually in his eyes, they weren't far away,' recalls Belbin.

In March 1977 we waved goodbye to Norman Stanley Fletcher in the final episode of *Porridge*. But this wasn't the last we saw of the old rascal. BBC executives invited Dick Clement and Ian La Frenais to lunch at Television Centre and discussions veered towards the future. Clement and La Frenais were interested in seeing what happened when Fletcher was released. The idea was favourably received and by February 1978 Barker was back on our screens in the first of six episodes, titled *Going Straight*, joined, again, by Richard Beckinsale and Patricia Brake, while there was an early screen outing for Nicholas Lyndhurst, as Fletcher's dense-looking son Raymond.

Considering the screening of *Going Straight*, some quarters felt strongly that any sequel would never recapture the magic and richness of its prison-based predecessor. Even though there was a logical progression, removing the jailbird from familiar surroundings into a new environment was no easy feat.

It was clear that Clement and La Frenais' new sitcom would be hard-pushed to ascend to the heights of its predecessor. Inside prison Fletcher was a winner, whereas outside he wrestled with the harsh realities of a life he was unaccustomed to. Opinions varied regarding the programme's success. Sydney Lotterby, who produced both sitcoms, views it as a mere shadow of *Porridge*. 'It lacked the flavour of the original series.' Although Ronnie Barker agreed the sequel didn't work as well, he enjoyed the experience nonetheless. 'It wasn't as good, but there were some great people working on it, and we had excellent stories, too.'

Inevitably, some viewers weren't convinced. When the BBC compiled an Audience Research Report after the screening of the opening story, 'Going Home', a small minority echoed the views of other critics, claiming they 'found it harder to adjust to Fletcher's new situation, feeling that the prison setting was ideal and that *Porridge* had a special quality of its own, which, they feared, would now be lost.'

Although no episode attracted the ratings of the most popular episode of *Porridge* – 'Desperate Hours' was watched by 20.8 million – *Going Straight* never dropped below 12 million during its six-episode run. It is an underestimated sitcom with plenty of inherent qualities, from the calibre of acting to the sleekness of the scripts. Despite being overshadowed by its big brother, it is a meritorious example of the sitcom genre and in 1978 picked up a BAFTA as 'Best Sitcom'.

Chapter 15

During the 1970s and 1980s it seemed as if anything Ronnie touched turned to gold. He was certainly hot property and able to command power and respect not only within the television industry but the entertainment world as a whole; his experience in the business had given him a cachet among his peers. He was seemingly never off the box, what with *The Two Ronnies*, *Open All Hours* and *Porridge* in full flow. But still he managed to squeeze additional projects in to an already chock-a-block timetable – as well as find time to dip into his enormous collection of Victoriana and postcards to publish a handful of books, including *Ronnie Barker's Book of Bathing Beauties* (1974), *Ronnie Barker's Book of Boudoir Beauties* (1975) and *Sauce* (1978).

Ronnie revisited the *Comedy Playhouse* format in 1974 when, on 23 April, he played Johnnie Wetherby in the Richard Waring scripted *Franklyn and Johnnie*, depicting two rivals who have the chance to reconcile lifelong grievances while attending the funeral of their only mutual friend. At loggerheads for four decades, their friend bequeaths his estate to the pair, leaving them to contemplate patching up their differences. The programme disappointed critics and viewers. The BBC's Audience Research Department's report revealed their respondees viewed the programme as ponderous, silly and disappointing, even with Ronnie Barker's presence.

The following year, Ronnie was back in a BBC *Play of the Month*, this time as Henry Ormonroyd, a photographer, in a version of J. B. Priestley's 1938 play *When We Are Married*, which he'd first performed at the start of his repertory days at the County Theatre, Aylesbury, twenty-seven years previously. The play, shown during the Christmas holidays, centres on triple silver wedding anniversaries where doubt is cast over the marriages' validity.

By the time the television play was screened, Ronnie had completed his penultimate film, *Robin and Marian*. Revisiting the

Robin Hood legend, twenty years on, the eponymous hero, played by Sean Connery, is returning to England after fighting for King Richard and soon reigniting his passion for Maid Marian (played by Audrey Hepburn). Produced by Columbia Pictures and Rastar Productions, the film meant that Ronnie spent the summer of 1975 in the intense heat of a northern plateau in Spain. Donning his habit, he played Friar Tuck, joining a star-studded line-up which included Richard Harris, Robert Shaw and Denholm Elliott.

Making the film, which took Ronnie away from his wife and children for ten weeks, wasn't the happiest experience for him. But being nearly 800 miles away from those he loved wasn't the only reason for his unhappiness: his general feelings about the picture contributed, too. Ronnie dedicated an entire chapter to the film in his autobiography, recalling disagreements among the cast, culminating in him becoming a sounding board for other artists who, at times, confided in him and sought his advice.

Producer Denis O'Dell says Ronnie was ideal to have around the set. 'He was a quiet man, in some ways. Usually, after shooting, all the actors went to the bar for a drink – never Ronnie, he'd go to his room. But he was a good influence with the actors on a day-to-day basis, because there was a lot of sitting around, not doing a lot. He was a great morale-booster.'

Denis cast Ronnie as Friar Tuck and has no regrets about his decision. He saw the role as needing a trace of humour, something Ronnie was more than qualified to deliver. 'It worked well. Ronnie was very good in it – an incredible talent. He didn't overplay the part or play it for comedy, simply with some humour; after all, we didn't want a stand-up comedian playing it.'

From reading Ronnie's account of the film, it's clear that his biggest bugbear stemmed from his dislike of horses. He was frightened of the animals and, on first seeing the script, back in London, had noticed that, understandably, his character was expected to ride a horse. According to Ronnie, he stressed that he wouldn't even be able to sit on a horse, let alone ride one. This was understood by the producer, but to protect himself Ronnie requested it be written in the contract. Today, thirty-five years later, producer Denis O'Dell recalls the conversation in which Barker stressed his congenital dislike, although he can't remember details of his contract. He says, 'Ronnie said to me, "The only thing is, can you keep me off a horse?" I said, "Yes, yes, I'll do that." I don't think we ever put him on a horse.'

When I mentioned to O'Dell, who wasn't on set every hour of the day, the first chapter of Ronnie's autobiography in which he writes that, reluctantly, he agreed eventually to sit on a horse, O'Dell was extremely surprised. He says, 'If I'd known, I would have backed Ronnie on it, naturally, because I'd given him my word.' In the film there is only one shot of Ronnie on a horse, prior to the battle in the closing scenes. It's noticeable that the horse's head is being held firmly by one of Robin's men. It's a fleeting shot and next time Ronnie is on camera he's standing alongside his steed.

Ronnie's fear of all things equine hadn't just surfaced: on another occasion, it arose while filming a scene for *The Two Ronnies*. Derek Ware, who ran his own team of stunt performers, worked as Ronnie's stunt and acting double for around fifteen years, having first met him in 1965 on rehearsals for *Come Spy with Me*, an ill-fated musical comedy which folded before it was performed, only to be successfully revived a few years later, starring Danny La Rue. Derek recalls the sequence in *The Two Ronnies*. 'He didn't like horses at all. We were doing a fox-hunt scene, where he and Ronnie C. had to sing a parody of traditional hunting songs, and he wouldn't get astride the quietest mount the local hunt had to offer. They tried filming him sitting on a five-bar gate, but the director complained he looked too static. So I suggested he threw his legs over my shoulders and I would make movements appropriate to a thoroughbred hunter anxious to join in the hunt. Ronnie agreed and we made for a very convincing pair. As I recall, I even threw in a whinny or two.'

Unfortunately, *Robin and Marian* director Richard Lester – who had worked with the Goons on radio, Spike Milligan and Peter Sellers on television and The Beatles in the cinema – didn't want to be interviewed for this book, but he has fond memories of working with Ronnie. And despite any annoyances and worries Ronnie experienced, it was clear fun was had by the team. Executive producer Richard Shepherd, along with Tony Reading (Assistant Art Director), Roy Charman (Sound Recordist) and Ronnie compiled a humorous document to help everyone remember the weeks spent in Spain. A collection of potted profiles make up part of the document, with Ronnie's including the line that his ambition was 'To form a National Naked Ladies' Choir, touring the country with it, bringing music to millions and enjoyment to the deaf'. He also recorded an audio tape for many of the team members, containing a droll poem about the making of the film.

Production manager Barrie Melrose, who explains that the Spanish plateau, with its oak forests, was chosen to replicate Nottingham because of its wonderful weather, thinks Ronnie found the film strenuous. 'But whenever he came down for dinner, he'd always have a few jokes. He was a polite, charming man.'

Reviewing films is, of course, subjective, but watching *Robin and Marian* today, while everyone's yeoman efforts are admirable, it's evident that the film was never going to become a blockbuster or big money-spinner at the cinemas. Geoff Brown, reviewing it for *Monthly Film Bulletin*, wrote that acting 'can only partially redeem the weaknesses of a script burdened with sagging dramatic tension and fuzzy characterisations – especially as the director himself provides insufficient support'[1].

One of the worst aspects of film-making for artists is the hanging around, idling away time until their next scene is shot. Boredom can set in and tempers fray during these long interludes. One good thing to come out of Ronnie's Spanish adventure is that he flew home with a manuscript in his suitcase, one which would come within a whisker of claiming the Golden Rose Trophy at the Montreux Television Festival.

No sooner had he touched down on home soil than the wheels were put in motion to make *The Picnic*, a wonderful little film which, in true Barker style, is dialogue free, save the usual grunts and groans. Terry Hughes, the inaugural director of *The Two Ronnies*, directed the thirty-minute picture, the idea for which had come when Bill Cotton visited a *Two Ronnies* rehearsal at Acton. 'In those days, Montreux was a big deal. The BBC had won it with, among others, *The Frost Report* and *The Two Ronnies* and Bill wanted to win again,' explains Hughes. 'He thought that the Ronnies, along with Morecambe and Wise, were the premier comedy acts on British television at the time and that they should

RICHARD WEBBER

try something. We all sat in the rehearsal room and Bill, looking at Ronnie B., said he'd like us to come up with something. Ronnie B. had played the squire-of-the-manor-type characters and we'd made silent films on the *Ronnies*, so it wasn't a big stretch for Barker to go away and create *The Picnic*.'

This time, it wasn't the Gerald Wiley or Jonathan Cobbald pen names Ronnie used: he opted for Dave Huggett and Larry Keith. One constant, though, was Ronnie's character: the General was a Lord Rustless-cum-General Futtock character in an amusing story in which he heads into the countryside for a picnic with friends and staff (played by, among others, Barbara New, Madge Hindle, Patricia Brake, Dennis Ramsden and Julie Crosthwaite) but, as expected, it's not long before chaos ensues. It was typical Barker humour, with myriad naughty postcard scenarios and plenty of short skirts and busty girls on show.

Filming took place near Dartington Hall in Devon, but atrocious weather caused a scheduling nightmare, as Terry Hughes recalls. 'It was terrible. We only had a short space of time to film, because of the cast's availability and we were rained out wherever we went. We were fighting the weather all the time. It wasn't fun because we never knew if we'd get it completed.' An already tight shooting schedule being affected by inclement climate meant filming *The Picnic* wasn't a ball. 'You're under such constraints because of the time schedules that you don't necessarily enjoy it when you're doing it; that comes after, when the pressure is off.'

Making the film was a serious business. There wasn't much room for laughter, production designer David Myerscough-Jones informed me. He recalled the time he was ticked off by Ronnie B. 'It was during a breakfast scene, with the swinging chandelier of the brooch in the yolk of an egg. That was repeated several times to get it right and was hysterical. I was killing myself with laughter and had to lie on the floor, because I couldn't control myself. Ronnie turned to me and said, sharply, "Stop laughing!"'

It was clear that this was, again, Ronnie's baby: he'd written the script and, therefore, had a clear idea in his mind of how the picture should look. As a result, Ronnie was frequently seen taking the lead in steering the project forward. 'He was very much in charge. He seemed to take over, but then that was his nature. Although it was very, very serious business, he was still funny at times and was an agreeable man,' stated Myerscough-Jones, who recalled one of his biggest challenges involving a bull, which was seen chasing a girl in the film. 'It didn't have any horns, so Bill Bonner, the prop man, and myself had two fake horns made, which we tried desperately to stick on it. That was a difficult job – and they kept falling off, so weren't ideal.'

Journalist Alexander Frater spent a day on set in deepest Devon, soaking up the atmosphere, and dodging the showers playing havoc with the schedules. He reported that when the sun peeped through the leaden clouds after lunch, Ronnie quickly donned his director's hat. 'Barker was very much in charge . . . and told Hughes they ought to be getting down to the river to start the actual picnic sequences.'[2]

Ronnie viewed the script as an extension of his *Futtocks End* format, a snapshot of a moment in time when families packed up proper picnic baskets and ventured into the country to sit on blankets and stuff themselves silly. He remarked that various themes had been considered, such as Christmas at Futtocks End and a day at the seaside, but were discarded – interestingly, though, the latter idea was revisited. 'We wanted something very English, you see, and thought then about a garden fete, but that would have meant hiring 200 extras. Then we decided on a picnic because a picnic is a nostalgic, pre-war, golden sort of occasion.'[3]

But it wasn't all work and no play; some of the cast were able to snatch a moment to pick mushrooms. Picnic scenes were shot in a field alongside the River Dart and each morning a fresh batch of mushrooms had popped up. Ronnie would harvest them, returning to the hotel with bags full for the kitchen staff to cook. Patricia Brake took some home for her family. 'Ronnie B. seemed to know all about mushrooms. He said they were completely safe and I trusted him. Once, I returned home on the train with a bag and made soup for my family. I could have killed them if Ronnie had been wrong.' But she placed her trust in Ronnie.

The Picnic was transmitted on New Year's Day 1976 and was well received. The blend of sight gags and comedic moments wrapped in a nostalgic celebration of saucy, McGill-style humour worked well. But when asked to rate *The Picnic*, director Terry Hughes says it was 'pretty successful, but not the best thing we did. It did well in terms of ratings, but creatively was OK.'

This entertaining silent-film approach was adopted by the Ronnies seven years later when they returned to an earlier rejected idea and spent a weekend at the seaside. The same characters were revived, although a couple of new faces joined the cast: but it was the same routines, although this time it was real seaside-postcard territory for Ronnie to exploit to the full.

Executive producer on the film was the experienced Michael Hurll, who recalls Ronnie suggesting ideas throughout the shooting schedule. 'You had to say "yes". It would be a silly director who said "no", because we'd reshoot a particular scene his way and it would be perfect. People didn't always work on my basis, which was: he knows all about comedy and what you did was what Ronnie B. wanted. You just agreed and he was always right.'

The scenes were shot around the Studland area of Dorset and, again, the team weren't blessed with reliable weather. Michael remembers the eagerness of Ronnie to get the job done, something he can appreciate. 'We were staying at this big hotel and I'm somebody who wakes up early and wants to get moving – just like Ronnie. I'd wake up and go for a walk and, sometimes, Ronnie would join me.' One morning under clear blue skies, Ronnie turned to Michael and asked why they weren't starting. 'He was keen to get going, but it was only 7 a.m. and the crew weren't arriving until 9 a.m. He said, "By 9 o'clock it will be raining." And it was. We'd have breakfast and down would come the rain. He looked at me and said, "You see. If we'd started at seven we would have had two hours in the can before the rain came."' Eager to keep the camera rolling, Ronnie even suggested shifting locations in order to chase the sun. Occasionally, he'd look across Poole Harbour and see Bournemouth basking in sunshine and suggest driving there to complete the beach scenes. 'Trouble was, we'd arrive just as the rain started and look back towards Studland, where the sun had come out – that happened a few times,' recalls Hurll.

Although many scenes were very derivative, almost carbon copies from the likes of *The Two Ronnies*, *The Picnic* et al., it was a humorous piece of television – or would be, once it was cut down to size. Too much material was gathered, resulting in a film excessively over length. Prudent editing was urgently required, something which irked Ronnie. But an hour and forty minutes – the duration after Ronnie and editor Ray Millichope had worked on it – was too much. When Jimmy Gilbert told Ronnie he wanted to cut it to fifty minutes, Ronnie was 'horrified'[4], says Ronnie Corbett, who agrees the cuts were necessary, but points out the importance of the project to his partner. 'It was the seaside postcard brought to life, his tribute to the world of McGill . . . it was probably, therefore, his most personal work of all, and I think for this reason he had probably been a bit self-indulgent.'[5]

Editor Ray Millichope remembers the special interest Ronnie took in editing the film at Millichope's editing suite in Bourchier Street in London's Soho. He was aware that Ronnie was desperate to retain as much material as possible. 'He knew it was over length and didn't want to lose anything, so wanted to make it into two episodes of forty-five minutes. I told him it would never work, because there wouldn't be enough.' Despite being aware that it was running too long and cuts would eventually be required, it didn't stop Ray enjoying his time working with Ronnie on the production. 'He wanted to know more about how editing worked and would turn up at 9.30 every morning – he was never late.' Such was his keenness, he'd often stop at the laboratory en route to pick up the rushes. 'He'd arrive and rush up the stairs, puffing and blowing, then spend all day with me. He'd even answer the phone, just like an assistant.' For further exemplification of this remark, Ray refers as well to the occasions they would go to a dubbing session at Television Centre. 'I'd walk in empty-handed, while Ronnie would stagger in carrying all these cans of film, putting on a bit of a show.'

Ray and Ronnie worked hard on the film, holing themselves up inside the editing suite for hours. They even sent out for food rather than taking breaks. 'Ronnie was supposed to be on a very strict diet, but I remember one day he wanted a battered sausage and chips. I thought that Mrs Barker wouldn't be at all impressed with this, but he had it, saying things like, "Do you know what wine goes with a battered sausage?" But, overall, he kept to his strict diet – I even remember him going on a fruit diet for a week.'

Ronnie was very partial to a fry-up. Ronnie C. says, 'A very nice chap who worked for me, Ron Waverley, would sometimes drive Ron home from the Palladium. He would often have a double portion of chips in the back of the car with all the windows open so that Joy wouldn't be able to tell he'd had them.'

When I discussed *By the Sea* with Jimmy Gilbert, he admitted it was the nearest he came to falling out with Ronnie. 'I'd always been against the idea that just because a show is funny at thirty minutes, it will be twice as funny if it lasts an hour; often it works the other way around. The first cut was over an hour and a half – at that length it would have been a total disaster.' Jimmy had a plan to save the film and turned to Alan J. W. Bell, who is best known for producing and directing *Last of the Summer Wine*. His idea was efficacious. 'Alan is very good and was the first person I thought of, because he's also an excellent film editor. Ronnie knew of him and when I said I was asking Alan to do a cut, he accepted it, although I'm not sure he realised it was going to be so radically cut.'

Soon, Bell was heading to Jimmy Gilbert's office. Settling down in a chair, Alan listened as Jimmy asked him for a favour. Holding a VHS tape, he wanted Alan to look at the film. Alan recalls, 'Jimmy said, "It's *By the Sea* with Ronnie Barker and it's a disaster!"' Alan asked what was wrong and Jimmy confirmed it was too long and unfunny. 'He asked me to watch it and salvage it,' says Alan, who was allocated a £10,000 budget for reshooting scenes with Ronnie, if necessary.

After watching the video at home, Alan agreed with Jimmy Gilbert that, as it stood, it wouldn't have viewers going into raptures. 'It was very bitty and didn't have any heart. As a viewer, you didn't get inside it. I knew I could reshoot, but was also aware that there was enough material to make a shorter episode.' Alan went back to Jimmy and told him he'd take it on, but instead of spending the ten grand on reshooting, he'd ask Ronnie Hazlehurst to write a music track. 'Music is a wonderful weld. If you put music to something it keeps it all together. But £10,000 only bought us thirty minutes of music. I re-cut it entirely,' explains Alan, who accepted the project with one proviso. 'I said to Jimmy, "The only stipulation I'll make is that Ronnie Barker doesn't come near and I don't have anything to do with him whatsoever, not because I don't like him, but if he's going to interfere we'd be back to where we started." This was agreed and I then went to Hong Kong for a week, where I got a call saying, "Ronnie is delighted you're going to do it, but would I mind using the film editor that he used, because he knows where all the bits of film are and where they came from?" I agreed.'

The job took around two months and was very taxing. 'I'd go home with terrible headaches after thinking so much about how to use the shots in a slightly different order or perhaps to extend them. In the end, it looked very good and Ronnie Hazlehurst wrote music for half of it. So I took the music, got it copied six times and went to a cutting room – there was no point in getting someone else to do it – and broke the music into sections. I relayed the music in a different order for the second half and made it fit.'

Jimmy Gilbert thinks Bell did a 'marvellous job'. He says, 'My heart sank when I saw the long version, because it cost a lot of money and I didn't think it was going to do anyone any good. Ronnie resisted the changes, and although there wasn't any heated exchange between us, there was a coolness, because I'm sure he thought the whole process had been too drastic.'

By the Sea was finally transmitted on Easter Monday 1982 and scored a huge hit in terms of ratings. Viewers quizzed for the BBC's Viewing Panel Report regarded it as ideal bank-holiday viewing and the report's author stressed the exceptionally positive response from virtually all respondees. Jimmy Gilbert, however, rates *Futtocks End* and *The Picnic* better than *By the Sea*. 'I guess this is partly because we'd gone through this lengthy process; plus there wasn't a central core. It was just a series of comic incidents, like an album of picture postcards. There wasn't anything holding it together until Alan imposed a musical score, which gave it continuity.'

Despite some venerable jokes and situations running through this enjoyable romp, W. Stephen Gilbert, writing in *Broadcast*, remarked, 'If any of the silent clowns had produced a feature as thin and uninventive as this, they wouldn't have lasted five minutes in Hollywood.'[6] James Murray in the *Daily Express*, meanwhile, thought that even fifty minutes was too long to sustain the viewers' interest, but acknowledged Barker's use of a plethora of seaside-postcard jokes, referring to Barker's collection in the process, summarising, 'I think he used them all in this one, with often hilarious results.'[7] But other critics were disappointed, flagging the unfunniness of the film. Ray Connolly in the *Evening Standard* thought that 'someone seemed to have forgotten to add the ingredient of humour . . . the jokes were extremely thin.'[8] And the *Sunday Telegraph*'s Philip Purser stated that 'most of the jokes were so heavily semaphored in advance that you could have nipped out to put the kettle on and still got back for the pay-off'[9].

It's fair to say many people, if pushed to make a decision, would opt for *The Picnic* as their preferred choice of these two amusing films. After *The Picnic*'s screening on 1 January 1976, Ronnie appeared in three more seasons of *The Two Ronnies* and a series of *Open All Hours* before the 1970s were out. He also said his farewells to Norman Stanley Fletcher, appearing in the third and final series of *Porridge*, before nursing him back into civvy street upon release from Slade Prison for the six-part sequel *Going Straight*. But that wasn't all: Ronnie also made a big-screen version of *Porridge*; he was on stage at the Palladium in the first of two stage versions of *The Two Ronnies*; spent a year Down Under; and he collected a well-deserved OBE from the Queen at Buckingham Palace – hardly a chance to draw breath.

It was February 1978 when the Ronnies were rewarded for their hard work and impeccable service in the entertainment arena and awarded OBEs by the Queen. Sydney Lotterby remembers the moment Ronnie B. announced over dinner that he was being presented with the medal. 'Ronnie took a few of us, including Richard Beckinsale and his wife, myself, my assistant and, of course, Joy to a meal. We were eating away at this restaurant in Kew, when Ronnie looked at his watch and said, "Ah, it will have been announced now, I can tell you all. Raise your glasses, because I've actually just got my OBE." Joy, who was sitting next to him, said, "What? You never told me!" He replied, "No, I thought I should keep it a secret." It was marvellous for him, so well deserved.'

At the ceremony, when the Queen asked the Ronnies what they were working on, they informed her that they were preparing to appear at the Palladium. It was the first of *The Two Ronnies* stage shows, which previewed at the Bristol Hippodrome in May 1978 before opening at the London Palladium in August and, at Christmas, being turned into a festive show at the Gaumont (now Mayflower Theatre) in Southampton.

The stage show was born when Harold Fielding approached the BBC about transferring *The Two Ronnies* to the stage. Terry Hughes was installed as director and recalls discussing the idea with the Ronnies. 'Harold thought the show would be very successful, so in one of our many meetings in my office at the BBC we discussed it and decided what material we'd do. Ronnie wrote a couple of special musical numbers, like the French cabaret routine, and we put it all together like a TV show. We enjoyed it enormously. In hindsight, I think it could have been better; perhaps it was a bit too glitzy, but it was the Palladium and the venue probably demanded that. We all enjoyed it enormously.'

The show, which included a *Porridge* sketch, was tested out at the Bristol Hippodrome before arriving in London. A member of the cast was Nelson E. Ward, who appeared in several sketches with the Rons. He'll never forget performing the *Porridge* sketch with Ronnie B. on the opening night. 'A section of the blackout canvas, which was stretched across the dome roof, came detached and fluttered down on to the third row of the stalls. The audience evacuated their seats and the theatre staff removed the canvas. All this happened during the *Porridge* sketch, which was stopped in its tracks. When the house lights finally went off again, Ronnie redoubled the laughter by turning to me – as the nearest "prisoner" in his cell – and saying, completely in his character of Fletcher, "Do you know, me old mate, they're even parachuting out of here now." This brilliant piece of ad-libbing showed just what a genius the man really was,' says Nelson.

His ability to think on his feet and ad-lib was something Roy Hudd noticed when working with Ronnie on radio. 'He was one of the great ad-libbers of all time, because he used to ad-lib in the character he was playing. Most of us, if we were going to ad-lib at all, would have to drop the particular character we were playing to concentrate on the ad-lib. But Ronnie could ad-lib in Irish, Scottish, whatever, and you couldn't see a join. He was brilliant at it.'

Nelson E. Ward remembers a piece of advice Ronnie proffered. 'He told me to never turn down a job. He said, "You'll learn more from performing in a room above a pub than holding a spear at the National. I've absorbed so much from all the work that I've done in those early days – that's why I look like a sponge now," he said jokingly, pointing to his stomach.'

The notices upon opening at the Palladium carried a similar thread, inasmuch as most critics saw the show as an enlarged version of a *Ronnies* television episode, purely for addicts of the duo. But then, as Milton Shulman stated in the *Evening Standard*, 'Fortunately for the Palladium, there are lots of them.'[10] Chris Dunkley, writing in the *Financial Times*, agreed that in truth it was a glorified and extended television episode: he noted that it was the familiarity which proved to be popular with the audience, who were enjoying the two-and-a-half-hour show. The *Daily Telegraph*'s John Barber, however, was very impressed, commenting that the show bore signs that it had actually been 'thought about'[11]. Despite what the reviewers said, the members of the public who packed the Palladium during its run loved it, regardless of whether or not they had seen the material before. Such was its popularity, the initial seven-week run was extended to three months, and within months would be staged on the other side of the world.

Beginning in May 1979 a fourteen-week run was planned in Australia. In fact, the Ronnies were heading Down Under for tax reasons, after it became apparent that it made sense for them to spend time out of the country. So it was decided to take the stage show to Australia, where they enjoyed a huge fan base. Both the Corbett and Barker families uprooted for the twelve-month period, and it was during this time that Charlotte Barker took her first steps towards following her father into the profession when she enrolled at a drama school.

Before travelling to Australia, Ronnie offered his house and car to Sydney Lotterby and Dick Clement/Ian La Frenais respectively. 'He asked me to look after his property,' says Sydney. 'I was thinking about selling my flat and he suggested I put it on the market and live in his place for the year, rent free. I declined, partly because if anything had happened it would have been my fault.'

Dick and Ian, however, didn't miss the opportunity of borrowing his treasured Jaguar. 'He gave it to me and Ian for the twelve months,' says Dick, smiling. 'I think I drove it on odd days and Ian on even ones.'

En route to Australia, the Ronnies stopped off at Los Angeles to appear in the American variety-based television programme *The Big Show*. Eventually, the Barkers arrived in Sydney, settling in to their house overlooking the city's Harbour Bridge. The self-enforced exile from Blighty wasn't just a success professionally: the Ronnies and their respective wives helped develop their friendships during this period; despite working together for over a decade, the Ronnies rarely socialised together, partly because of different interests, and also because they lived in different parts of the capital. Now, though, in unfamiliar territory, they had plenty of opportunity to spend time together.

The Ronnies made a further visit to Australia in 1986, to make the second of their one-hour television shows on Kerry Packer's Channel 9, reliving many of the sketches performed back home, which hadn't been seen in Australia. (Barker and Corbett had asked the BBC not to sell their shows to the Australian market for a year in order to ensure the material they used on Channel 9 was fresh.) This time, Ronnie travelled without Joy and the children, who planned to visit during the summer holidays, so he spent time on his own. Michael Hurll, executive producer and producer on the latter series of *The Two Ronnies*, travelled Down Under as well, and spent much time with Ronnie B. 'I'd go home with him after rehearsals and pop round in the evening. We'd sit and talk about comedy and he explained to me how a joke has rhythm to it – he taught me so much about comedy.' There was also another reason Ronnie enjoyed Michael visiting the house in Rose Bay, which had been provided by Kerry Packer – to move his car for him. 'He had a big car – a Mercedes, I think – but the trouble was his house was on a hill. He hated doing a hill start and then turning the car around on the hill to drive back to rehearsals, so at the end of the day he'd say, "Michael, can you come back to the house, because I'd like to discuss something about tomorrow." So I'd follow him and he'd park his car up the hill and we'd have a chat. But he'd always say, "Just one thing, Michael, could you turn my car around so it's facing down the hill?"'

While Ronnie B. was in Australia in the late 1970s on his first visit – leaving behind economic and political turmoil during the infamous Winter of Discontent, which, ultimately, saw the fall of James Callaghan's Labour government – the big-screen version of *Porridge* arrived on the cinema circuit.

During the Seventies there was a vogue for making movies out of successful television sitcoms. From *On the Buses* and *Bless This House* to *Are You Being Served?* and *Man About the House,* hardly a show was spared. Sadly, most offerings were flimsy versions of the small-screen originals, lacking the pace and intensity which originally made the show a success. Most of the film plots left a lot to be desired, resembling over-stretched episodes, agonisingly spread over ninety minutes. But there were exceptions and, although many of the reviewers in the British press didn't agree, *Porridge* stood out from the crowd.

Released in 1979, it received its first television outing on BBC1 on Friday, 31 December 1982. Initially, Clement, La Frenais and producer Allan McKeown had discussed the film project with Columbia, but when a deal couldn't be struck, McKeown met executives at ITC, most notably Lew Grade. The British film company snapped up the chance to transfer Clement and La Frenais' runaway success to the big screen, and assigned the project to its low-cost production wing, Black Lion Films.

Dick Clement, meanwhile, relished the chance of directing the picture. 'Everyone we spoke to, including Ronnie, was interested, so we sat down here in California and wrote a script very quickly, then cut it down to size.'

Just like its small-screen forerunner, locations would play a vital part, and Allan McKeown couldn't believe his luck when a friend happened to mention that Chelmsford Prison was temporarily empty. Other than the occasional scene – such as the escape sequence shot in Buckinghamshire, and a glimpse of prison gates at Maidstone – the entire film was set in prison, so the chance of filming in a *real* jail was too good to ignore. McKeown sought permission. 'There had been a fire inside one of the wings, so all the prisoners were moved out whilst the prison was refurbished. Fortunately, parts remained intact and didn't need decorating; it was these areas I wanted to borrow.'

A meeting was convened with a Home Office official, and proceedings couldn't have started better when Allan discovered the head of the Prison Service was an ardent fan of the sitcom. 'The great thing about *Porridge* was that everywhere you went people had such incredibly strong feelings for the series and the characters. Luckily, we were granted permission.'

The movie's release received plenty of attention from the British media, but in line with most examples within this genre, the conversion from small to big screen didn't impress the majority of critics. And although he was pleased with the result, Ronnie admitted to me that the cinema wasn't his favourite medium. 'With films there's lots of stopping and starting, which makes it disjointed: one minute you're working on an early scene, then you jump to another at the end of the film; it wasn't as enjoyable as the situation comedy. It suited a half-hour slot better.'

A new decade was approaching and yet more success for Ronnie, but there were some surprises and important announcements, too.

Chapter 16

Failure wasn't a word you would associate with Ronnie Barker. After plying his trade in repertory theatre, he progressed to the West End and steadily forged a solid, successful career. The 1970s and 1980s marked the acme of his acting life, with a relentless stream of hit shows, most notably *The Two Ronnies*, *Porridge* and *Open All Hours*, meaning Ronnie was rarely off the screen. But no one's career runs entirely smoothly, especially one which has already spanned more than three decades; it was, therefore, almost inevitable that Ronnie would experience a flop at some point.

That blot on an otherwise exemplary professional life came a year and a half after the Ronnies had returned to the Palladium for yet another successful, money-spinning theatre show. It arrived in the shape of Plantagenet Evans, an outspoken, hectoring Welsh photographer in Roy Clarke's sitcom *The Magnificent Evans*. One six-part series ran during the autumn of 1984 and, unfortunately, was largely panned by the critics.

Even the beautiful Welsh countryside couldn't save the sitcom. 'It was filmed in a lovely part of the country – Powys,' says Welsh-born actress Sharon Morgan, who played Rachel, Evans' assistant and long-time fiancée, a woman desperate to hear the chime of wedding bells. While the exterior of the photographer's shop was shot in Llanwrtyd Wells, filming frequently took place in the surrounding countryside. At the end of each day's filming, the cast returned to the Metropole Hotel at Llandrindod Wells. Sadly, though, the filming created such a stir in the region that Ronnie was forced to switch to the Lake Hotel in nearby Llangammarch Wells. Sharon explains, 'We'd be sitting outside and people would be driving past, taking photographs of him. Once, we visited the Albert Hall in the town to see Hinge & Bracket and ended up having to huddle around Ronnie; not that he minded, it just meant he found it difficult doing anything.'

Sharon Morgan was already in London – attending a wig fitting for a S4C drama documentary – when she auditioned at BBC Television Centre for the role of Rachel. She found the atmosphere 'relaxed', with Ronnie putting her at ease immediately. 'I was wearing a big, woolly lilac polo neck with lilac corduroy plus fours and red ankle boots. Ronnie remarked, "You do a lot of leg work, do you?" He was as charming at the audition as he was making the programme.' But when offered the job, Sharon had to think twice before accepting. 'I'm a feminist, nationalist and socialist and thought the part was sexist. I have two children, but don't believe in the marriage institution. Rachel was just a sex object.' But despite being an avowed feminist, she decided to accept the part. 'I, perhaps, made her softer or more fluffy, identifying this innocence in her and the fact she was madly in love with this guy.'

Once she had accepted the role, Sharon decided not to mention her politics to Ronnie. But as it transpired, they shared many robust discussions on the subject. 'We'd spend lots of time in between filming and during the evening talking politics and arguing about feminism. He was wonderful, though, and professionally I learnt so much from him, because he knew why something would get a laugh and how you could do it slightly different to get an even better reaction.'

Ronnie, again, was involved in the construction of the television show. When it came to shooting a particular scene, producer-director Sydney Lotterby – who had already worked with Barker on *Porridge* and *Open All Hours* – had formulated a system which seemed to work, as he explains. 'When filming a scene, he'd say, "How are you going to shoot this?" I'd tell him and he'd respond, "Don't you think you ought to shoot it this way?" So I'd always reply, "Tell you what, why don't we shoot it two ways and then in editing I'll have a look and see which works best." Sometimes it was his, sometimes mine,' says Sydney, whose only falling out with Ronnie occurred on this programme. 'The script required a black pig, but I couldn't find one. Eventually, a farmer said I should dye one. I didn't realise you could do that, but he assured me it was possible and agreed to do it. When the pig turned up, it had been sweating and much of the black dye had come off or started running.

It looked very silly, so, in the end, we had to use a black spotted pig. Ronnie and I fell out over it. He stated, "The script says a black pig, so it should have been a black pig." I told him I couldn't get one – thankfully, it was only a five-minute falling out.'

Sydney Lotterby admits there were problems with *The Magnificent Evans*. 'Ronnie got hold of the character and wanted to do it in a particular way, and it's very difficult fighting somebody of his stature. Eventually, it's the same old thing: if he thinks he can do something better his way, you might as well let him try. The sad thing is that it was too exaggerated, while the stories were all on the same premise – they never had any breadth.'

Ronnie explained that although he realised the sitcom had its faults – such as an ambling pace and too much concentration on the countryside, slowing the pace even further – he did, nonetheless, enjoy playing the flamboyant snapper. Of course, no one knows for sure if a sense of impending disappointment in terms of the programme filtered through to those working on it, including Ronnie. This is a question posed by cameraman Rex Maidment. 'Ronnie was a talented man, there's no doubt about that, but he wasn't someone I warmed to or found the easiest to work with. But perhaps he realised the show wasn't as good as he thought it would be and was, therefore, not the happiest of men. I remember we were filming in a graveyard and the recordist, while tracking through, hit one of the headstones with a boom. Ronnie had a moan about the incompetency and it wasn't necessary,' says Rex, who also recalls the time he turned up at the wrap party dressed as a gangster. 'It was a costume affair, so I went along as a gangster and one of the make-up ladies as my moll. Wardrobe provided me with a blazer and I got a toy machine gun and we strolled in. Ronnie happened to be there wearing a similar blazer and it didn't go down too well – perhaps because it was his own blazer!'

Although there was an odd voice or two in the wilderness, most of the Press reaction was scathing as the first few episodes – which attracted, on average, seven million viewers – were transmitted from 13 September. Patrick Stoddart in *Broadcast* classed it 'boring'[1], while a reviewer in the *News of the World* rated the show as the 'biggest disappointment of the week'[2]. He added, 'How can Ronnie

. . . inflict this tedious torture on us?'[3] Margaret Forwood in the *Sunday People* said it took until the end of the series to summon the courage to admit the show 'simply didn't make me laugh'[4].

The eccentric photographer was rude – not what had come to be expected from a Barker character, and it didn't endear him to viewers. Evans was different from anything Ronnie had played on screen before – the character simply didn't click, as the BBC discovered when an Audience Reaction Report was conducted. The majority of viewers were disappointed and thought Ronnie had been grossly miscast, some commenting that he didn't make a particularly effective Welshman, either. The show's writer is frank about his creation. 'Ronnie played this small-town photographer, but it didn't work. I think we got too extravagant with him: if we'd played him looking seedy like Piggy Malone in *The Two Ronnies* it might have worked, but he was too extravagantly dressed and had this little Louis Napoléon beard – it all became too fanciful for people.'

The sitcom may have been a comedic damp squib, but it wasn't going to dent Ronnie's hard-earned reputation, especially as more instalments of *The Two Ronnies* and the final series of *Open All Hours*, screened during the autumn of 1985, had audiences guffawing once again.

Sadly, it wasn't just Ronnie's penultimate sitcom which failed to deliver: his final sitcom left many fans and critics disappointed. *Clarence* was a one-off series shown between 4 January and 8 February 1988. It was meant to be Ronnie's swansong, but the farewell sitcom didn't live up to expectations. Coming at the end of his career – or so everyone thought – the central premise was one he promised himself he'd revisit some time. The seriously myopic removals man had previously appeared with his pebble-thick glasses in a Hugh Leonard-written episode of *Six Dates With Barker*. 'I always thought it would make a good series, so we bought the first episode and I rewrote it, so it would flow into the rest of the series I wrote,' said Barker. 'I enjoyed making *Clarence*, partly because it was filmed around Oxfordshire. The cottage featured in the series was built specially. It was beautiful and several people wanted to buy it.'

Working on *Clarence* was a 'gift for a designer', says John Bristow, who recalls many local residents stopping to ask about the cottage. It was built a few miles from Ronnie's home, which by then was a secluded, Grade 2-listed watermill near Chipping Norton, set in acres of Oxfordshire countryside. 'Some said they'd been driving up and down the road for thirty years and couldn't decide whether it was new or not. We built it in an area which had been a stone quarry, on a bend in the road, and it sat very nicely within the landscape.' It was meant to be made from corrugated iron, although John and his team used largely corrugated PVC on a scaffolding frame. 'I put some real corrugated iron into the structure, so that Ronnie could get the noise when he tapped on the side of the house.'

John liked the fact Ronnie knew exactly what he wanted in terms of design, as well as being very precise. 'We dressed the cottage and tried hard to preserve the nettles and wild plants around it, because it was supposed to have been empty for six months or so. Then the film crew came along and squashed everything flat, which was a shame, so I dropped some flowers in amongst the remaining weeds to resemble an overgrown garden. Ronnie asked, "What kind of flowers are these?" I replied, "They're yellow flowers, Ronnie." He said, "We need to be a bit more precise than that." I'd also put an artificial wisteria around the door and he thought there was too much blossom, because they only bloom on trimmed wood or new growth, so we had to adjust things.'

As on other shows, Ronnie had created, written and was starring in the programme, so retained a clear vision of how everything should look and pan out. 'He was charm itself, but steely underneath. He was sure of what he wanted and determined to have it,' states John, who wasn't entirely happy with how the interior scenes in the studio worked out. 'It had been a fairly long shoot and the turnaround in the studio was quite quick. We'd all worked hard on it, but then Ronnie came and changed things around a bit, which I didn't find easy. But there was no way the producer-director was going to back me against him. To be honest, it wasn't any great shakes. I'd dressed the interiors by following the scripts, but Ronnie thought I'd got the balance wrong between dressing the cottage and the little one-room flat his character lived in.'

The sitcom's director was Mike Stephens, who'd already directed, among others, *Dear Ladies*. He acknowledges the assiduous research and effort which went in to making the setting as accurate as possible. 'John [Bristow] and I did lots of recces to find the right site. There were lots of rape fields in the area, which wasn't period, while if you wanted cows around you couldn't have Friesians, because there weren't many in the country then. We tried to be as accurate as possible to give it the right flavour, treating it like a drama series.'

One thing the director liked about Ronnie was that he displayed magnanimity when he realised he had been hasty or wrong, such as the time Mike and his team spent two hours dressing a Cheltenham square with Coronation bunting and erecting railings at the side of the road through which Stephens planned to shoot; the director thought it would provide some depth to the opening sequence. Ronnie, however, didn't agree and went off to have his breakfast. Before long, Mike received a call: Ronnie wanted to see him. 'He was sitting in his caravan eating breakfast. He asked if I'd had anything and when I said I wasn't going to bother, he told me to get a roll and a coffee and join him. He said, "I'm really sorry. You're absolutely right. I've just been thinking about that shot and it's a brilliant idea."'

Stephens was a relatively new producer to London, having moved from BBC Manchester, but he was fully prepared for working with Ronnie, aware that he was a stickler for detail – in fact, he'd already been warned by the man himself. 'Ronnie said to me, "You'll find me very, very picky on things, but that's why I've lasted so long. I just want to get things right. I'm not being awkward and will always give you good reason if I want to do or change something." He just knew the business back-to-front. I'd worked on a few comedies before that, but he was light years ahead of me.'

Over the years, many people were content to let Ronnie take charge. But he was happy to listen and consider accommodating other people's ideas and views, like the occasion when the director noticed the lights were reflecting off Clarence's glasses. 'They were specially made. In theory, they were back-to-front glasses. They should have had flat fronts and round backs, so they were convex facing the eye. When I noticed the lights reflecting off them, we swapped them around; the only problem was that Ronnie couldn't see a damned thing – he really had to feel his way around the place.'

Averaging 8.5 million viewers for each of the six episodes transmitted in early 1988, *Clarence* hardly set the televisual world on fire. It may have been a little too twee, but the series did possess a cosiness and was warmly amusing and nostalgic, each instalment brimming with a genuine 1930s feel, thanks to meticulous research and attention to detail by all concerned, not just Ronnie. One problem with the series, though, was that once it was established it didn't have anywhere to go. It was stuck in its own little bubble and lacked a plot weaving through the episodes. The premise was better suited to a three-part mini-series or extended film like *The Picnic*; running over three hours' worth of episodes stretched the joke of the visually impaired clot too thinly and, at times, the programme became repetitive – after all, how many times can you laugh at Clarence bumping into tables or using salt in his tea instead of sugar? And the setting, although beautifully rural, constricted the comedic opportunities: an urban location for Clarence Sales' property would have opened up many more possibilities for amusing situations, such as having to negotiate traffic and busy pavements.

The Press picked up on this from the beginning. The *Daily Mirror*'s critic wrote, 'What a clot Ronnie Barker was to think *Clarence* . . . was more than a comic motion for a *Two Ronnies'* sketch. I can't see many people sticking with it.'[5] The reviewer in the *Financial Times* concurred with the tabloid scribe, writing, '*Clarence* needs to improve enormously if Ronnie Barker is to make anything of it.'[6] And while acknowledging he chuckled throughout the second episode of the series, the *Daily Express'* Ian Christie was worried about remaining episodes sustaining the humour on 'the basis of just two themes – Clarence's short-sightedness and his desire to get Jane into bed'[7].

When the series was at the planning stage, Sydney Lotterby was asked to direct it, but declined the offer. 'I didn't like the idea,' he admits, frankly. 'I didn't think it was that good and couldn't see it going anywhere. I was proved right. When you've made programmes like *Porridge*, *Open All Hours* and *Yes, Prime Minister* you get some idea of what is good. Then, if an idea comes along which you don't think is to that standard, it's difficult to accept it. I couldn't believe in the idea.'

Editor Chris Wadsworth was surprised he didn't have Ronnie Barker sitting alongside him in the editing suite, bearing in mind his interest in the job. 'I thought that strange considering he wrote it; nor was an edit ever rejected because it wasn't what Ronnie or the director wanted.' His absence was all the more noticeable when Chris considers his experiences working on other programmes. 'I can remember times when, for example, it seemed slightly odd to have a close-up at a particular point. I'd comment and the director, on whatever show it was, would say, "Oh no, Ronnie would like that covered at that point." There were also instances when I'd offer alternatives and be told, "Oh, we'd better keep that because Ronnie really liked it." But I can understand that: after all, people were tuning in to see Ronnie, rather than a programme edited by Chris Wadsworth or directed by Syd Lotterby. Ronnie's comedy track record was one of the best we've had in the last century and you had to respect what he thought and how he was going to play it. Any director worth his salt would respect Ronnie's experience and talent.'

Working alongside Ronnie again was his good friend Josephine Tewson, who played Jane Travers in the original episode, *1937: The Removals Person.* She knew Ronnie was keen to revisit the characters they had played in 1971, and remembers the morning phone call at her home, just off London's Oxford Street, informing her that he was turning it into a series. 'He said he'd written it with me in mind and asked if I'd be available in three months' time. I was thrilled to bits and said I'd make myself available.' Then Ronnie dropped a bombshell. 'He said, "By the way, when I've done that series I'm going to pack up and retire."' Josephine was still reeling from the shock when she responded. 'I said, "What do you mean, retire? You can't." He said, "Yes, I've done everything I want to do. But don't tell anyone, it's a great secret. I've told the BBC and little Ron; and I'm telling you because I don't want you to get any ideas there's going to be a second series."'

Of course, Josephine respected Ronnie's decision not to mention his impending retirement, although she hoped someone would encourage him to rethink. 'People were saying we could do the series for ever. The war would come along and the characters could have evacuees – everyone was suggesting these wonderful plots.' She smiled wryly. 'But all the time I was thinking, I hope someone persuades him. But no, he couldn't be persuaded.'

Ronnie may not have been as active in the editing suite for this series but he was still offering guidance and making suggestions in other respects. Josephine recalls a particular scene in which he rendered some valuable advice. 'We'd rehearsed a couple of times and were going to do a take, when suddenly he said, "Can I say something to you? It's not up to performance pitch, the pitch you'll be with a live audience in the studio." He meant that the filming was at a lower temperature, which is fine if everything is going to be filmed, because every scene would match. But in a studio, where there's more adrenalin, everything is at a higher pitch. I hadn't thought about that before. It's a marvellous piece of advice and I've tried remembering it every time I'm filming – you've got to pretend there is an audience watching.'

Prior to the transmission of *Clarence*, just a select few knew that Ronnie was calling it a day, including Ronnie Corbett, who had been informed during the summer of 1986. While the two Ronnies were filming at Lulworth Cove in Dorset for a *Two Ronnies* episode, Ronnie B. confided in his long-time partner and friend. Ronnie Corbett recalls, 'We were having breakfast in the caravan and he said, "I'd better tell you that the year after next, it will be my last *Two Ronnies*. I can't remember what I said. Nothing very much, probably. I knew that a little vacuum would appear in my life, but then we'd probably wrung *The Two Ronnies* dry anyway. I knew Ronnie wasn't feeling well. He worried about his heart in Australia and had had a funny incident in the swimming pool, so perhaps he was concerned about it. I think he felt a little bit less than sound. I was grateful to him, though, for giving me a year and a half of warning.'

Ronnie had decided to retire in late 1985, soon after Sir Peter Hall had tried continually to persuade him to play Falstaff. Despite a concerted effort over several years, he never got his man, something which saddens Hall. 'He made me a promise that he'd one day play Falstaff. Alas, it's one of my great regrets that he never got there. He became too weak to take on something like that.' As for Ronnie retiring at the height of his career, while only in his late fifties, Sir Peter says, 'It was his career, his talent, his life. I think he would have become one of our greatest stage actors. I don't think we should criticise Ronnie, just be sad that the theatre didn't get more of him.'

Although work schedules may have played a part in preventing Ronnie from taking up Hall's offer, what led to him eventually declining the chance to play the role was the thought of travelling across London, battling against the traffic and the stress that comes with commuting. He didn't want the hassle of enduring that every day. Also, he knew that if he had begun taking such matters into consideration when he'd just been offered what many would regard as one of the best stage roles around, then it must be time to call it a day.

But several factors were behind Ronnie's decision to retire. He told me, 'I'd run out of ideas and, to be honest, I'd done everything I wanted to do. And, I'm sorry to say, the material coming through wasn't such good quality.' He'd also become unimpressed with the standard of programming. He said at the time, 'I find it difficult to laugh at shows nowadays. Some are too vulgar. Unnecessary language in scripts can turn people away and much of it isn't needed.

'I remember having a meal in the BBC canteen and sitting next to Rowan Atkinson when they were doing *Not the Nine O'Clock News*, and said, "I don't know why you guys feel the need to have a lot of the language you have in. I saw one of your shows the other night and if you gave me that script and let me cut four words out of it, you'd have three million more viewers." You don't need it.

'One of the problems is that everyone wants to write their own scripts now. The performers write and feel they have to resort to lines concerning bodily functions.' This was something Ronnie found both repugnant and unnecessary. 'Producers are trying desperately to appeal to younger viewers, but they're not watching television, they're out with their chums. Producers should concentrate on older viewers if they want to increase audience figures.'

After creating and writing so many sketches, jokes and even a complete series during his career, Ronnie's creative juices were starting to run dry. He once told a journalist that the ideas weren't arriving as fast as they had done when he began writing. Often the pain writers endure when trying to pen more sketches or scripts is underestimated. As Ronnie once explained, he didn't find the task easy at the best of times. 'If it went well I loved the result and was very satisfied . . . but the actual physical thing of getting it on the paper I used to find very painful and very tiring. I used to go in at nine o'clock into the room and there was the blank sheet of paper and a pen. I would try and come out at five o'clock with something performable, and mostly I did.'[8]

Once he had made up his mind and told Ronnie C. about his retirement plans, there were plenty of other people to be informed. On a sunny morning he arrived at BBC Television Centre and took the lift to the fourth floor. As well as informing Michael Grade and Gareth Gwenlan, Ronnie also sat in the office of Jim Moir, the then Head of Light Entertainment. 'I wondered why he wanted to see me and had a kind of foreboding that there was going to be sad news; but it was announced in a very straightforward, gentlemanly fashion,' says Moir. 'Courteously, he explained, although he didn't go into much detail. He said that he'd decided to smell the roses and that it had come to a natural finish. I think he'd been considering his overall financial position and knew that with the work he'd done, plus the likelihood of repeats, he'd be sound in that area.

'We shared a joke about our girths and he gave me a leaving present: one of his suits, it was green and presented in a plastic suit bag. Sadly, it was a tad small for me, so I was unable to use it. Subsequently, I made efforts to ask him to make the odd guest appearance on stuff we were doing. He wrote me a lovely note, saying, "Thank you very much for your very kind invitation, but I cannot attend due to a previous retirement."'

Regrettably, Moir knew there was nothing he could do to change Ronnie's mind. 'When a man of that stature and decisiveness says he's going to do it, you'd better understand that's what he's going to do. So with sadness I accepted the situation.' Moir wonders if Ronnie's heart had gone out of the business. 'Perhaps he'd heard enough applause. These are delicate things and affect the mechanism of creativity in a man's heart and mind. If you've lost the thirst for it, you'll want to stop.'

When his retirement was announced officially, there was press speculation that after the deaths of Tommy Cooper and Eric Morecambe, who had passed away in April and May 1984, respectively, Ronnie had been so shocked that he became concerned about his own health. Although he stated that their deaths – though deeply upsetting – were not a factor in his decision, it's clear his health concerned him. Producer Michael Hurll recalls making the twelfth and final series of *The Two Ronnies* in 1985, and how Ronnie's health was beginning to affect his performance. 'He couldn't rehearse for long in the studio, but he was a very proud man and would never show that to anyone else. He'd say to me, "Sorry, I can't do the filming. I can't do that." So we'd have to scrap a piece of filming and find something else, perhaps with Ronnie C. The last series was a struggle for him. He could still perform, but you knew he was ill.' Michael thinks his way of working was beginning to take its toll. 'He was involved in everything: how the set looked, the props, costumes, make-up, whatever. The only way he knew how to work was to make the decisions. It weighed heavy on him.'

For some time Ronnie denied his health was a contributing factor. Concerning claims that he quit *Open All Hours* due to health problems, he pointed out that, yes, he'd had a blood-pressure problem for some years, but that was controlled by drugs. His doctor had ordered him to lose weight but, again, what was unusual about that? His hard work and brilliant career had rewarded him handsomely and he could afford to retire and, to him, work wasn't the be-all and end-all.

The fact that *The Two Ronnies* had probably run its course made Ronnie confront the decision, too, and he knew he wanted to enjoy some years at his home in the Cotswolds, which he originally bought as a holiday home in 1981, with his wife and family around him; after all, he'd led an incredibly hectic professional life for over forty years, and so deserved to relax and unwind at the mill house with its tranquil garden, listening to the trickle of the streams winding their way along.

The final *Two Ronnies* was the Christmas Day show in 1987, an emotional time for the Rons, although the retirement news wasn't yet in the public domain. But even here, the man who had achieved so much and knew so many luminaries remained a very modest man at heart, someone who could still become starstruck himself. Take the moment Charlton Heston appeared in the studio to make a guest appearance on the Christmas show. Weeks earlier, cameraman Keith Burton had filmed the movie star at his Hollywood home for another project and had developed a good relationship. Keith remembers how nervous Ronnie was about meeting Heston. 'When he arrived, Charlton recognised me immediately. He came over, but I was slightly embarrassed because I had to introduce him to the director and Ronnie. I'll never forget, Ronnie said to me, "Would you mind asking Mr Heston if I can have a photograph with him?" I asked and Charlton – or Chuck as he wanted me to call him – didn't mind at all.'

Keith Burton recalls Ronnie showing generosity towards others working on the production. 'When we started filming, we were away on location and it's customary at lunchtime for the sparks, in particular, to go down the pub and have a drink. On the first day, we were shooting a gangster sequence and Ronnie gave me a £10 note. I asked him, jokingly, if he was betting on something, such as the shot not working, and he replied, "No, take the lads down the pub and buy them a drink on me." I thought it was a wonderful gesture.'

Keith enjoyed a smooth working relationship with Ronnie. 'To say he was a man who wouldn't suffer fools gladly is fair, but he was always open to new ideas, if he felt they were genuine and practical.'

On the final show, Ronnie Barker considered, momentarily, signing off not with the customary, 'And it's goodnight from him,' but with 'And it's goodbye from him.' He resisted the temptation, though. After the usual drinks in Gerald Wiley's dressing room, the Ronnies and their wives slipped out into the cold night air and, keeping up with tradition, enjoyed a meal at their usual Indian restaurant in Westbourne Grove. There had been no fanfare, no farewell drinks with the rest of the team.

Ronnie didn't formally announce his retirement plans to the world. He chose simply to leave a message on his answerphone, which used to tell callers they were through to Dean Miller Associates, a fictitious name which people thought belonged to his agent. On New Year's Eve, Ronnie altered the message to inform any callers that as of 1 January he had retired from professional and public life and wouldn't be accepting any further commitments. After thanking everyone he'd ever worked with, he closed with, 'So it's a big thank you from me and it's goodbye from him. Goodbye.'

Soon the news broke and the national newspapers were clamouring to be the first to tell the rest of the world. Ronnie's friends and contemporaries were just as shocked as the general public to hear the news. Barry Cryer says, 'We couldn't believe it, this man who loved his work. But he'd had the gypsy's warning: his doctor, apparently, asked, "Is your job worth killing yourself for?" Like Eric Morecambe, a direct parallel, he poured everything in to whatever he did. They both worried a lot and a lot of stress and energy went into his work.'

Ronnie Corbett once commented, 'People had been going younger than us – Eric Morecambe and Tommy Cooper – so if you're not feeling strong, not feeling vigorous, you don't kill yourself with work.'[9] Although Ronnie B. had for some while maintained that his decision to wave goodbye to the entertainment business had no connection whatsoever with his well-being, it wasn't strictly the case. He had a heart condition and needed to slow down and reduce the pressures he was under while working. His constant drive for perfection took its toll and he had to ease off. His condition was regularly monitored until, eventually, in June 1996, he underwent a heart bypass operation; while the fatality rate was 3 per cent, waiting another twelve months would see the rate rocket to 30 per cent – there was no time to waste.

The operation was a success and Ronnie made a steady recovery, only to be knocked back nine months later when he developed a pulmonary embolism, a blood clot, this time on the lungs. It could have been a fatal condition and such was the concern for his well-being, his family gathered around his bed, fearing the worst. Thankfully, Ronnie pulled through.

Ronnie knew exactly where he was going to spend his retirement: in his beloved home. From time to time he received requests from hopeful directors, offering opportunities to return, such as Sydney Lotterby being asked to phone him to see if he'd play a comedy role in a Shakespeare series the BBC were planning, which he declined politely.

Barry Cryer felt Ronnie coped with retirement surprisingly well. 'I thought he might get awful withdrawal symptoms, but he didn't. He adapted to it brilliantly. The solid family life was to do with that: he really had something to go home to. He wasn't a workaholic who went back to four walls and a room and thought, "Oh god, who shall I ring, where shall I go?"'

Ronnie's retirement was far from inactive. He spent some time writing. While his autobiography *It's Hello – from him!* was published around the time he retired, he wrote other books during his years of retirement, including another volume of memoirs in 1993, *Dancing in the Moonlight,* which concentrated on his early years on the stage.

Another major piece of writing he undertook during his 'retirement years' involved trying his hand at being a playwright. In 1998 he wrote a play, *Mum*, which was designed to showcase the talents of his actress daughter Charlotte – to give her career a boost. It was staged at the King's Head Theatre, Islington, for a month in the autumn of 1998. Charlotte played the lead, Alison, a desperate, lonely thirty-something cleaner with little in her life, who spends much of her time talking out loud, aiming her conversation towards the chair where her deceased mother used to sit. Virtually a monologue, it took Ronnie about two weeks to write the script, which is full of melancholy, earthiness and well-constructed dialogue. Unfortunately for both writer and performer, the critics weren't impressed; although Charlotte's performance was complimented by many, the general consensus was that the play lacked tension, ambled along and one critic even questioned the point of it. Sadly, it didn't provide the career boost the Barkers had wanted.

Locally, he made the occasional appearance, such as appearing at two performances of old-time music hall at The Theatre, Chipping Norton, to raise funds for repairs to the building. He did two turns, one performing a song he'd written, a parody of a comic song, *They Tell Me There's A Lot Of It About*, and an appearance as a Chelsea Pensioner. Later, he became patron of a new charity in Chipping Norton, the Lawrence Home Nursing Team, which provides nursing care at home for the terminally ill.

Various documentaries and entertainment shows, such as *The Two Ronnies Night*, popped up on our screens. He sat in the audience for *An Audience with Ronnie Corbett* and the BBC presented him with a Lifetime Achievement Award in 1996. But after deciding to quit, it must have come as something of a relief to slip away from the public gaze to live a life free of the stresses and strains associated with the world of television. He had never felt comfortable with the baggage which accompanies such a public persona, especially the loss of anonymity, but now he could relax and look back on a staggeringly successful career with pride. 'I've been so lucky. To get a job where the only thing you have to do in your career is make people laugh – it's the best job in the world.'[10] He had no regrets about calling it a day at fifty-eight. 'I've never regretted it. I did everything I wanted to do, I had no ambitions left.'[11]

So, Ronnie disappeared off the professional radar and dedicated some of his time to running an antiques shop he opened in the high street of the Oxfordshire town of Chipping Norton. He christened it The Emporium and treated it as an extension of his hobby of collecting antiques, memorabilia and Victoriana, a real passion of his, especially as his postcard collection extended to over 53,000 items.

Unfortunately, running the shop didn't always go smoothly for Ronnie and on two separate occasions he found himself in the headlines of the national press and media – exactly the kind of thing from which he had wanted to escape. On the morning of 15 December 1988 *The Sun* newspaper ran a story, written by journalists Sue Evison and Mark Chadbourn, informing its readers that Evison, posing as a member of the public, had taken a silver salver – which a leading auction house had valued at around £1,000 – into Ronnie's shop enquiring if he wanted to buy it. When he offered £20, they ran a story highlighting the difference between its value and Barker's low offer.

The BBC was keen to hear Ronnie's side of the story and frantic arrangements were made to persuade him to appear on that evening's *Wogan* show. Eventually, he was persuaded and at an hour's notice Bill Wyman – the planned guest – was happy to step down to make way for Ronnie, who marched on to the set in front of the studio audience carrying two weighty *Sun* awards he'd been given during his career – both of which he planned to sell for scrap or to the highest bid, which would go to charity.

Ronnie, visibly riled by the story, told Terry Wogan that both he and his wife thought the woman looked shifty and were worried she had stolen the item. Ronnie realised the piece was valuable, but thought that by offering a ridiculous amount it would send her packing. Apparently, she said she would need to check with her mother and Ronnie suggested leaving the piece with them, which she refused to do. It would have given him time to call the police. Later, two men carrying the silver salver walked into the shop. Before long, the men – reporter Mark Chadbourn and a photographer – announced they were from *The Sun* and proceeded to take Ronnie's picture. Thinking it was a scam, Ronnie rushed to the back of his shop.

Barker accused *The Sun*, which visited other antiques shops in an investigation into the fairness of high-street dealers, of running a spoiler story, because the *Daily Mail* were publishing extracts from his autobiography. Three days later *The Sun* hadn't let the story go and were running a competition in which its readers had the chance to win the salver.

I tracked down Mark Chadbourn, now a successful writer of fantasy and horror novels. Even today, twenty-two years after the story ran in the tabloid, he remembers clearly the day they walked in to The Emporium. He says, 'I can categorically state that there was no internal discussion at *The Sun* that this would be a spoiler for the *Daily Mail* series. Ronnie was only really an after-thought to the on-going antiques investigation, which was a much bigger deal at the time. It's worth restating that Ronnie was extremely well-liked by *Sun* executives, reporters and – importantly – readers. There was no desire to upset him, far from it, but journalistically it was impossible to ignore his actions in his shop that day.'

Mark says Sue Evison was charged with taking the salver into a range of antiques shops across the Midlands and the south-east to get it valued. 'When the hallmarks were checked, there was no way anyone could say it was worth very little. I was then asked to go in with a photographer, after Sue had got the valuation, to get the reaction of the owners. I had some very tense confrontations with some of the antiques dealers, who had clearly appeared to try to cheat Sue, but we all expected the visit to Ronnie would be a pleasant wrap-up. But when Ronnie checked the hallmarks and compared it to those in a reference book, he made one of the lowest offers, as I recall. We were all shocked – this wasn't how it was meant to turn out. When I walked into the shop to ask Ronnie about it, he made an initial excuse, and then fled into the back and wouldn't talk to us any further. Personally, I found it a very dismal affair.'

Mark was disappointed about Ronnie appearing on *Wogan* to, in his words, 'blame *The Sun* for somehow trying to stitch him up. I'm no defender of that paper, but on that occasion I can attest that the investigation was completely above board, and with no secret agenda. I can understand why he did it, but it was very sad nonetheless.'

Five years later, in 1993, Ronnie found himself in the headlines again, this time after unwittingly buying an antique cabinet for £50 from a man who turned out to be a convict. The crook was, apparently, dressed in his blue prison uniform and home on leave when he duped Barker into buying the item of furniture, which resulted in Ronnie being questioned by police before being released without charge. Such a situation is an occupational hazard for those in the trade, who, understandably, won't know the history of every item they're offered. The risk must have been higher for someone like Ronnie Barker, who, after all, saw antiques and collectibles as just a hobby; here was no trained expert, just someone who had become increasingly interested in collecting items from a bygone era.

The Barkers ran their little shop for a further six years until, in the autumn of 1999, with Ronnie wanting to take things easier, they closed the doors for the final time. Ronnie's spell of being an antiques dealer was at an end.

Chapter 17

Ronnie's retirement didn't stop hopeful producers and directors testing the water to see if they could entice this great national icon to return to the screen for one last time – or two. But Ronnie politely declined any such requests; that was, until the offer to play David Inches, Churchill's butler, came along. The 2002 film – a joint production between HBO Films, BBC Films and Ridley Scott's production company Scott Free – exuded talent of the calibre of Albert Finney as Churchill, Vanessa Redgrave as Clemmie Churchill and Derek Jacobi as Prime Minister Stanley Baldwin.

The screenplay was written by Hugh Whitemore and directed by Richard Loncraine, focusing on Churchill in the years leading up to World War Two. The role of Inches was going to prove a challenge for casting director Irene Lamb, as she explains. 'It was an incredibly difficult part to cast, because we wanted someone with humour, but who wasn't going to be over the top.' While talking to top agent Ros Chatto, the conversation turned to the role of Inches. 'I said, "Oh god, this part is so difficult." Ros suddenly replied, "What about Ronnie Barker?" I said, "Ronnie Barker? He's retired." She told me that he'd approached her, because he might want to work again, but only in certain things.' Irene admits that she went 'berserk'. She explains, with a smile on her face, that in response to her, 'Oh, Ronnie, Ronnie, how fantastic – that would be great!', Ros had to calm her down, stating that he'd only put his toe in the water and wasn't really sure yet. In the meantime, an excited Irene Lamb spoke to Richard Loncraine and producer Frank Doelger, both of whom shared her understandable enthusiasm.

Uncertainty remained, though, about Ronnie accepting the part, so with the BBC not wanting to let the opportunity slip, writer Hugh Whitemore was asked to drop Ronnie a line, encouraging him to consider the role. 'It was a strange coincidence that my father and his worked in the same office during the 1930s –

ShellMex. When Ronnie became famous my father used to say, "Just think, he used to sit on my knee." So I wrote to him, saying I'd love him to play the role, telling him about the wonderful cast we were assembling and mentioning the fact our fathers had worked together at City Gate House. Then Ronnie phoned me, joking, "We've got to keep the City Gate House boys together." It was a typical Ronnie remark.'

When asked to write a script about Churchill, Whitemore wasn't overly enthused. The BBC had a script they wanted him to rewrite, but when he declined it was offered to another writer; eventually, though, they returned and asked him to write a script from scratch. 'There had been about a thousand books on Churchill and I didn't think I'd have anything new to say. They kept on at me, so finally I agreed to have a go. I wrote a couple of scenes and discovered I liked writing about the man, so off we went.'

Hugh had no doubts about Ronnie, who, although having played his fair share of dramatic roles in the early part of his career was largely known as a comedy actor. 'He was absolutely wonderful. I'd seen him acting, years before, in a Peter Hall production of *Camino Real*. Even in a tiny part he had the presence and charisma that made him stand out – not in an offensive, show-off way, he just seemed to inhabit the part perfectly.' And that's what he did with Inches, says Hugh. 'He withdrew himself and became the character in a marvellous, modest way. He could so easily have hogged the whole thing and ran away with a dazzling little cameo, but chose to be part of the ensemble.'

What impressed Hugh Whitemore most of all was that Ronnie – seventy-two when he made the film – was a gifted performer technically. 'His technique was formidable. I've never known a more technically talented actor in any field of drama in my life.' And he was such a modest, down-to-earth, friendly chap, as was proven when Ronnie and Joy accompanied Hugh and his wife Rohan to the preview of their next project *My House in Umbria*. Hugh says, 'When we came out of the Curzon Cinema two young men suddenly saw Ronnie and said, "Oh look, it's Ronnie Barker." One of them took out his phone, dialled his mum and turned to Ronnie, saying, "Mr Barker, could you just talk to my mum? She's a huge fan of yours." He thrust his mobile phone at Ronnie, who was unbeliev-ably wonderful. Instead of saying "Bugger off!" he took the phone and spoke to her – it was a marvellous, one-man show, standing on the pavement in Curzon Street.'

Ronnie's experience on film was limited to a handful of big-screen appearances and the comedy serials which became an integral part of the *Two Ronnies* series. In some respects, it wasn't a favourite medium or one in which he'd excelled; but his performance in *The Gathering Storm* proved that he could compete alongside any of the movie greats. 'Ronnie could stand up to anyone on screen. He was a star in his own right,' says director Richard Loncraine. 'Ronnie knew how to deal with the power on screen that someone like Albert Finney or Maggie Smith had and was a perfect foil for them.'

Richard enjoyed working with Ronnie. 'He wasn't a greedy actor. He'd listen to notes and ideas, but tell you if he thought you were wrong, if something wouldn't work or wasn't structured right. Ninety-nine per cent of the time he was right. Directing is largely about man-management, getting on with people and getting the best out of them, so a lot of the time it's about listening to them. You'd be foolish not to listen to someone who's come as far as Ronnie. They're not always right and they can be complicated people, but you always listen. As Churchill's butler, Ronnie was wonderful.'

The film was screened on BBC2 on Friday, 12 July 2002 to glowing reviews, with Ronnie's return causing excitement among the reviewers, emphasising the high regard in which he was still held. When asked by a journalist what had tempted him out of retirement, he replied simply that it was a worthy script and he knew it was something he wanted to do. He admitted, however, that he had first-day nerves. 'The feeling of being on the set was very new and strange to me at first. I was a bit nervous about doing it again, but the first day, I fitted in fine once I got there.'[1]

Although Matthew Sweet in the *Independent on Sunday* thought that his 'much-vaunted return to the screen was lost on the periph-eries'[2], he congratulated the overall production, while other reviews were complimentary about Ronnie's performance: Paul Hoggart in *The Times* encapsulated many people's view that it was 'delightful to see Ronnie Barker back on screen'[3].

After making *The Gathering Storm*, Ronnie told director Richard Loncraine that he wouldn't do another film for anyone else, and he didn't. Two years later, though, he was seen playing The General in Loncraine's next project with HBO – *My House in Umbria*, an adaptation of William Trevor's novella. The screenplay was, again, penned by Hugh Whitemore and told the story of a romance writer who survives a terrorist bomb on a train and invites the other three survivors from her carriage to her villa in Umbria to recover – although, in reality, a suitable villa couldn't be found in the region, so they nipped over the border to Tuscany.

The film saw Ronnie meet up with Maggie Smith one more time, but as Richard Loncraine reveals, there had been some initial resistance within HBO about the casting of Ronnie as The General. 'I can't remember who from, but because he was the comic relief in the Churchill film, to a degree, they worried whether he could play it completely straight. It wasn't a big battle I had to fight, but it was one I certainly remember having. I just had to tell them I thought he'd be perfect and if you want it to be sad, he'll make it sad.'

Loncraine concurs with Hugh Whitemore about Ronnie being a fine technician. 'His work was truthful and honest. He didn't push it. He knew that less is often more in acting. He knew what would work on film, understood the power of a close-up and how you had to control the size of a performance.'

By now, Ronnie was becoming frail, but as Richard Loncraine says, 'He had such pluck.' His declining health didn't cause the production any problems. 'We just took it easy and made sure he had a place to sit in the cool and was looked after. It wasn't hard to do, because he was a gentleman. We just wanted to make sure he had a nice time, wasn't working ridiculous hours and had a couple of hours off in the day for a kip if he wanted it, but usually he didn't. He was a man in his twilight years.'

His failing health didn't prevent him appearing at the BBC's moving hour-long BAFTA tribute, which was screened on 7 February 2004, in which Barker's five decades in the entertainment business were celebrated, with friends and colleagues, including David Jason and Richard Briers, sharing memories and thoughts of Ronnie, a comedy genius. It was a tearful occasion for Ronnie; flanked by his two greatest pals, Ronnie Corbett and David Jason, he was looking gaunt, but could still raise a smile and lift the spirits of the millions watching, despite shedding a few tears. Ronnie retained his humour to the very end, even when away from the spotlight.

Professor Ronald Spiers, who retired to Chipping Norton in 1998, managed to secure Ronnie as a patron of a then newly formed charity, The Lawrence Home Nursing Team. He remembers seeing Ronnie at the local branch of Barclays Bank, just months before he died. He was, as ever, witty and engaging on that bright morning. 'He was naturally funny. I was waiting in a queue when Ronnie came out from an office with a young, attractive manageress, who had a bundle of files under her arm. She was leading the way and just as they got level with me, although I don't think he saw me, she turned to Ronnie, saying, "I'm afraid this is something we'll have to go upstairs for." Ronnie replied, "Oh, it's a long time since anyone said that to me!" The whole queue erupted.'

The rapturous reception which greeted Ronnie Barker at the BAFTA tribute, as well as the satisfying audience figures, proved just how much love and affection the general public held for not only Ronnie B. but his diminutive partner Ronnie C., too. Executive producer Beatrice Ballard, whose department had organised the tribute, witnessed the 'fantastic' atmosphere that evening and became fundamental in bringing together the two Rons for their last ever shows: *The Two Ronnies Sketchbook* and the *Christmas Sketchbook*, both screened during 2005. She recalls a phone call from Ronnie, the morning after the BAFTA tribute. 'He rang to say thank you and to tell me how much he'd enjoyed it.' She grasped the opportunity, saying, 'It was wonderful seeing you and Ronnie C. together again – we really must try and cook something up together where we bring you two back together for a project.' Ronnie showed interest from the beginning and between them hatched the idea of reflecting on old sketches, under the *Sketchbook* title, which Ronnie coined. It was one of the easiest shows to get commissioned, says Beatrice.

The structure mirrored the form of an old *Ronnies* show, beginning with headlines before moving into 'quickies' and longer sketches, all carefully selected. 'Some people might think it was just a ragbag of sketches thrown together, but it wasn't like that,' says Ballard. They were carefully chosen: initially, Ballard's production team assembled a short list of material, based on discussions with Ronnie, for his viewing. 'I loved production meetings with him, because I'd drive to his house in the Cotswolds and he'd make a nice cup of tea, and we'd sit in the back sitting room – it was very pleasant. Then we'd go out for a fantastic Italian meal in the village. It was great fun.'

Some of the selected sketches were considered too long compared to the standards at that time, so discussions took place about how they could be trimmed without losing their rhythm and brilliance. While the sketches were old, new material was added in the form of links and quips.

Such was the popularity of the initial *Sketchbook* series, it came as no surprise when a one-off *Christmas Sketchbook* was planned. Beatrice, however, was aware that Ronnie was even weaker by this stage. 'He knew he was coming to the end of his life, which made it all so terribly poignant. Recording that last show was very sad.'

'It was a very emotional ending,' admits Ronnie C., 'because Ron realised he wouldn't be able to do any more, and he was seriously ill. I was surprised he was up for doing it, but I'm glad he was.'

Many people had mixed feelings when they heard the Ronnies were returning to television, including David Renwick, who assumed they had been railroaded into the decision by some 'opportunistic producer'. 'But to my surprise Ronnie told me he'd been trying to sell the idea of a comeback for some time. The idea of them introducing a selection of their best work from behind the old news desk was sweet enough in itself, and the warmth bestowed on them by the studio audience was palpable. But the truth was that Ronnie B. was, inevitably, becoming a pale shadow of his old self, and while Ronnie C. still had plenty of bounce and attack about him it was sad to watch Ronnie B. stumbling here and there over the jokes he used to deliver with such breathtaking dexterity.'

Fellow writer Peter Vincent says, 'I think the *Sketchbook* series was a terrible mistake. Ronnie B. looked so old and didn't have much energy. I don't know why they did it – why not just repeat the old shows?' Barry Cryer was concerned for his long-standing friend. 'He didn't look well. We were all worried for him.'

So, too, was actress Lynda Baron, 'I knew he wasn't very well and the second I saw him doing the *Sketchbook* series I thought, you're too thin, you've never managed that on a diet before – his diets had always spectacularly failed.' Ronnie was always trying to lose weight. His size even became a tool to exploit, even in the warm-up when an episode of *The Two Ronnies* was being recorded. Ronnie C. would come on and use his skill at patter, before introducing his partner, enthusing, 'You've heard of a man who's built like a Greek god. Now for a man who's built like a Greek restaurant.' On came Ronnie B. and the show would begin.

At the end of the *Christmas Sketchbook*, Ronnie B. strolled over to the studio audience and announced this was the last show he'd make for the BBC. It was the last he'd make for anyone. It was a sad moment, but not unexpected, given his obvious decline in health. 'When they made the Christmas special of *The Two Ronnies Sketchbook* I'd heard that Ronnie was very anxious to record it in the summer, and the implication was that after that he wouldn't be well enough to go through with it. But still I had no idea the end was imminent,' says David Renwick. By the time the *Christmas* instalment was screened on Christmas Day 2005 Ronnie Barker had gone. Attracting the third biggest audience figure during the festive period, it was a perfect tribute to a fine actor.

Chapter 18

On 3 October 2005 Ronald William George Barker died at Katharine House Hospice in Adderbury, Oxfordshire, a tranquil setting amid lush countryside close to the Oxfordshire-Northamptonshire border. He was seventy-six. His death was notified to the General Register Office by his daughter Charlotte two days later. The doctor certifying the death recorded heart disease and diabetes as the causes of death. When Ronnie's will was published the following September, it revealed that he had left £465,664, reduced to £300,337 after liabilities.

After Ronnie's farewell appearance the previous Christmas, his decline was swift. He wasn't able to enjoy his food or sleep properly – he realised it was time to go. Ronnie Corbett and his wife wanted to visit their friend just one more time, having last seen him at the BBC while making the *Christmas Sketchbook*, but Ronnie Barker wasn't allowing visitors. Richard Briers – desperately worried – wanted to see his friend, too. 'I knew he was ill. I rang and said I'd love to see him, but he told me I couldn't. He'd lost so much weight that he didn't want people to see him. It was a sobering conversation. I was on the phone around three minutes. We talked about illness and he talked about dying and quite rightly said, "It will happen to all of us." It was very tragic to talk to him like that, but he realised the end was near. I said, "Keep hoping and we'll all hope and pray for you." He replied, "I think the game's up and I don't want you to see me looking like this." It was about ten days before he died.'

After two days in the hospice Ronnie Barker passed away, peacefully. Charlotte Barker called Ronnie C. to break the news. The people closest to Ronnie were being told before it was announced to the media. David Renwick had already been informed by Corbett that Ronnie wasn't seeing anyone. A few days later, the phone rang again – it was Michael Hurll, the Ronnies' former executive producer at the Beeb. 'He told me that Ronnie had died that morning, but they weren't releasing the news until the next day. It was just the most awful body blow, and so very strange to spend a full twenty-four hours aware that he had gone, seeing nothing reported, just waiting for the whole thing to break. It seemed unreal then and it still does. The following summer, Joy generously threw another summer party for old times' sake, and Ronnie Corbett's voice fell away in swallowed tears as he stood up and proposed a toast for his former partner. It was a terribly, deeply moving moment.'

As soon as Ronnie's passing was made public, the coverage was immense, spanning all media: every newspaper carried the shattering news, many splashing it across their front pages; radio reports, interviews, television items, every one deeply saddened by the tragic news, and wanting to reflect and celebrate the enormous pleasure he bestowed on the nation.

Reflecting on the huge outpouring of grief which swept across the British Isles and beyond, Ronnie Corbett feels a reason for the reaction was 'there was something in Ron's personality that made you think he was speaking directly to you, that you knew him, that you were part of his family, and he part of yours.'[1]

Some of the biggest names paid tribute. David Jason called Ronnie 'a dear friend and someone for whom I had the greatest respect'. Peter Kay stated that Barker's death would 'leave a huge hole in our lives'. Michael Palin, meanwhile, said, 'Ronnie was a straightforward man who had this extraordinary ability to make the nation laugh.' Tributes continued to flood in.

A quiet funeral was held at Banbury Crematorium, close to his home in the peaceful hamlet of Dean, on 13 October, ten days after his death, with around twenty family members and close friends attending. Joy was accompanied by her daughter, Charlotte, and elder son, Larry. Sadly, but predictably in the circumstances, her younger son, Adam, was not present. He had disappeared after failing to surrender to bail on 24 June 2004, following his arrest for allegedly being in possession of indecent images of children.

Police were present at the funeral to keep the press at bay, while family and close friends paid their respects and said their final good-byes. Aware of the myriad fellow performers and fans who would like to remember the man they had come to love, a memorial service was held at Westminster Abbey on 3 March 2006, six months after his death. On a nippy day in London streams of people, including directors, writers, performers and fans of the great comedy actor, made their way through the biting wind to the Abbey.

During the singing of the first hymn, four choirboys headed the clergy procession bearing four candles – setting the tone for the rest of the service. It wasn't long before ripples of laughter spread through the 2,500-strong congregation. It was a poignant moment, a touch of humour symbolising the man whose life everyone had turned up to celebrate. 'After the four choirboys carrying four enormous candles – around two-foot high – the length of Westminster Abbey, the laughter gradually spread as people caught on to the fact it was *the* four candles,' says Richard Briers, smiling. 'They produced that joke – in this dignified place – out of great respect. But he was very well loved and gave millions genuine enjoyment and laughter. He lifted the spirits of millions of people. It's very touching when you go along as a fellow actor and see this amazing turnout and affection.'

Hymns, prayers, readings from Briers and Josephine Tewson, contributions from Michael Grade and Peter Kay and soon the tones of Ronnie Barker in a sketch in which he delivered a sermon in rhyming slang echoed around the abbey's vaulted roof. And then it was left to Ronnie Corbett – who in forty years had never had an argument with Ronnie B. – to pay his final tribute, reflecting on the many moments of happiness his partner and friend had brought.

'It was a wonderful service – and very funny, too,' says John Sullivan. 'It was a great celebration of comedy. The bells rang out, and I thought, God almighty, that's the way to go. They were ringing the bells all over London for you. You were that good, that talented.'

It was a fitting send off for a man who had given so much to so many for so long.

Notes

Apart from those listed below, all the quotes used throughout this book were taken from interviews carried out by the author.

(Note: WAC = BBC Written Archives Centre, Caversham, Berkshire.)

CHAPTER 1

1 Ronnie Barker, *It's Hello – from him!*, p.10.
2 Ibid.
3 Ibid. p.9.
4 Ibid. p.15.
5 Ibid. p.21.
6 Bob McCabe, *Ronnie Barker: The Authorised Biography*, p.16.

CHAPTER 2

1 Printed in an incomplete Manchester Repertory Company's programme for production beginning Monday, 31 May 1948.
2 Ronnie Barker, *It's Hello – from him!*, p.34.
3 Note from W. Armitage Owen in the Manchester Repertory Company's programme for *He Walked in Her Sleep*, which ran for a week from 25 April 1949.
4 Ronnie Barker, *Dancing in the Moonlight*, p.63.

CHAPTER 3

1 Ronnie Barker, *It's Hello – from him!*, p.46.
2 Review in *Stockport Express* (2/11/50), critic's name unknown.
3 Review in *Stockport Express* (12/1/51), critic's name unknown.
4 Review in *Stockport Express* (22/2/51), critic's name unknown.
5 Review in *Stockport Express* (2/3/51), critic's name unknown.

6 Review in *Stockport Express* (3/5/51), critic's name unknown.

7 'Tudor Personality – 4', published in the *Stockport Express* (28/6/51).

8 Article in *Stockport Express* (2/9/51).

9 The Director's Summary, written by Frank Shelley in March 1951.

10 Letter dated 9/3/95 from Ronnie Barker to Don Chapman.

11 Ibid.

12 Ibid.

13 Ibid.

14 Ibid.

15 Ibid.

16 Ibid.

17 Ibid.

18 Review by S. P. B. Mais in the *Oxford Mail* (16/10/51).

19 Ronnie Barker, *Dancing in the Moonlight*, p.130.

CHAPTER 4

1 Review by S. P. B. Mais in the *Oxford Mail* (12/51).

2 Ibid.

3 Review in *The Oxford Magazine* (27/11/52).

4 Review by Patrick Dromgoole (27/1/53), publication unknown.

5 Extract from the Oxford Playhouse programme for *Don't Listen, Ladies!*, staged for twelve nights from 5 April 1954.

6 Review in *The Oxford Magazine* (20/4/54).

7 Review by H. H. H. in *Cambridge Daily News* (5/54).

8 Ibid.

9 Review by Montague Haltrecht in the *North Berkshire Herald* (20/4/54).

10 Review in *Cambridge Daily News* (5/54).

11 Review by S. P. B. M. in the *Oxford Mail* (6/10/54).

12 Barker interviewed on *Ronnie Barker: A Life in Comedy* (24/8/97).

13 Article by Laurence Marks in the *Oxford Mail* (7/1/55).

14 Article in *The Oxford Magazine*, writer and date unknown.

15 Article in the *Southend-on-Sea and County Pictorial* (11/2/55).

16 Review in the *Southend-on-Sea and County Pictorial* (11/2/55).

CHAPTER 5

1 Review in *The Times* (10/6/55).
2 Ibid.
3 Review by Milton Shulman in the *Evening Standard* (10/11/55).
4 Review by John Barber in the *Daily Express* (10/11/55).
5 Ibid.
6 Sir Peter Hall interviewed for a BBC tribute show (4/10/05).
7 Review by W. A. Darlington in the *Daily Telegraph* (17/12/55).
8 Review in *Punch* (28/12/55).
9 Review by C. W. in the *Daily Mail* (17/12/55).
10 Ronnie Barker, *It's Hello – from him!*, p.76.
11 An interview with Charlotte Barker was shown on *Heroes of Comedy*, transmitted by Channel 4 (28/12/00).
12 Ibid.
13 Article by Philip Oakes in the *Radio Times* (*c.* 10/75).
14 Review by Cecil Wilson in the *Daily Mail* (15/11/56).
15 Review by Patrick Gibbs in the *Daily Telegraph* (15/11/56).

CHAPTER 6

1 Review in *The Times* (14/4/57).
2 Article by Tim Ewbank in *The Sun* (3/12/83).
3 Article by Philip Oakes in the *Radio Times* (*c.* 10/75).
4 Article by Cecil Wilson in the *Daily Mail* (9/4/57).
5 Article in *The Times* (17/5/57).
6 Review by W. A. Darlington in the *Daily Telegraph* (9/4/57).
7 Review in the *Daily Sketch* (24/4/57).
8 Review in *Punch* (17/4/57).
9 Review by Thomas Wiseman in the *Evening Standard* (18/9/57).
10 Review by Cecil Wilson in the *Daily Mail* (18/9/57).
11 Ronnie Barker, *It's Hello – from him!*, p.93.
12 Review in the *Observer* (27/12/57).
13 Review by John Barber in *Daily Express* (27/12/57).
14 Ibid.
15 Review by Patrick Gibbs in the *Daily Telegraph* (18/7/58).
16 Review in *The Times* (18/7/58).
17 Review by T. C. Worsley in the *Financial Times* (18/7/58).
18 Ronnie Barker, *It's Hello – from him!*, p.82.

19 Article by Mike Bygrave in the *Radio Times* (22/3/73).
20 Ronnie Barker, *It's Hello – from him!*, p.86.
21 Bob McCabe, *Ronnie Barker: The Authorised Biography*, p.52.
22 Memo from Alastair Scott-Johnston to H. L. E. (S), 7.10.58, subject: 'Programme Suggestion: *The Navy Lark*'. Held at WAC.
23 Ibid.
24 Leslie Phillips, *Hello*, p.202.
25 Laurie Wyman's original synopsis for *The Navy Lark*, held at WAC.
26 Ibid.
27 Memo from R. E. Gregson to H. L. E. (S), 6/5/59, subject: *The Navy Lark*. Held at WAC.
28 Ibid.
29 Ibid.

CHAPTER 7

 1 Review in *The Sunday Times* (16/10/60).
 2 Review in *Tatler* by Anthony Cookman (26/10/60).
 3 Audience Research Report dated 8/12/60, regarding an episode transmitted 12/11/60. Held at WAC.
 4 Audience Research Report dated 9/2/61, regarding an episode transmitted 21/1/61. Held at WAC.
 5 June Whitfield, . . . *and June Whitfield*, p.138.
 6 Review in *The Times* (13/4/61).
 7 Review by W. A. Darlington in the *Daily Telegraph* (13/4/61).
 8 Review in the *Daily Mail* (13/4/61).
 9 Amanda Barrie, *It's Not a Rehearsal*, p.105.
10 Ibid.
11 Ibid.
12 Review by Peter Black in the *Daily Mail* (15/12/61).
13 Review by Philip Purser in the *Sunday Telegraph* (19/11/61).
14 Review by Peter Black in the *Daily Mail* (16/11/62).

CHAPTER 8

 1 Article in the *Radio Times* (*c.* 1975).
 2 Ronnie Barker, *It's Hello – from him!*, p.80.

3 Review by Eric Shorter in the *Daily Telegraph* (25/1/62).

4 Review in *The Times* (25/1/62).

5 Ibid.

6 Review by Robert Muller in the *Daily Mail* (25/1/62).

7 Review by Nina Hibbin in the *Daily Worker* (12/1/63).

8 Review by Margaret Hinxman in the *Daily Herald* (12/1/63).

9 Memo from Scott-Johnston to A. H. L. E. (Sound), 26/2/63.

10 Interviewed by Ernest Thomson in the *Radio Times* (19/9/63).

11 Ibid.

12 Ibid.

13 Comment reported in an Audience Research Report, dated 7/1/64, held at BBC WAC.

14 Memo from Alastair Scott-Johnston to H. L. E. (S), dated 22/1/64.

15 Letter from C. J. Mahoney to Evans and Collyer, dated 9/7/64.

16 Letter from producer John Bridges to Barker, dated 22/6/65.

17 Article in the *Radio Times* (23/7/64).

18 Audience Research Report dated 16/2/65, retained at WAC.

19 Ibid.

20 Memo from Ted Taylor to Roy Rich dated 22/1/65, titled 'Let's Face It'.

21 Ibid.

22 Memo from Roy Rich to John Fawcett Wilson dated 3/2/65, titled 'Let's Face It – Warm Up'.

23 Review by Eric Shorter in the *Daily Telegraph* (17/3/64).

24 Review in *The Times* (17/3/64).

25 Review by Eric Shorter in the *Daily Telegraph* (17/3/64).

26 Review in *The Times* (17/3/64).

27 Review by Eric Shorter in the *Daily Mail* (7/8/64).

28 Review in the *Sunday Telegraph* (9/8/64).

29 Interview by Philip Oakes in the *Radio Times*, date unknown.

30 Eric Sykes being interviewed for the Telegram DVD *And It's Goodnight From Him – The Very Best of Ronnie Barker*, 1996.

31 Review in the *Monthly Film Bulletin* (1/6/64).

32 Review by Ernest Betts in the *Sunday People* (26/4/64).

33 Review by Ann Pacey in the *Daily Herald* (24/4/64).

34 Review by Dilys Powell in the *Sunday Times* (26/4/64).

35 Review by Nina Hibbin in the *Daily Worker* (25/4/64).
36 Peter Graham Scott, *British Television – An Insider's History*, p.150.
37 Review in *Monthly Film Bulletin* (3/65).

CHAPTER 9

1 Bob McCabe, *Ronnie Barker: The Authorised Biography*, p.85.
2 Review by Lyn Lockwood in the *Daily Telegraph* (8/3/65).
3 Anonymous review in *The Times* (8/3/65).
4 Bob McCabe, *Ronnie Barker: The Authorised Biography*, p.73.
5 Comment from BBC Audience Research Report (29/3/66). Held at WAC.
6 Report by David Griffiths in the *Radio Times* (3/3/66).
7 Interview for *Heroes of Comedy*, transmitted on Channel 4 on 28/12/00.
8 Review by Richard Last in the *Sun* (5/5/67).
9 Anonymous review in *The Times* (24/9/66).
10 Review by Philip Purser in the *Sunday Telegraph* (18/9/66).
11 Review by W. A. Darlington in the *Daily Telegraph* (18/6/68).
12 Review by Harold Hobson in the *Sunday Times* (23/6/68).

CHAPTER 10

1 Michael Palin interview shown on the documentary *Heroes of Comedy* (28/12/00).
2 Review by James Thomas in the *Daily Express* (5/1/70).
3 Ibid.
4 Ibid.
5 Review by Sylvia Clayton in the *Daily Telegraph* (25/7/70).
6 Review by Mike Kerrington in the *Daily Mirror* (26/4/69).
7 Review by Sylvia Clayton in the *Daily Telegraph* (24/11/69).
8 Anonymous review in the *Monthly Film Bulletin* (5/70).
9 Review by Brian Boss in the *Daily Sketch* (8/1/71).

CHAPTER 11

1 Bill Cotton interviewed on *The Two Ronnies Night* (16/7/99).
2 Audience Research Report, dated 5/4/71, held at WAC.
3 Ibid.

4 Review in the *Birmingham Evening Mail* (17/12/71).
5 The BBC's Audience Research Report, dated 21/4/71, held at WAC.
6 Ibid.

CHAPTER 12
1 Interview for *Ronnie Barker – A Life in Comedy*, transmitted 28/8/97.
2 Interview with Michael Parkinson on BBC's *Parkinson*, date unknown.

CHAPTER 13
1 Comment in the BBC's Audience Research Report, dated 13/5/71. Held at WAC.
2 Review by Peter Fiddick in the *Guardian* (12/4/71).
3 Barker interview appeared in the documentary *Ronnie Barker – A Life in Comedy*, transmitted 28/8/97.
4 Review by Stewart Lane in the *Morning Star* (14/4/71).
5 Review by Virginia Ironside in the *Daily Mail* (30/7/71).
6 Barker interview appeared in the documentary *Ronnie Barker – A Life in Comedy*, transmitted 28/8/97.
7 Anonymous review in the *Daily Mail* (6/11/72).
8 David Renwick interview, featured on *Comedy Connections* (11/4/05).

CHAPTER 14
1 Ronnie Barker interview shown on documentary *Heroes of Comedy* (28/12/00).
2 Interview by Gordon Burn in the *Radio Times* (23/9/71).
3 Review by Sylvia Clayton in the *Daily Telegraph* (27/9/71).
4 Review by Henry Raynor in *The Times* (27/9/71).
5 Interview in the *Radio Times* (1/6/72).
6 Review by Peter Black in the *Daily Mail* (5/7/72).
7 Review by Philip Purser in the *Sunday Telegraph* (25/6/72).
8 Interviewed for *Heroes of Comedy* (28/12/00).

CHAPTER 15
1 Review by Geoff Brown in *Monthly Film Bulletin* (date unknown).
2 Article by Alexander Frater in the *Daily Telegraph* (19/12/75).

3 Ibid.
4 Ronnie Corbett, *And it's goodnight from him . . .*, p. 217.
5 Ibid.
6 Review by W. Stephen Gilbert in *Broadcast* (26/4/82).
7 Review by James Murray in the *Daily Express* (17/4/82).
8 Review by Ray Connolly in the *Evening Standard* (13/4/82).
9 Review by Philip Purser in the *Sunday Telegraph* (18/4/82).
10 Review by Milton Shulman in the *Evening Standard* (26/5/78).
11 Review by John Barber in the *Daily Telegraph* (27/5/78).

Chapter 16

1 Review by Patrick Stoddart in *Broadcast* (28/9/84).
2 Anonymous review in the *News of the World* (9/9/84).
3 Ibid.
4 Review by Margaret Forwood in the *Sunday People* (14/10/84).
5 Anonymous review in the *Daily Mirror* (9/1/88).
6 Anonymous review in the *Financial Times* (13/1/88).
7 Review by Ian Christie in the *Daily Express* (12/1/88).
8 Interview appeared in the documentary *Heroes of Comedy*, 28/12/00.
9 Interview with Ronnie Corbett appeared in the documentary *Comedy Connections*, transmitted 11/4/05.
10 Interview with Ronnie Barker, ibid.
11 Ibid.

Chapter 17

1 Ronnie Barker interviewed by Judy Leighton, source and date unconfirmed.
2 Review by Matthew Sweet in the *Independent on Sunday* (14/7/02).
3 Review by Paul Hoggart in *The Times* (15/7/02).

Chapter 18

1 Ronnie Corbett, *And it's goodnight from him . . .*, p.291.

Career at a Glance

(Note: although I've tried to include as many professional stage, radio, television and film credits as possible, there may be some productions I have overlooked or situations where I've been unable to confirm as much detail as I would have liked. Any comments or additions from readers are, therefore, very welcome. Please write to me c/o the publisher.)

THEATRE

Between November 1948 and April 1949 Ronnie was employed by the Manchester Repertory Company, based at the County Theatre, Aylesbury.

Productions:

15/11/48: *Quality Street*, played Lieutenant Spicer
22/11/48: *Ladies in Retirement*, not on the cast list
29/11/48: *When We Are Married*, played Gerald Forbes
6/12/48: *Maria Marten*, no programme in the archives
13/12/48: *They Walk Alone*, not on the cast list
27/12/48: *Little Red Riding Hood*, played Trunch, a village constable
3/1/49: *Treasure Island*, no programme held in the archives
10/1/49: *Are You A Mason?*, played Ernest Morrison
17/1/49: *The Guinea Pig*, played Read
24/1/49: *Sweeney Todd*, played Daft Dickie
31/1/49: *Third Time Lucky*, played Vincent
7/2/49: *Miranda*, played Charles
14/2/49: *Pride and Prejudice*, played Mr Wickham
21/2/49: *Dracula*, played R. M. Renfield

28/2/49: *Is Your Honeymoon Really Necessary?*, played James Hicks, a lawyer's clerk

7/3/49: *Arms and the Man*, played Nicola

14/3/49: *East Lynne*, no programme held in the archives

21/3/49: *The Rotters*, played Police Inspector Wick

28/3/49: *Eden End*, not on the cast list

4/4/49: *The Guinea Pig*, reprised his role as Read at the Pavilion Theatre, Rhyl, North Wales, where a branch of the Manchester Repertory Company was performing

11/4/49: *Pygmalion*, not on the cast list

18/4/49: *Just William*, played Egbert Huggins

25/4/49: *He Walked in Her Sleep*, played Geoffrey Deacon

January 1950 – April 1950
Ronnie toured with the Mime Theatre Company, touring Wales and South West England

May 1950 – August 1951
Ronnie worked with Frank H. Fortescue's Famous Players, based at the Tudor Theatre, Bramhall, Cheshire

Productions:

(Note: no programmes or cast lists are held in the archives, so the following is a list of the productions staged within Ronnie's spell with the company. It can be assumed that he appeared in most – if not all – the shows.)

1/5/50: *The Shop at Sly Corner*

8/5/50: *The First Mrs Fraser*

15/5/50: *Painted Sparrows*

22/5/50: *Lovely to Look At*

29/5/50: *Rookery Nook*

5/6/50: *To Have and To Hold*

12/6/50: *Is Your Honeymoon Really Necessary?*

19/6/50: *Rebecca*

26/6/50: *Separate Rooms*

3/7/50: *The Family Upstairs*

10/7/50: *The Dominant Sex*
17/7/50: *The Paragon*
24/7/50: *Wishing Well*
31/7/50: *Wearing the Pants*
7/8/50: *Bed, Board and Romance*
14/8/50: *The Late Edwina Black*
21/8/50: *Her First Affair*
28/8/50: *Random Harvest*
4/9/50: *Young Wives' Tale*
11/9/50: *What A Woman Wants*
18/9/50: *Pink String and Sealing Wax*
25/9/50: *Eliza Comes to Stay*
2/10/50: *The Girl Who Couldn't Quite*
9/10/50: *Fresh Fields*
16/10/50: *Smiling Through*
23/10/50: *See How They Run*
30/10/50: *Secret Lives*
6/11/50: *Ma's Bit o' Brass*
13/11/50: *Dr Brent's Household*
20/11/50: *Arsenic and Old Lace*
27/11/50: *Apron Strings*
4/12/50: *Scandal Mongers*
11/12/50: *Meet the Wife*
18/12/50: *The Magic Cracker*

1/1/51: *Little Women*
8/1/51: *Mountain Air*
15/1/51: *The Night Was Our Friend*
22/1/51: *My Mother Had Three Sons*
29/1/51: *Travellers' Joy*
5/2/51: *A Lady Mislaid*
12/2/51: *They Fly By Twilight*
19/2/51: *Love in Idleness*
26/2/51: *There's Always Tomorrow*
5/3/51: *Black Chiffon*
12/3/51: *School for Husbands*
19/3/51: *Love in A Mist*

26/3/51: *Harvey*
2/4/51: *Castle in the Air*
9/4/51: (This week, the Brookdale Amateur Operatic Society performed *The Gondoliers*.)
16/4/51: *Mary's Other Husband*
23/4/51: *The Third Visitor*
30/4/51: *What Anne Brought Home*
7/5/51: *The Eleventh Hour*
14/5/51: *Mice Will Play*
21/5/51: *Home at Seven*
28/5/51: *Sleeping Out*
4/6/51: *Three Birds*
11/6/51: *Deep As A Well*
18/6/51: *When Peace Broke Out*
25/6/51: *The Shining Hour*
2/7/51: *Jane Steps Out*
9/7/51: *Man in Grey*
16/7/51: *The Constant Sinner*
23/7/51: *The Naughty Wife*
30/7/51: *September Tide*
6/8/51: *Families Supplied*
13/8/51: *The Unfair Sex*
20/8/51: *The House of Tomorrow*
27/8/51: *Too Young to Marry*

October 1951 – January 1955
Ronnie was a member of the Oxford Playhouse Company, a fortnightly repertory company based at the Playhouse Theatre, Oxford

Productions:

1/10/51: *The Sport of Kings*, walk-on
15/10/51: *Pick-Up Girl*, played Peter Marti
12/11/51: *Who is Sylvia?*, played Denis
26/11/51: *The Cat and the Canary*, played Hendricks

10/12/51: *Larger Than Life*, played the Stage Manager
26/12/51: *Charley's Aunt*, played Brassett, a college scout

4/2/52: *A Hundred Years Old*, played Manuel
18/2/52: *He Who Gets Slapped*, played Polly
10/3/52: *His Excellency*, played Captain Jacono de Piero
24/3/52: *Harvey*, played E. J. Lofgren, a cabman
7/4/52: *The Heiress*, played Arthur Townsend, Marian's fiancé
21/4/52: *Golden Boy*, played Siggie
5/5/52: *The Lady's Not For Burning*, played Matthew Skipps
19/5/52: *Point of Departure*, played Orphée
2/6/52: *Maria Marten*, played Flatcatcher, a showman at the fair
16/6/52: *Random Harvest*, played Truslove, a solicitor
4/8/52: *Black Coffee*, played Hercule Poirot
18/8/52: *One Wild Oat*, played Mr Pepys
1/9/52: *A Cuckoo in the Nest*, played Alfred, the barman at the Stag and Hunt
15/9/52: *Peril at End House*, played Hercule Poirot
29/9/52: *The Seventh Veil*, played James, Nicholas Cunningham's footman
13/10/52: *Queen Elizabeth Slept Here*, played Professor Douglas, a neighbour
27/10/52: *The Case of the Frightened Lady*, played Sergeant Totty
10/11/52: *The Top Box*, played Robbins (Devil)
24/11/52: *Housemaster*, played Old Crump
8/12/52: *Present Laughter*, played Fred
26/12/52: *The Cinderella Story*, played 'Enery Loam, Major Graves and Don Unamustachio Candelabra de Tapioca

26/1/53: *See How They Run*, played The Intruder
9/2/53: *Night Must Fall*, played Dan (for the second week of the production)
23/3/53: *Major Barbara*, played Snobby
6/4/53: *You Never Can Tell*, played Mr Bohun, QC
20/4/53: *The Hollow*, played Inspector Colquhoun, CID
4/5/53: *Rookery Nook*, played Putz
18/5/53: *Charley's Aunt*, played Brassett, a college scout

(Between 25 May and the end of July the main Playhouse company staged a six-week Coronation summer season at the Theatre Royal, Norwich. Performances were *Charley's Aunt*, *Rookery Nook*, *Night Must Fall*, *The Housemaster*, *Rebecca* and *Black Coffee*. The cast was the same as at Oxford.)

3/8/53: *Peg O' My Heart*, played Alaric, Mrs Chichester's son
17/8/53: *Alibi*, played Hercule Poirot
31/8/53: *Wishing Well*, played Morgan Morgan
14/9/53: *The Unguarded Hour*, played Metcalfe
28/9/53: *Too Young to Marry*, played Sam Green
12/10/53: *The Love of Four Colonels*, played Colonel Alexander Ikonenko before, in the second week, taking over Frank Shelley's role as one of the two Miserable Immortals, after Shelley scratched his eyeball
26/10/53: *Aurora*, played John Strang, a scientist
9/11/53: *The Deep Blue Sea*, played Philip Welch
23/11/53: *The Cherry Orchard*, played Yepihodov, a clerk on the estate
30/11/53: *The Holly and the Ivy*, played Mick
22/12/53: *Ambrose Applejohn's Adventure*, played Mr Pengard

18/1/54: *The Private Secretary*, played Robert Spalding
1/2/54: *Ten Little Niggers*, played William Blore
15/2/54: *Journey's End*, played 2nd Lieutenant Trotter
8/3/54: *The Dover Road*, played Nicholas
5/4/54: *Don't Listen, Ladies!*, played Baron de Charancay
17/4/54: *Carrington, VC*, played Sergeant Crane, Royal Artillery
3/5/54: *The Government Inspector*, played Yosif
1/6/54: *Who Goes There?*, played Langley
29/6/54: *A Man About the House*, played Ronnie Sanctuary
13/7/54: *The Letter*, played Chung Hi
27/7/54: *Arsenic and Old Lace*, played Dr Einstein
24/8/54: *Youth at the Helm*, played Fitch
7/9/54: *The Amazing Dr Clitterhouse*, played 'Pal' Green
21/9/54: *The Corn is Green*, played Old Tom
5/10/54: *Saloon Bar*, played Joe Harris
1/11/54: *The Public Prosecutor*, played Sanson

15/11/54: *Theatre 1900*, played Moses Mendoza in *A London Actress* and the Chairman in *The Cave of Harmony*

15/12/54: *Listen to the Wind*, played Gypsy Man and Popple

1955

Jan – May: toured in *Hot Water*, played Mr Seymour

June: *Mourning Becomes Electra*, Arts Theatre, London, played the Chantyman and Joe Silva (ran 9 June–31 July)

Nov: *Summertime*, Apollo Theatre, London, played the Farmer (ran 9 November–18 February 1956)

Dec: *Listen to the Wind*, Arts Theatre, London, played the Gypsy Man (ran 16 December–21 January 1956)

1956

Nov: *Double Image*, Savoy Theatre, London, played Mr Thwaites (ran 13 November–23 February 1957; transferred to St James's Theatre and ran 4 March–13 April 1957)

1957

April: *Camino Real*, Phoenix Theatre, London, played the servant, Sancho Panza, Nursie and Bum (ran 8 April–1 June)

Sept: *Nekrassov*, Royal Court Theatre, London, played Perigord (ran 17 September–26 October)

Dec: *Lysistrata*, Royal Court Theatre, London, played Drakes, True Leader and an Old Man (ran 26 December–8 February 1958, transferred to Duke of York's Theatre and ran 18 February–10 May 1958)

1958

July: *Irma La Douce*, Lyric Theatre, London, played Robertoles-Diams (ran 17 July–3 March 1962)

1960

Oct: *Platonov*, Royal Court Theatre, London, played Nikolai Triletski (ran 13 October–closing date unconfirmed)

1961

After a pre-London tour in the revue *On the Brighter Side*, Ronnie appeared at the Phoenix Theatre and Comedy Theatre, London, as a member of the ensemble. (Ran 12 April–closing date unconfirmed, but also staged at the Comedy Theatre between 15 August–23 September 1961)

1962

Jan: *A Midsummer Night's Dream*, Royal Court Theatre, London, played Quince (ran 24 January–17 March)

1964

March: *All in Love*, Mayfair Theatre, London, played Bob Acres (ran 16 March–closing date unconfirmed)

Aug: *Mr Whatnot*, Arts Theatre, London, played Lord Slingsby-Craddock (ran 6–29 August)

1966

Feb: *Sweet Fanny Adams*, Theatre Royal at Stratford East, London, played Alf Always (ran 7–19 February)

1968

June: *The Real Inspector Hound*, Criterion Theatre, London, played Birdboot (ran 17 June–7 December)
1971

Dec: *Good Time Johnny*, Birmingham Repertory Theatre, played Sir John (ran 16 December–*c.* 15 February 1972)

1978

The Two Ronnies Stage Show previewed at the Bristol Hippodrome in May before opening at the London Palladium in August. Between December 1978 and January 1979, it was performed as a Christmas show at the Gaumont (now Mayflower Theatre) in Southampton

1983

The Two Ronnies Stage Show was staged in Southampton before opening at the London Palladium on 18 February, running until 21 May

FILM

1958

Wonderful Things!, played a Head Waiter in an uncredited role

1962

Kill or Cure, played Burton, assistant to Detective Inspector Hook

1963

Doctor in Distress, played Man at Railway Station

The Cracksman, played Yossle

1964

A Home of Your Own, played the Cement Mixer

Father Came Too!, played Josh

The Bargee, played Ronnie
1965

Runaway Railway, played Mr Galore

1968

The Man Outside, played George Venaxas

Ghost of a Chance, played Mr Prendergast

1970

Futtocks End, played General Futtock

1971

The Magnificent Seven Deadly Sins, appeared in the 'Sloth' segment

1976

Robin and Marian, played Friar Tuck

1979

Porridge, played Norman Stanley Fletcher

TELEVISION
(Note: tx = transmission date)

1956

Sailor of Fortune, played an uncredited waiter

Nom de Plume, played Monsieur Fleury in episode 4: 'Child of Her Time', tx 8 June

1959

I'm Not Bothered, played two characters, including a patient

The State of Prisons, played Bob the Turnkey
1960–64

It's a Square World, various roles

1961

The Seven Faces of Jim, played Ron and various roles, tx 16 November–28 December

Citizen James, appeared in episode 7, tx 13 November

1962

Six More Faces of Jim, played Ron and various roles, tx 15 November–20 December

Tonight, appeared in 'Evelyn', a comic strip during the show

Drama 61–67, appeared in the episode, 'Drama '62: The Frightened Sky', played Harrison, tx 7 October

The Benny Hill Show, appeared in episode 2, played a chef, tx 2 March

Suddenly It's Jim, tx 9 June

Brothers in Law, appeared in episode nine, played Mr Butler, tx 12 June

The Rag Trade, appeared in episode 13, tx 29 June

Play of the Week: The Second Chef, played Bundles in the ITV show, tx 2 October

Citizen James, appeared in episode, 'The Librarian', tx 9 November

Christmas Night with the Stars, tx 25 December, in the segment *The Christmas Night with Jim*

1963

The Sunday Play: The Holly Road Rig, played Henry Wallace, tx 14 April

More Faces of Jim, Ron and various roles, tx 28 June–9 August

1964

Bold as Brass, played Mr Oakroyd in five episodes, tx 18 April–13 June (fortnightly)

How to Be an Alien, (voice only), six episodes, tx 12 February–18 March

Sykes and A . . ., played a tramp in the episode, 'Sykes and a Log Cabin', tx 31 March

1965

Crackerjack, tx 12 February

The Walrus and the Carpenter, appeared in Episode 4 of series, tx 23 March

A Tale of Two Cities, played Jerry Cruncher in seven out of ten episodes, tx 11 April–17 June

Armchair Theatre – The Keys of the Café, playing Grimwood, tx 7 March

Gaslight Theatre, played various roles in all six episodes, tx 31 July–4 September

Not Only . . . But Also . . ., appeared in the 'Poet's Cornered' segment within Series 1, tx fortnightly 9 January–3 April

Theatre 625 – Portraits from the North: Bruno, played Crowther Rimington in the third of three plays set in the North, tx 19 December

Home is the Sailor, tx 3 December

1966

The Frost Report, played various roles in Series 1, tx 10 March–9 June

Foreign Affairs, played Grischa Petrovich in all six episodes, tx 16 September–21 October

The Saint, played Alphonse in the episode, 'The Better Mousetrap', tx 25 November

1967

Before the Fringe, appeared in two episodes, series ran 30 January–20 March

The Avengers, played Edwin Cheshire in the episode, 'The Hidden Tiger', tx 4 March

Frost Over England, various roles in special episode, tx 26 March

The Frost Report, played various roles in Series 2, tx 6 April–29 June

Crackerjack, appeared in one episode

Frost Over Christmas, various roles, tx 26 December

The Gamblers, appeared in one episode, 'The Glory of Llewellyn Smiley', tx 30 December

1968

Once More with Felix, guest appearance, tx 3 February

Late Night Line-Up, interviewed by Noel Picarda on 19 May

The Ronnie Barker Playhouse, various roles, tx 3 April–8 May

Frost on Sunday, various roles, Series 1, tx 4 August–5 January 1969

1969

Hark at Barker, played Lord Rustless in Series 1, tx 11 April–30 May

Play of the Month: Charley's Aunt, played Stephen Spettigue, tx 23 November

Noel Coward Revue, tx 26 December

1970

Frost on Sunday, various roles, tx 4 January–29 March

Hark at Barker, played Lord Rustless in Series 2, tx 10 July–21 August

Not Only . . . But Also, guest appearance in Series 3, tx 18 February–13 May (fortnightly)

Wiltons' – The Handsomest Hall in Town, played a Music Hall Performer, tx 26 December

Put A Bit of British On It, a sixty-minute special show (a collection of the best sketches) for US television

1971

Six Dates with Barker, various roles, tx 8 January–12 February

Play of the Month: A Midsummer Night's Dream, played Bottom, tx 26 September

The Ronnie Barker Yearbook, various roles, 20 March

Ronnie Corbett in Bed, various roles, 27 March

The Two Ronnies, various roles, Series 1, tx 10 April–29 May

Christmas Night with the Stars, short special of *The Two Ronnies*, tx 25 December

1972

Comedy Playhouse: Idle at Work, played George Idle, tx 14 January

His Lordship Entertains, played Lord Rustless, tx 5 June–17 July

The Two Ronnies, various roles, Series 2, tx 16 September–4 November

Christmas Night with the Stars, short special of *The Two Ronnies*, tx 25 December

1973

Seven of One, various roles, tx 25 March–6 May

The Two Ronnies, various roles, Series 3, tx 27 September–3 January

The Two Ronnies Old-Fashioned Christmas Mystery, sixty-minute special, tx 26 December

1974

Comedy Playhouse: Franklyn and Johnnie, played Johnnie Wetherby, tx 23 April

Porridge, played Norman Stanley Fletcher, Series 1, tx 5 September–10 October

1975

The Two Ronnies, various roles, Series 4, tx 2 January–20 February

Porridge, played Norman Stanley Fletcher, Series 2, tx 24 October–28 November

Play of the Month: When We Are Married, played Henry Ormonroyd, a photographer, tx 29 December

1976

The Picnic, played The General, tx 1 January

Open All Hours, played Arkwright, Series 1, tx 20 February–26 March

The Two Ronnies, various roles, Series 5, tx 4 September–23 October

Porridge, played Norman Stanley Fletcher in Special episode, tx 24 December

1977

Porridge, played Norman Stanley Fletcher, Series 3, tx 18 February–25 March

The Two Ronnies, various roles, Series 6, tx 12 November–7 January

1978

Going Straight, played Norman Stanley Fletcher, tx 24 February–7 April

The Two Ronnies, various roles, Series 7, tx 26 December–10 February '79

1980

The Two Ronnies, various roles, Series 8, tx 1 November – 13 December

The Two Ronnies, various roles in special Christmas show, tx 26 December

1981

Open All Hours, played Arkwright, Series 2, tx 1 March–19 April

The Two Ronnies, various roles, Series 9, tx 5 December–23 January

The Two Ronnies, special Christmas show, various roles, tx 25 December

1982

Open All Hours, played Arkwright, Series 3, tx 21 March–25 April

By the Sea, played The General, tx 12 April

The Two Ronnies, various roles in special Christmas show, tx 25 December

1983

Pebble Mill at One, interviewed on 9 December

The Two Ronnies, various roles, Series 10, tx 10 December–14 January 1984

1984

The Magnificent Evans, played Plantagenet Evans, tx 13 September–11 October

The Two Ronnies, special Christmas show, various roles, tx 25 December

1985

The Two Ronnies, various roles, Series 11, tx 13 February–20 March

Open All Hours, played Arkwright, Series 4, tx 1 September–6 October

The Two Ronnies, various roles, Series 12, tx 25 December–1 February 1986

1986

The Two Ronnies in Australia, various roles

1987

The Two Ronnies, special Christmas show, various roles, tx 25 December

1988

Clarence, played Clarence Sale, tx 4 January–8 February

1999

The Two Ronnies Night, various roles, special two-hour programme, tx 16 July

2000

The Nearly Complete and Utter History of Everything, played the Renaissance Man, tx 2 January

2002

The Gathering Storm, played David Inches, tx 12 July

2003

Life Beyond the Box: Norman Stanley Fletcher, tx 29 December

2004

Ronnie Barker: A BAFTA Tribute, tx 7 February

My House in Umbria, played The General, tx 26 November

2005

The Two Ronnies Sketchbook, introduced by Barker and Corbett, tx 18 March–22 April

The Two Ronnies Christmas Sketchbook, introduced by Barker and Corbett, tx 25 December

Radio

1956

The Floggits, played various roles in Series 1, tx 17 August–30 November; Christmas edition, 25 December

1957

The Floggits, played various roles in six programmes, tx July–August

The Trouble with Toby, tx 1 August

Variety Playhouse, various roles, 5 October–29 March 1958

1958

The Floggits, various roles in Series 2, tx 8 April–5 August

Fine Goings On, a Frankie Howerd show, appeared in seven episodes, tx July–August

Pantomania, a Frankie Howerd Christmas show, tx 25 December

Variety Playhouse, various roles, tx 27 December–8 July 1959

1959–67

The Navy Lark, playing various characters over the years, including 'Fatso' Johnson, Lt-Commander Stanton, Mr Merrivale and 'Snogger' Pettigreaves

1961

Round the Bend, tx May–August

Variety Playhouse, various roles, tx 23 September–30 December

1962

It's a Stereophonic World, Network 3 broadcast, tx 22 September

Discord in Three Flats, Home Service broadcast, tx 22 September

Variety Playhouse, various roles, tx 6 October–29 December

1963

Variety Playhouse, various roles, tx 5 January–25 May

The Arthur Haynes Show, tx 7 January

The TV Lark, tx 29 March–19 April

Star Parade – Crowther's Crowd, various characters, tx 4 July

Crowther's Crowd, various characters, tx 21 September–21 December

1964

Not to Worry, various characters, tx 31 July–25 September

Variety Playhouse, various characters, ten programmes tx March–May

Variety Playhouse, various characters, thirteen programmes, tx 19 September–12 December

Afternoon Theatre: Round Trip, Home Service radio broadcast, tx 18 November, played Max Brayling

Comedy Parade – The Merchant of Little Venice, North West One, tx 10 December

1965

Let's Face It, various characters, tx 8 January–5 March

This is Your Jim, various characters, seven programmes, tx 27 May–8 July

Let's Face It, various characters, ten programmes, tx March–May

Listen to This Space, tx 20 June

1966

The Embassy Lark, tx 15 March–7 June

Crowther's Crowd, various characters, tx 17 April–17 July

1967

Call My Bluff, tx 1 August

The Young Pioneers, a Light Programme broadcast, tx 3 August, a chronicle of Australian frontier days in the 1850s with Ronnie playing Andy Winters

1971

Lines From My Grandfather's Forehead, played various characters, Series 1, tx 15 February–5 April

Lines From My Grandfather's Christmas Forehead, played various characters, tx 24 December

1972

Lines From My Grandfather's Forehead, played various characters, Series 2, tx 9 July–26 August

Bibliography

Baddeley, John, *Double Take* (Ken House Press, 2009)

Barker, Ronnie, *Dancing in the Moonlight* (Hodder & Stoughton, 1993)

Barker, Ronnie, *It's Hello – from him!* (New English Library, 1988)

Barrie, Amanda, *It's Not a Rehearsal* (Headline, 2002)

Chapman, Don, *Oxford Playhouse: High and Low Drama in a University City* (University of Hertfordshire Press with the Society for Theatre Research, 2008)

Corbett, Ronnie, *And it's goodnight from him . . .* (Michael Joseph, 2006)

Donovan, Paul, *The Radio Companion* (Grafton, 1992)

Frost, David, *David Frost: An Autobiography* (HarperCollins, 1993)

Graham, Malcolm, *Oxfordshire at War* (Sutton Publishing, 1994)

Graham Scott, Peter, *British Television: An Insider's History* (McFarland, 2000)

Lewisohn, Mark, *Radio Times Guide to TV Comedy* (BBC Books, 1998)

McCabe, Bob, *Ronnie Barker: The Authorised Biography* (BBC Books, 2004)

Phillips, Leslie, *Hello* (Orion, 2006)

Webber, Richard, *Porridge: The Inside Story* (Headline, 2001)

Whitfield, June, *. . . and June Whitfield* (Bantam Press, 2000)

Some excellent websites were extremely useful during the writing of this book, including whirligig-tv.co.uk, imdb.com, televisionheaven.co.uk and navylark.org.uk